WE
ARE
LIFEBEATERS

PROPHET ALLYSON MICHAEL D'ESPYNE

abbott press

Abbott Press books may be ordered through booksellers or by contacting:

Abbott Press
1663 Liberty Drive
Bloomington, IN 47403
www.abbottpress.com
Phone: 1 (866) 697-5310

All scripture quotations taken from the King James Version of the Bible.

ISBN: 978-1-4582-2240-4 (sc)
ISBN: 978-1-4582-2239-8 (hc)
ISBN: 978-1-4582-2238-1 (e)

Library of Congress Control Number: 2019909494

Print information available on the last page.

Abbott Press rev. date: 07/16/2019

This book is dedicated to my deceased parents
Livingston and Phyllis D'Espyne. They had spent
their lives making every sacrifice necessary for the
well-being and spiritual growth of the family.

WE ARE LIFEBEATERS

1. The Journey

It is Sunday morning, in the spring of May, 2016. Homeless for Jesus as I slept on the steps of St. Mark's Episcopal Cathedral, Shreveport, Louisiana. When suddenly, I heard the voice of Jesus, our Lord and Savior saying in a loud voice that "We are Lifebeaters." Simultaneously, seeing Him walking pass by me, I opened my big brown eyes and stared at the rising sun beholding no one but just footsteps in the moving light.

I opened my briefcase and reached for my light, black, sponge shoe cleaner and polished my black boots and tidied myself reminiscing on God's Vision. I stood up and prayed my early morning's prayer, the Lord's Prayer, the Our Father. Picking up my long black umbrella and placing my black hat on my head, I proceeded to McDonald's to have breakfast.

Journeying with Jesus is a wonderful gift especially when He dwells in you and speaks to you all day and all night. We are in conversation as I made my way to the restaurant. Of course, Jesus is doing all the talking and I am doing all the listening as He is teaching me on the subject of Our Time, The End Times.

It is now six o'clock as I entered the building making my way to the counter. Then Jesus will say to me, that you meaning myself, will order black coffee and three hot cakes without the sausage. Waiting time 15 minutes tops. Taking my seat, Jesus will tell me to take out my Bible from my strapped-leather bag. Go to 2 Timothy 1:7, which reads That God does not bring a Spirit of Fear. He brings Love, A Sound Mind and Power.

PROPHET ALLYSON MICHAEL D'ESPYNE

Sipping my hot cup of coffee and enjoying my hot cakes with Jesus discussing with me about fear, in a world of fear, and trembling is not the best of topics. Because Jesus looks at it in a way like no other mortal can perceive. Taking my thoughts and speaking them as though I am verbally speaking while He is speaking to me. Jesus knows our profound thoughts which are as deep as an iceberg. Some icebergs have depths of thousands and tens of thousands that human beings cannot get to no matter how hard they try. Because God the Father, God the Son, and God the Holy Spirit would not allow them to achieve such depths.

I closed my Bible staring at the TV, as I listened to the News of the day. People are moving and fleeing from the Middle-Eastern countries by the tens of thousands. People from Syria, Lebanon and surrounding countries are making their way to France, Germany, Netherlands and Belgium. People seeking asylum. Families torn apart. Once again a world in utter chaos.

CNN reporters are broadcasting the events of the day-to-day happenings as the world unfolds its ugly face. ISIS a Radical Islamic regime is creating havoc in the Middle East. Isis wants total control of every country in the region, by any means necessary. The world looks at America to solve this crisis. To solve the failures of society who chooses other gods besides Jesus. And the failings of nations to respect each other life styles in a world that was given to Our Lord Jesus Christ by His Heavenly Father. The question that everyone must ask themselves is: Were you there when God the Father and God the Son created this world for His only begotten Son, Jesus?

As soon as I have had my third cup of coffee, I wended my way to St. Vincent Mall to do what the Lord will ask of me to do for Him. The walk took ten minutes. I looked at my cell phone and it was 12:55 p.m. So I paid the bathroom a visit. After 15 minutes, I walked through the mall window shopping, as I passed by. The smell of French fries consumed the air.

This daybeing Sunday, the mall opened at 12 noon and closed at six in the evening. Some people were still at church as I made my way to have a seat in front of Dillard;s. Before I could sit down, I noticed a white man coming my way all suited up and smiling. He said, "excuse me young man are you just coming out of church?" I replied, "no Sir." "You looked so distinguished and spiffy in your black three-piece suit." I retorted that, "I am a Pastor, Prophet and Hymnist."

Consequently, I made my way to the other end of the mall passing men and women shoe stores on my right and my left. Strolling past the "Piccadilly" restaurant, you could smell the savor of fried chicken and fried fish filling the walk paths of sweet-scented bodies of men and women and children. Stylish shoes adorned the windows of the men stores. While at the same time adorable spike-heeled women shoes, and fashionable dresses adorned the windows of the women stores throughout the mall. It was three o'clock, as the millennia shoppers were slowly coming through the revolving doors.

I took my seat obliquely in front of Sears, the last store in the mall. Sears like Dillard's is a conglomerate. Before I could open my Bible, I heard someone said, "Prophet" with a loud voice. The face I knew, but the name I could not recall. I shook his hand vigorously and he was so happy to see me. His face was full of laughter, as he turned to introduce me to his lovely wife Barbara. In 2004-2006, I had lived in a tiny town called "Vivian" (which is about fifty miles North of Shreveport). There I had ministered to him.

Immediately, I started to tell him about his life as the Spirit of the Lord drilled through him. I remembered saying to him to expect a miracle. And in the year 2017, God will remove some scars in his life to turn him around, so that his past bad days will now be good days. His wife stood motionless, as she was consumed with the fire of love permeating her eyes, her cheekbones and her lips. He gave me forty dollars.

Reflecting on what I saw on CNN, Jesus began to enlighten me as to why the world is going through perilous times. Every now and again Jesus would take me to the bottom of the ocean floors to show me the injustices of a world not wanting to accept and embrace the new shift of "Apocalypse"—the end times.

The whole Muslim world is oblivious of the Book of Revelation especially Radical Islam. The disclosure of what is to come in the future torments their souls. The one who is to come, the only one true begotten Son of the Living God is causing rift in the Middle East. And the dawn of Revelation Preachers have caused an alarm for those muslms, who have embraced Jesus in their faith. The Jihardis and the Radical Islamic Muslims are one and the samepeople that do not want peace in the world.

And in the Christian world, there are inner fighting between preachers of the last days and preachers of the end times. Because they have found out that the book of revelation belongs to end time preachers. And not just end time preachers, but to those who are obedient to His Every Word. Interpretation of the very book is only acceptable coming from the mouths of anointed preachers of God rather than the status quo.

A walk with Jesus is a walk with Truth. And the houses of religion, Jesus has already began to tear down those walls of injustices, those walls of sugar-coated truth, those walls of deprivation and those walls of pride. Jesus reminds us that He will be coming like a thief in the night. Jesus has allowed the plague of Ebola to come into this world on account of the many misdeeds of homo sapiens.

For those of you who are repeatedly stealing His Fame and His Glory you will no longer live to see age 40. Obedient children of God will be living past 120 years. For the children of these end times must continue to live in hope thus saith the Lord. Banquets will become a thing of the past. Miracles will become more widespread. More volcanic eruptions will take place in the Arctic and the Antarctic regions of the world.

This means a renewing of gold, silver and tin. More food in abundance will be spreading throughout these virgin lands. Lands that will be more succulent; richer than those running alongside the River Nile. Fruits that were thought to be extinct will be springing up along the borders of these new found lands.

From the year 2017, more people will be seeing angels descending and ascending continually both day and night. Glimpses of a New Heaven and a New Earth will be shown to the children of the earth. This will continue throughout human existence.

It was now six o'clock. The doors of Sears are closed and the shutters of every store come sliding down. I got up and proceeded to the nearest exit. In the cool of the evening Jesus is conversing with me on the inside, as I soliloquy to myself. Jesus is describing Isis as one of the ancient Gods of Sodom and Gomorrah that ravished the hearts of men and women. A god that children wore in lockets around their ankles in Medieval Times is still in practice today.

On entering McDonald's, I took my place in the line of three persons of different colors and ethnicity, and waited my turn. When I got to the counter, I humbly and politely greeted the young lady with a good evening and do have a good day and she smiled. She answered and said, "you do have a beautiful accent." I said, "thank you very much" and asked the young lady her name, which she said in a feigning low voice "Alisha.' I told her that "I am a Prophet" and in the same breath, I ordered a spicy chicken burger and small fries and a large diet coke. I swiped my credit card to the tune of $3.26.

I headed to the nearest vacant seat and placed my umbrella alongside the leather seat and my "Kenneth Cole" briefcase and leather-strapped bag beside me. Before I could settle in my seat, my ticket number "201" was called. I ushered to the counter and took the waiter with my food and two honey mustard condiments and six packs of ketchup. At the fountain, I got some ice and placed my empty cup under the diet coke faucet, filling it to the top. Then I grabbed a handful of tissues and headed to my seat.

Spreading the ketchup on the hot French fries with a little salt and black pepper for added ingredients, I slowly started to eat and drink the beverage of Jesus's choice. CNN was rolling back the news over and over again concerning the spiraling number of refugees by the hundreds of thousands from Syria, Lebanon and other countries of the surrounding hemisphere. The whole world was now upside down.

Isis is not just another god or the name of a warring Radical Islamic country. No Isis is an entire world Order on the uprise in the form of cells. Cells are distributed throughout the world by satellite. Cellsare encouraging young people to come and join this new fad, which is cool among young people. Look around you and open the eye of wisdom and see that every new generation is a wave of change in the world. Change can go in any direction.

Christians are required to stand up for Jesus. Now is the time to show their great love for the only one True Son of the Living God, who gave His life for their inheritance of HEAVEN. Jesus is the bridge. Jesus is the only I AM. Jesus is the Solid Rock. Jesus is the Lamb of God. Jesus is the High Priest. This is what Christians cannot give up for any other gods on the face of the earth. This is your gold, because your hands will be formed out of this precious element when you inhabit heaven.

As I was eating Jesus is still talking to me. I opened my sandwich and spread the entire two packs of honey mustard dressing on the spicy chicken on one side of the bread. Still warm and chewing slowly Jesus is telling me everything about people as they pass me by. And of course there is a humor side of Jesus that keeps me smiling through the events of the day.

An empty cup raised me from my seat to get another free refill of diet coke and a handful of tissue. It was now nine in the evening and the lobby was getting empty by the hour as closing time draws near. The manager found out that there is a Prophet in the restaurant and block me in the aisle. Brenda, the manager, who is filled with the Holy Spirit wanted to get a word from me. I walked her through her academic disciplines and achievements at High School. She was pierced through her side by the words that emanated from my mouth.

Periodically, I paid a two-minute visit to the bathroom; drying my eyes, as I focused on the news on the120-inch television set. It is disheartening when you see people of no faith, because people of faith do not worry about anything. An influx of tens of thousands of refugees coming into France is not a worrisome thing. If you have ever paid a visit to Paris, which is indeed another wonder of the world, then what is the problem? God the Father, God the Son, and God the Holy Spirit has blessed you.

So open the flood gates of heaven to refugees from all walks of life.

It was 10 p.m. when astonishing news about the refugee non-admittance to some countries were reported. And more so, conflicting positions taken by so-called democratic countries, talking about there are no room or no more roomin there beautiful countries. Jesus always knows how to show them up with His Word. Much is given to you, much more is demanded of you. So Belgium, a beacon of light, could do much more than you are doing right now.

The Netherlands, you who flourish in the land of milk and cheese and organic products, Jesus does expect you to build apartment buildings for the influx of his children fleeing from Syria. And, don't you stoop to the cries of your people. A people typical of those who think only of themselves. Because when you do Jesus, good always return in the form of favor.

Belgium, a booming and a blossoming country, follow in the footsteps of France and open your doors to your neighbors. God knows that you are lovers of yourselves. One day Jesus is going to come like a thief in the night and pay a visit to those who have passed the laws of same sex marriage in your country. Jesus is saying that Enough is definitely Enough.

Sweden, a land of the affluent, Jesus is holding you hostage from the many deals that you have made in the past with Satan, the devil. You, who continually hide rich people in the covers of your spreading wings. Jesus is saying with a double-edge sword, beware of falling meteors on your land. Because like a volcano. Jesus can and will split all of Sweden into two separate countries.

England, it is time to release Australia to its own. Because like the bubbles in the bathtub I will spit you out of my mouth for generations to come. For Psalm 23 says: The Lord is my shepherd; I shall not want. Jesus hears the cries of the suffering masses of poor people, who have come to know the Lord Jesus and have accepted Him as their Lord and Savior. Jesus will not relent. Jesus will not turn away from His children in their hour of need.

The lobby doors of the restaurant closed at eleven this night. I, Allyson D'Espyne, the Prophet left and headed for St. Mark's Episcopal Cathedral. At the top of the steps I rolled out a light cloth to lie down. It was indeed another long day for me. Jesus woke me up at five o'clock in the morning. The birds were singing and flying around. I prayed my morning prayer and showered myself with perfume. Then I fetched my belongings and off to McDonald's.

A breath of fresh air is a wonderful thing that some people take for granted. That Monday morning was busy with cars and trucks entering the city of Shreveport. The blowing of horns from cars and trucks and the occasional loud siren sounds coming from the ambulances filled the air with the noise of its first work day. It took me about five minutes to get to the restaurant. Seeing that there was no line, and saying good morning to everybody, I paused for a moment. Everybody was just two people. Three quarter of the morning staff just did not turn out for work. Waiting time for my breakfast, three hot cakes and a senior's cup of coffee totaled $3.46, was thirty minutes.

I took my ticket and had a seat, as usual near the window. The news of the refugees plastered the television set twenty-four seven. CNN rolled it in as the empty seats started to fill up at McDonald's. Gradually, workers one by one showed up grumbling. Long lines of cars bumper to bumper rolled in alongside the building causing a gridlock situation. My food was brought over to me at my table. The coffee was very hot. I took the cover off the hot cakes and plastered the fresh butter over the top one. Then, I opened the two syrup containers and poured all of the liquid over the mountain. I slowly began to cut down the mountain.

It was seven o'clock, when I got up to ask for another refill of black coffee with three Equal packs of sugars. My friend Alisha, one of the employees that were so sweet to me, saw me coming towards her and took the cup out of my hand and filled it up with caffeinated coffee. Taking my three sugars, I returned to my seat with my focus on Jesus. By this time, the sun was piercing through the glass windowsas the sweat kept pouring all over my face. The tissues were all soaked up by now, as Jesus kept my eyes on Him.

Some customers would greet me by saying, "top of the morning to you Sir," before taking their seats. They were dressed in white long sleeve shirts, ties and slacks filling the empty seats and tables around me, staring at the news. Women, who were not dressed in appropriate uniforms, would be dressed sophisticatedly. Eventually, the dining room was almost filled up. Tables were decorated with meals of all varieties: biscuits and sausages with orange juice; scramble eggs with two biscuits and coffee with three containers of milk and six sugars; two biscuits with ham and eggs and mocha coffee.

The temperature was rising as the sun was lifting itself off the glass windows. Whitney, one of the employees that cleans the tables and sweeps the floors was going around asking the customers if they needed more coffee. I nodded my head to her indicating a yes. She filled me up once again to the brim. Meanwhile, the good Lord Jesus is repeating scriptures to me as He keeps me focus on Him.

Armageddon: the movie that features destruction in the way that the producer and director reeled it out was not in any way what Jesus meant. Revelation 16:16 reads as follows: and he gathered them together into a place called in the Hebrew tongue Armageddon. Firstly, the people that wrote the script are not anointed men of God. Secondly, did God mandate the brothers to do this film? Being zealous is not the criteria!

Obedience is the answer to the Book of Revelation. Everybody wants to know precisely what Jesus is thinking. Some distrustfully so; some want Jesus to magnificently come to them, so that they can touch Him and hold Him in their arms. Before we get together into a place, eyes have not seen and ears have not heard the Glory of the Lord. This comes first.

The angels of heaven have to come down from heaven to minister unto the children of God. Myriad of things have to come to pass.

More meteorites have to fall from heaven to the earth. The sun will increase in a way that has not been seen before. Darkness will decrease, because satan hides in darkness. A staircase has to be built from the earth straight to heaven for the souls of mankind to come on all up.

It was now 12 noon. I picked up my belongings and headed out to St. Vincent Mall. The weather was set to rain. Going through the revolving doors, I perambulated the aisles of Dillards store that led to the entrance of the interior of the mall. Taking my seat, I sank into the leather chair and opened my Bible to read. Then suddenly, Joe the white man that stared at me, giving me kind remarks on the last occasion was seated on the opposite side. Before I could look him in the eye, someone passing by called his name out aloud. And this is how I knew his name.

He came over to me to ask a question. Knowing his question before he could pose it, I told him that God has mandated me to preach out of the Book of Revelation. He being Jewish, and wrestling with his faith, had a question about Jesus Holy Spirit. And, how do I perceive the Word of God in the book of revelation? For God so Loved the world that He gave His only begotten Son is something that some Jewish people of faith cannot deal with. Nobody wants to accept Jesus as His only begotten Son. Apparently, God owes them something. Jesus owes you nothing.

Jesus is the Alpha and the Omega. He is the Light of the world. He is the one who is to come. He laid down His life for everyone.

We spoke for about two hours. By then, I realized by the power of Jesus Holy Spirit, that he never got it. I left him to continue his discourse of a trouble mind. One whose only purpose in mind was to convince you and to enunciate his words of rhetoric. In other words, win you over to his beliefs.

I made it to the end of the mall at 3:05 p.m. Realizing in that moment in time, that Sears and all the other stores in the mall would be opened till 9 p.m. At this time, I decided to peruse the men's department section of sears. The men's suit section were very limited. They showcased two different styles of three-piece suits. Too little to choose from--not accommodating. I decided to go over to the shoe section. Lots of shoes to choose from but my income was limited.

Jesus always says that He does not give you more than you can bear. As soon as you could look up to the mountains in faith, then you would be very happy to go take a walk with Jesus. Jesus is continuously waiting for someone to come take a walk with Him. But humankind could not stay still for too long. Everybody wants to be a Movie Star. But to be a movie star just does not happen by conjecture.

So it was for the refugees fleeing from their countries to some other land. They got to give up their homes, their jobs, their cars and to some degree something that could not be replaced. Yes, some countries would welcome them with open arms. But would it ever be the same. The point is that when you have never been through something, through some situation, you definitely cannot help anyone at their hour of need.

Yes, some people have been drifters in their own countries. Whilst on the other hand, others could not keep their jobs, if their lives were dependent on it. But these would be very few. But then again, Jesus wants you out there to give these jobs, big jobs to Pastors who were homeless. Great men of God who had to take one loaf of bread and a pound of butter and divide it up for ten children together with husband and wife. Men of God, who had to flee from their country and sojourn in another man's country due to war should come first. Give these jobs to these anointed people of God! And God the Father, God the Son, and God the Holy Spirit will be pleased and pour out a blessing.

Look at the rainbow! Tell me what you see! Jesus knows exactly what you will say, but can you see all of the colors that is represented on the face of the earth. Well that is what you are missing the truth that God is Real, Real, Real. You must give up yourself. You must lose yourself when accommodating others, who are placed in your care. And be careful not to speak first. Let them do the talking whilst you do the listening.

PROPHET ALLYSON MICHAEL D'ESPYNE

It was six o'clock, when I left the mall to go to McDonald's for my dinner. Jesus does the ordering. When I got to the counter Jesus had already told me that we would be eating large French fries and a large diet coke. This was what I ordered. Surprise! No waiting time, I asked the young lady for a waiter and took my food over to the side of the soda machine. There I fetched three small cups and placed them one by one under the nozzle of the ketchup machine. Afterwards I took a handful of tissues.

Walking to my table, I laid down all of my things on the side of me, before I began to eat. Watching the news and eating hot French fries and drinking diet soda and listening to Jesus became my pastime. Darkness was consuming the earth and the news remained the same. On reflection, I could hear Jesus saying that "We are Lifebeaters."

One thing that I do not do is to question Jesus, not even for a moment. The dining room was now filling up somehow with families having a night out. At the restaurant, couples sat side by side or facing each other enjoying their meal in soft conversation. Burgers and large French fries with a large soda were the order of the evening and the night. Children came in droves to enjoy their kid's meal. And the cars and trucks in the drive through were slowly moving.

Christians question God too much. And they got to be told the same thing over and over. Grow up! Jesus is the same today and forevermore. When you want to be used by Jesus just let Him know that you are available. His journeying will be long and there will be steep mountains to climb. Take nothing for your journey! Jesus will not leave you alone. Jesus will not abandon you.

It is the same thing as the mustard seed. Jesus is that small mustard seed. Jesus will bury the smallest of seeds in the world. That is what He wants to do. Now let Him come and do the watering and the plowing and the pruning. In spring time the flowers will come out and the fruits will bear and they will be good.

My last refill was nine o'clock, an hour from closing time. An employee started to clean the lobby. At this time, McDonald's was practically empty. The place was swept up real clean. The chairs were placed in their proper places and the tables were wiped. There were no cars in the drive through. I decided to pick up my brief case, my parasol and my hat. It was time to leave. As I opened the door, gosh it was raining. I pressed the button on the umbrella and noticed small pools of water on the pavement.

I jumped over the pools of water and headed out to St. Mark's Episcopal Cathedral just five minutes away. My concrete bed was not wet. Leaving my light long coat on, I fell asleep. God the Father, God the Son and God the Holy Spirit surrounded me with his love. Visions filled my soul all night long. Attacks by satan, the devil filled the night. But Jesus kept me strong. Jesus keeps telling me over and over again that when morning break, we will be going to Brookshire's Food Store.

It was five in the morning, when Jesus woke me up. After my usual morning prayer, I stretched out my arms and yawned. That Tuesday morning I was heading out to brookshire's. Putting my hat on my head and spraying down my clothes with perfume, I proceeded to the food store after making sure that I had left nothing behind.

My parasol became my walking stick as I walked down the side streets leading to the super market. Residential houses stood side by side on either side of the streets. One, two or three cars were parked in the respective driveways. There also were cars and trucks parked on the streets in front of these houses. Brookshire's opened at half past the hour of six in the mornings. It was precisely six thirty.

Drawing the push cart in front of me, I picked up two cans of sardines in the third aisle. In the second aisle, I picked up a can of green beans and a con of peel potatoes. To my right, almost to the entrance of the grocery, I bagged two rolls at 25 cents a roll. Thereafter, I proceeded to the cashier. All alone in the line, the cashier totaled the food to the tune of $4.00.

Almost obliquely opposite the food store was a Laundromat. There I sat and ate my cold food.

It was eleven o'clock, when I left the laundromat. I headed in the direction of Kings Highway. I walked past Family Dollar and came to Byrd High School at the top of the hill. Crossing Lyons Ave. I passed a bunch of lawyers' offices. The dew point was low as a cool breeze blew my hat off my head. I retrieved it in the middle of the highway. Tightly fitting my hat unto my head, I came in view of St. Vincent Mall.

I quickened the pace so that I can use the bathroom. Fifteen minutes tops. Combing my hair and shaving only took but a few minutes. Tucking my black body fitting shirt in my slacks and adjusting my black suspenders, I ran out of the restroom. All this time Jesus is still talking to me. I took my seat at center court almost parallel to Piccadilly Restaurant. Meanwhile, a small cake store was baking cookies as I wrestled with the indulgence.

It was evening, when I saw the security officers perambulating the floors. They were dressed in white shirts and blue trousers with black shoes. Sometimes, they walked in pairs and sometimes in single file. Mothers with babies in arms passed me by. Small groups of families with parcels in their hands would suddenly stop and take a seat to try on their brand new shoes that they have just purchased. Oftentimes one would see children running and playing in the mall only to be chastened by their parents.

Still in the center of the mall, I made my way to sit and play the game angry birds. It was the only free amusement. Before I could take my seat, a strong scent of sweet perfume aroused me and filled the air. Beside me to my right stood a beautiful young lady that the good Lord allowed me to have the pleasure of meeting. Her name was "April." She was a very pretty young lady, who was polite and courteous. The Lord Jesus moved in me to let her know that, "she would not be successful on her previous interview." She told me that, "she felt the same way too and that she was going to the store opposite us for an interview shortly."

At this time, Jesus is telling me to let her know that her future would be bright. Jesus took me through her high school academic years. Her scholastic achievements and good grades were stupendous. April needed much confidence. Is she filled with the Holy Spirit? Yes she got Jesus. Time had run out for us, but I knew that one day we would meet again.

My friend Rose entered my spirit, so I decided to give her a call. Still in mourning for her deceased mother Jesus has allowed me to take her out of mourning. Life is but a short time. Gone are the days, when people lived for 1,000 years. Gone are the days, when the angels would leave heaven and paid a visit to humankind. Gone are the days, when you could leave your cars open and no one would run off with your vehicle. Gone ae the days, when you and your family would fall asleep with the doors and windows opened and no one would come in and steal and kill everybody. Gone are them days.

In 2014, Debratold me that the doctor diagnosed her mother with cancer. Before she could finish the sentence, the good Lord Jesus told me to tell her to let her mother eat spinach. So I told her. A few weeks later, I enquired about her health. Debra replied to me that her "Mama will not eat spinach daily." We tried to get her to eat the spinach, but it was to no avail. Jesus is the doctor.

I left the mall about six in the evening. The humidity had begun to kick in. I took my sweet time to walk over to McDonald's. Traffic was light. Crossing was easy. The drive through was congested. Someone coming out the door let me in. About six people were ahead of me standing in the line. Jesus is talking to me and letting me know that we would be eating large French fries and drinking a large diet coke. After giving my order, I went to the fountain and filled up my cup with ice and soda. Then I filled up three small cups with ketchup. Taking a handful of napkins, I headed for my favorite seat.

Five minutes later, my meal was brought over to me on a waiter. Thanking Lakisha, I spread the ketchup all over the French fries, whilst sprinkling a little salt and pepper over them. As a senior, you need all the potassium you could get. Jesus also is eating my food as we both dine together. Jesus keeps me healthy all year round like the perennial flowers in the field.

There is always something on the news that will toss your mind around. It is not Jesus. Jesus is the Light of the World. When Jesus comes to you, He will at all times give His name, before you see Him. During the conversation, He will call His name out loud. Jesus is the Alpha and the Omega. No man cometh unto the Father except by Him, that is why His name is Jesus. If you have seen me you have seen the Father.

Beware of wolves in sheep clothing! In these end times, you have to be careful, who you entertain in the home. The home is your castle and in your castle are your children. So beware of who you bring in the home. Beware of the time you go to sleep! Time is God the Father, God the Son, and God the Holy Spirit. Remember your children are Jesus children too.

Jesus is the Rock of all ages. Refilling my cup with diet coke and listening to Jesus is something that I didn't ask Jesus for. He just gave it to me. Some people would come and introduce themselves to me. Some people the Spirit of the Lord sends them to me. And some people that have already known me, whenever they see me would come to ask me a question. It is all of Jesus doing.

Jesus gives us the Lord's Prayer, Luke 11:2. How many of us are praying the Our Father? We all have mountains in our lives. All of us need to remove these mountains. But, do we have faith? Satan too would continually be there to comfort you. That is why he is a roaring lion.

During the time while I sat in the dining room of the restaurant to have a meal, it was not just a meal, but Our Lord Jesus Christ is teaching me the shortcomings of everyone. When I am focused on the TV, Jesus is teaching me the misgivings of an entire world. Wake up my fellow brothers and sisters! You have been sleeping far too long. When you go home Sunday mornings, where do you go Sunday evenings?

Are you looking at the NFL game? Or are you viewing the NBA game? Don't you care about your soul? Could you tell me the last time you have prayed the Our Father? Jesus is looking; looking at you. Where is your Bible, sitting on the mantelpiece? Jesus is looking; looking at you. There is a window in every corner of Heaven looking at you. God does not remove His eyes off you. God is looking at you.

As the chairs began to shuffle all around me, I knew that it was closing time. Time for me to get up out of here. I left the restaurant feeling good. I negotiated the street behind Cane's restaurant and headed in the direction of the steps of the cathedral. I put away my umbrella and my hat and fell asleep. Every hour on the hour until five o'clock in the morning, Jesus woke me up. He kept on talking, talking, talking. Simultaneously, the sparrows kept on singing all night long.

At fifteen minutes after five in the morning, I traced my way to Brookshire's food store. The morning was nice, cool and breezy. The stars were becoming invisible. I was the only pedestrian; the only black man on the streets. Highland area was indeed a beautiful neighborhood. Lighted porches and garages could be seen in the distance. Lawns were cut and barking dogs were harnessed, thus making my walk a very splendid thing.

I stood outside the super market for fifteen minutes, before the doors were opened. Drawing my push cart and placing all my belongings into the trolley. Jesus is selecting my breakfast as usual. I picked up a can of peeled potatoes, a can of lima beans and two tins of sardines. Then I rolled around the store looking for a small cup of ice cream. My favorite ice cream was pecan chocolate. And Jesus says that's enough. They totaled about $6.00.

It was now thirty minutes after seven in the morning. The sunlight was just raising his head and striking me in my eyes. Jesus was guiding me to Colombia Park, which was a block away from the super market. Colombia Park took up at least three blocks. Sitting in the center of the hall, I placed all of my belongings on the wide wooden table. I prayed the blessing over the food and began to remove the caps off the tins of the cans of all the food. It was a sumptuous meal.

Meanwhile, white people with their dogs unleashed came through jogging or walking. Parents brought their children to the park to have some fun. Children were swinging, climbing and chasing each other, thus reminding me of my past childhood good days. High school students used the park as a short cut to Byrd High School.

Tiding myself at the water fountain, Jesus took me by the hand and stared me to Kings Highway. It was about 12 noon, when I crossed over Lyons Ave. Passing the lawyers' offices on my left, always let me know that I was in striking distance of St. Vincent Mall.

As soon as I got to the Mall, Jesus decided for me to do some window shopping, thus preventing me from falling asleep on myself. My shopping began at Dillard's men department. I tried out their hats. Their suits were well over $300. The shirt was $60. The slacks was $70. The total cost for everything would be about $700. At Burlington Store, I would get everything, shoes included for less than $300.

On leaving Dillard's, I strolled through the mall conversing with Jesus my Lord. Living with Jesus deep down in your belly is worth more than silver and gold. Wherever you are, Jesus is flowing in you like a river. Until you remove the mountain in your life, God the Father, God the Son, and God the Holy Spirit cannot put you to work. Jesus cannot use you. Just look around you and you would see a whole lot of dead people passing you by.

99.99 per cent of the entire world has gone left. No faith. People are caught in a stronghold of trying to live out somebodies' dreams. Live your own life! Be your own man! Be your own woman! Jesus is the tunnel to heaven. Jesus is able to give you that Rolls Royce. Jesus is able to give you that beautiful house. Jesus is able to give you that nice dress. Where is your faith?

Stop the gambling! You do not need the drugs. You have lost focus. The world is a big round circle and it is 360 degrees. How much of the circle have you conquered? Not much, because you have been running away from the One True Living God. That is why you got caught in the net, like the fishes in the sea.

Examine 1 Timothy 5:18 which reads: and, Thelabourer is worthy of his reward. Anytime you rob God by not paying your tithes and offerings, you end up in the strongholds of gambling and misuse of drugs. Now you are feeling sorry for yourself. You have stopped attending classes at the university. You have begun to miss days on the job. Your tardiness has turned to filthiness. You gave up quickly. God the Father, God the Son, and God the Holy Spirit lives by his own rules. Who do you think you are?

As you pray, ask Jesus for wisdom and understanding? Jesus will one day give it all to you. You need the gift of wisdom and understanding in your daily lives. It is your greatest weapon for Satan, the devil. Because as soon as the evil one comes to you, Jesus will put His Word into your mouth to defeat the devil. You must bear witness for Jesus to take care of you and your family.

Stop the doubting! This too is a defeatist attitude. Watch your mouth! You do not have to leave your own family to see evil display at its best. Running your mouth is not a sign of humility. Jesus comes to us in the midnight hour. But, where are we in the midnight hour? Or what are we doing during the midnight hour? Nothing that Jesus will be doing. Jesus will always come in His own time. Not ours.

As I am pacing the floors of the mall, Jesus is saying pray unceasingly. This means empty yourself. Cut out the foolishness! And begin to live by faith. Jesus alone can put it together. Jesus does not need your help. Lay down your burdens at His feet! Jesus alone can fix them. Jesus owes us nothing. Once we believe this then we are on our way to His Glory.

Render your heart and not your garments! This is as good a time to give away some of your clothes. But do it in the name of Jesus. He is our friend, our very best friend. Do not take him for granted! In everything you do, please remember to say thank you Jesus.

Thank Jesus for your empty pockets. Thank Jesus for the holes in your shoes. Thank Jesus for your nakedness. Thank Jesus for the loss of your home.

In my Father's house there are many mansions.

Jesus wants your heart. Jesus knows that there is and will be peer pressure.

I left the mall soliloquy with myself. It was 6:15 p.m. The rain had just fallen and McDonalds was almost filled. The lines were long at the cashiers. It took me about fifteen minutes to place the order. Waiting time was fifteen minutes. The lobby had to be mopped up quickly with slippery floor signs at every corner of the restaurant. I did not get my usual seat. As soon as my number was called, I got up and made my way to the counter. Retrieving the waiter, I headed to the fountain area. I ordered large French fries and a large diet coke.

After taking care of business, I took my seat almost too close to the TV. Everybody is conversing with their partner, as I spread the ketchup on my large hot French fries. The television set featured a movie that did not catch my fancy. The fries were good. There was one problem—no napkins. I had to police the area. It took about fifteen to twenty minutes to refill the napkin holder.

Some people would not stop what they are doing to lend an ear to someone else, especially Sons of God. Then they wonder why nothing go right for them. They keep on searching for their truth no matter what. Feet that are continuously taking you to do evil, would always be dirty. You need to clean them feet. When your feet are taking you to steal, you need to clean them feet. When your feet are taking you to cause mischief, you need to clean them feet. When your feet are taking you to war against your fellowman, you need to clean them feet.

Feet that are not clean cannot enter the kingdom of heaven. Feet that are not clean cannot see happiness. Feet that are not clean cannot live to see generations of blessings. Feet that are not clean cannot build bridges. Feet that are not clean cannot climb over mountain tops. Feet that are not clean cannot rise from the earth to heaven. Feet that are not clean cannot see the Face of God.

There are many mountains to climb. But you cannot get there without the love of Jesus. Many have gone to serve other gods and have become very successful. Where is there happiness? They generate meanest even to their dearest ones. Never have a good word to say to anyone. They are very diplomatic when answering questions. They would not speak the truth no matter if it would save their very own lives.

Jesus is our happiness. Jesus is our rock and fortress. We need to find our rest in Him. We allow Satan, the devil to steal our focus. We do not dedicate our lives in service to Our Lord and Savior Jesus Christ. John 3:16 reads, For God so loved the world, that he gave his only begotten Son, that whosoever believeth in him should not perish, but have everlasting life.

All the animals in the wilderness, the birds and the bees, depends on Jesus to provide for themselves and their offspring. Are we really depending on Jesus to provide everything for us? We say yes, but do we really mean what we say.

The animals in the wilderness give birth to their young ones. Jesus delivers those babies; a doctor delivers your sons and your daughters. The bees make honey. It is the only food that they can eat. Human beings have to depend on each other until they can stand for themselves.

It was ten o'clock, as I made my way out of the doors of McDonalds. I already had three refills of diet coke, before the hour of closing. The pavements were still wet as I negotiated the corner that led to the church. Using my parasol as a walking stick, I had to jump over large pools of water.

Jesus called me to preach His Word in the year 1998. I answered the call. Since then, Jesus has had me all over the world of America. In my 18 years, I have travelled the greater part of those years by greyhound. Life with Jesus has been enormous.

Reminiscing on the safety and safekeeping of Jesus is an awesome thing. Jesus is the only one, who can keep you and wake you up early for you to keep an appointment. Jesus is never late. Jesus is never hurry. Jesus takes his sweet time to do anything for anyone and He is no respecter of persons.

I retired on my concrete bed somewhere in the vicinity of midnight. Jesus is still talking even in my sleep. Jesus protects me as he covers me with his angels and his saints.

It was Thursday morning and the Lord Jesus is anointing me deeply. Meanwhile, His Holy Spirit is performing surgery on my body. Jesus is forever strengthening me for the journey. So will He strengthen you for your uphill walk. Jesus knows that the body is frail. Jesus knows that you want to finish the work that he has laid out for you to do. God wants your all.

Every knee shall bend and every heart shall confess that Jesus Christ is Lord. The whole wide world has been wrestling with the Word every knee. Isis's knee; Iran's knee; North Korea's knee. They will be the cradle of evil that surrounds the Christian world for centuries to come.

Christians must learn to loose themselves in God the Father, God the Son, and God the Holy Spirit. Stop playing church!

2. To Bring Hope

Psalm 39:7 And now, Lord what wait I for? My hope is in thee. Surely heaven and earth will pass away but my Word will live forever.

In the year 2002, the Lord Jesus led me to San Francisco, a City that I would have never gone to in my right mind. In obedience to Jesus I left. I boarded the Greyhound Bus in the City of Valdosta, Georgia about 1:30 p.m. It was in the beginning of summer.

San Francisco, a city known by me since a child, was a city of gays and lesbians. I remembered the catholic priest, in the island of Trinidad and Tobago emphasizing that San Francisco is liken to Sodom and Gomorrah. A city that God the Father destroyed for their homosexual behavior. Born in Trinidad and being catholic, the Catholic Church preached that sermon with a mighty and firm hand every year.

After making many stops the greyhound bus overnighted at Los Angeles, the City of Angels, California. We left early the following day, and about three in the afternoon, I recalled the driver saying "Welcome to Sin City." I retrieved my luggage which consists of five brand new three-piece suits, bow ties, ten pairs of Stacey Adams black shoes and one pair of white shoes. Not forgetting ten brand new black body-fitting cuffed shirts with a variety of cuff links.

It did not take me much time to get the tone of the city. Pulling my luggage along the side walk, I met Rose. A homeless, but pretty woman, who told me to follow this road throughout for the next three miles; I would see the building that would keep my luggage for free.

PROPHET ALLYSON MICHAEL D'ESPYNE

Ascending the wide staircase, the woman at the counter checked my things out and she said, "Sir, you sure do have new beautiful clothes here. I would have to keep my eyes on them for you, because they will steal them." I told her that, "I am a Pastor and a Prophet." She told me that her name is "Sandra." I thanked her very much.

Walking back to the station gave me a sense of delightfulness. For the first time, I came to realize how big the station really was? It was two stories and housed a large number of homeless people everywhere. Long benches lined the interior. It was a boarding area for in-coming and out-going passengers in the surrounding counties of the city of San Francisco. The peninsula is seven square miles and houses well over a million people.

The clatter of shoes woke me up letting me know that it was morning. With a backpack on my back, I went to the bathroom. Gosh! No doors in the bathrooms. Seriously. No privacy. Brushing my teeth, washing my face and combing my hair, was done quickly. Got to go now! Rose and her sister Barbara beckoned me to join them on the other side of the building, where coffee was served with donuts. I obliged.

Before you knew it, it was lunch time. Rose and her sister Barbara took me out to theTender Loin area, where the catholic church served a good meal to the homeless. Long lines of people standing in single file were waiting for the doors to open to enjoy a meal with Jesus. Sometimes workers in shirts and ties would stand in line for a free meal, or take a brown bag lunch, because time was of the essence.

Jesus is the author of hope. Jesus is building dreams wherever he goes. Jesus is putting smiles on their faces, when their lovers have turned them away.

It was 12:30 p.m. My new found sisters and I went to the nearby park obliquely opposite the library. The air was nice and clean and breezy. San Francisco claimed to be the cleanest city of all America. The city designated three days a year as clean-air days. On these days, people are advised to leave their vehicles at home and take the city transit to and from work. It was all free to the general public. It opened 24/7.

When you have the love of Jesus deep in your heart, the fire of love burns deeper within you that causes you to tremble. Jesus is always looking for lifebeaters. A dedicated few to finish his work here on the earth. Thousands of people do not go to a city just for the fun of it. What is the purpose for anyone—hope?

Some people go to sleep everyday and have never borne witness to their fellowmen. They resigned in their own little world, safe and secure, free from harm. When Jesus is inviting them to have a meal with him, they will not listen to the voice of the Lord. A meal that will break down barriers. A meal that will free them from their worrisomeness. A meal that will free them from the status quo. A meal that would remove strife, which is stuck deep down in their heart. You got to live your live for Jesus.

At nightfall, we decided to go back to the greyhound station for our night cap. Rose was originally from Florida. She buried her mother as a child and could not bear the thought of her mother's death. Barbara on the other hand, was born in Arizona. Mother of four, divorced, and drifted away from her children. Rose a very beautiful woman has been homeless for the past ten years. Barbara has been homeless for five years. They are not biological sisters. But Barbara defends her small frame sister Rose in any battle on the streets.

They called me the Prophet. They would continually bring others to me for prayer and to foretell their futures. Sometimes late at night, the police would come through yielding batons and striking the long benches hard to wake you up simply because you are homeless. Then we would all flee to the streets and cuddled under the arch of a store front. Jesus always remembers.

Sometimes we would have two hot cakes and coffee for the price of $1.00 from a group of good Samaritans. This was served at seven o'clock in the mornings above the catholic center. Jesus is constantly showing me that keeping hope alive is truly a wonderful thing.

The library opened at nine in the morning. A superbly beautiful, architectural, modernday designed structure. Second only to the beautiful edifices that lined the streets of Paris. I would secure myself on the third floor reading the World Book with a dictionary close by. But my sleepless eyes would not allow me to read. The police could be very brutal; they would pull the chair from under me and care less what would happen to me. Jesus is there for me at all times.

At lunch time I would break for lunch and there I would meet my friends Rose and Barbara. The line stretched all around the corner serving hundreds of meals a day. In the window of the building the menu for the week was posted. Meals were freshly prepared on a daily basis. Students from schools volunteered to help in the kitchen. Sometimes parishioners join the line to show their love.

After lunch, I returned to the library to continue from where I stopped. I would research whatever Jesus place in my head to take a look at. And I would read the World Book for added information.

On Sundays the good Lord Jesus Christ would actually take me to church. Jesus would choose the church by taking me for walks and reading the menu boards. Then Jesus would wake me up early for church. I remembered having church at a Missionary Baptist Church. I got there in time for the service. The Pastor, a wonderful man of God, was well into his eighties. He was fully absorbed with my story. At the end of the service, he gave me a Sunday to bring the Word.

People are sometimes fascinated by my story. I would tell them that it is not about me. It is all about Jesus. Jesus is the almighty conqueror. We must always remember to give Jesus the Glory. Don't you ever forget it! Jesus is our knight in shining armor. Jesus is our refuge.

I have met preachers on the streets of San Francisco strung out on drugs. Held by Satan, the devil in a stronghold. Jesus refers me to Psalm 105:15 Saying, Touch not mine anointed, and do my prophets no harm. Because when Jesus sends his Sons out in the wilderness without hotel or motel money they have already done their job. Who are you to judge my Sons?

It was not unusual to see long lines of people gathered in front of the theatre on Market Street. It was not unusual to see a man or a woman feeding the pigeons on the side walk. It was not unusual to see a great influx of visitors with a tour guide. It was not unusual to see the vagrant pushing a go-cart with empty cans or bottles and taking them to a nearby sight to be paid for their hard earned work.

Romans 12: 2 And be not conformed to this world: at night, when you roam the streets of San Francisco, you bear witness to Jesus like no other. I remembered as clear as the sun rises in the morning and the sun sets in the evening, sitting in the restaurant having a fish burger, French fries and coffee. It was two in the morning. Nodding over my food, I was awakened by voices. A young man, neatly dressed with a black jacket and slacks, weighing about 150 pounds. He sat in front of me with three women giving out drugs to each one of them to go sell.

I knew that he was armed. I also knew that he knew that I was the prophet. Because he sat at ease, no care in the world. He was carrying out his transactions as though he was at his house. It was pungent. On reflection, I recalled a night at a McDonalds in Washington, Seattle. Before I could say Jesus, I was surrounded by the police. It was a sting operation. The police questioned my profusely. It told them that, "I am a preacher and a prophet and that I am homeless." In my hand was the Bible. They immediately left me to search a young woman, who apparently they had their eyes on.

Drugs permeate the city and county of San Francisco. Both the young and the old sell drugs on the streets in frisco. Young ladies are naked on the streets. Heroin is everywhere.

Jesus is saying to the psychic millionaires that your free ride are on the verge of destruction. You have been running from the name of Jesus. You have been poisoning my sheep far too long. You have been exploiting my children and putting them in the abyss of Hell. One day and a glorious day it will be, Jesus will descend upon you with a ball of fire in his hand. Jesus will open your mouth and place the fire therein. And woe will be your name.

Christians have spent billions of dollars playing scratch. Christians have spent billions of dollars playing the lotto. Christians have spent billions of dollars gambling horses. Christians have spent billions of dollars going to the boat to no avail.

Jesus is still saying, where is your love? How many times must I come to you in the midnight hour to show you that I care? How many times must I send prophets and prophetess to your home to tell you to change your ways? To stop burning candles; To seek my face; To speak to your neighbors; To lay the hammer down; To denounce revenge; Are you listening?

The drugs do not have to stay with you forever. Take a walk to the Pacific Ocean! See how calm the ocean is! Take up your Bible and begin to read the true Living Word of God! Jesus will always be around. Look to no other! There is no other.

At nighttime I would passed drums, tall drums, filled up with fresh bread decorating the outsides of hotels. Jesus is speaking to the owners of these hotels. You do not have to throw away all that bread. Come to Jesus! Jesus will teach you wisdom.

Jesus sends someone to knock on your door. Jesus sends someone that you do not know. Jesus sends someone that you have never met. Jesus wants you to open the door and attend to their needs. That person did not knock your door by accident. There are no accidents in Jesus. The name of Jesus is universal.

You open your door one morning and you see a family walking down the road. You know that the family is homeless. Invite them in and have a fun day with them. Please, do not give them a bottle of water. Much is given to you. Much more is demanded of you.

In the sky there are zillions of stars way up above. God the Father, God the Son, and God the Holy Spirit will be using them to build his New Earth.

One morning, I remembered the sign a preacher was holding up at the side of the metro station in San Francisco. The gist of the story was that one day God will destroy San Francisco. After spending four years on this beautiful peninsula, God gave me a Word that he would not destroy this city. The answer is ten just men.

I have had the good fortune to walk all over the city. I have met generations of native people who educated me on the good old days. The days when the natives of frisco would be well-dressed going to the theaters or to the movies. The native people do not say, "San Francisco," they say "frisco." They are black people with long, soft, black beautifully curled hair that extends to their hips. They really missed those nightly good old days.

You could hear the sadness in their voices. Broken pieces of bottle adorned the sidewalks. The windshields of expensive cars were smashed up almost nightly. Pieces of bottle scattered all over the streets. The gays and lesbians were constantly doing everything to take over this beautiful peninsula of Jesus. They got their gay bars, towns and shops.

They walked the inner cities all dressed up in expensive designed clothing. Cross-dressed walking hand in hand, as they exchanged kisses in public. Jesus is saying Enough is Enough. Jesus is saying take a look at yourself. What you see is definitely who you are? Having operations to change your sex, would not change your gender. Getting married would be considered BLASPHEMY.

Satan is who you got. Jesus knows that you can remove the mountain of homosexuality that harbors your body. Jesus expects you to pray. Jesus expects you to pray constantly. Jesus expects to lose yourself in Him. Jesus expects you to change your Pastor, if he did not have the gift to deliver satan out of you. Stop lying to yourself! Speak the truth! Let Jesus in!

People like you behave as though God the Father, God the Son, and God the Holy Spirit owes you something. Jesus died for you to have a place in my Father's House. God owes nobody anything.

In these End Times God the Father, God the Son, and God the Holy Spirit is not playing with anybody. The devil is already losing ground. Jesus knows what time it is. The devil will grow weaker and weaker and weaker as time goes by. Jesus rules Supreme. Jesus is not holding back. Jesus expects you to gain more confidence in your daily lives.

Jesus wants families to honor their mothers and their fathers. Take them out of Nursing Homes! It is your mother and your father. Wash the sheets and the pillow cases with the love of Jesus in your heart! Sweep their room first with the love of Jesus in your heart! Bathe them first with the love of Jesus in your heart! Sing their favorite hymns aloud with the love of Jesus in your heart! No one else could show them love but you.

When you did not do what you were told to do, you have allowed the devil to come in and control your home. Then you wonder why the new car did not come your way. You just held back your blessing. You placed it on a back burner and now you vex with Jesus. Jesus did not do that. You did that. We blame Jesus for everything. There was no money in the house. We blame Jesus. There was no insurance on the car. We blame Jesus. There was no food in the refrigerator. We blame Jesus. There was no money to pay the rent. We blame Jesus. Yes Jesus alone can fix it. But this one was on you, because you doubted Jesus.

Jesus is speaking to me since we spend too much time doing nothing. We pick and choose who to go visit at the hospital. And when we do go, we go empty handed. We forget our Bible. We stand there wondering, what to pray. All we have to say is "speak Lord your servant is listening."

We do not go to the prisons. The excuse is that the place is too far. The excuse is that I need gas money. You have a Pastor, use him. You cannot say that you love Jesus, when you cannot love your own. Wake up! You have been sleeping too long. You want Jesus to bless you, then go take the suffering. Charity suffers long and is kind. Thank God for the gift of longsuffering. It is a fruit of the Spirit.

For those of you who have not the means to get to the prisons. These are the guide lines for you to follow:

1. You should buy a set of envelopes and stamps and placed them in your favorite top drawer.
2. You should read Psalm 1 in its entirety before you write any form of literature.
3. Your letter should contain a litany of forgiveness and hope.
4. You should cherish your lover with a holy kiss.
5. And please do not remind him or her of their past.

Suffice it to say, that we must not abandon our dearly beloved brothers and sisters, husbands and wives at the penitentiary. It is all well and good to say lock him up and throw away the key. Beware of sheep in wolf clothing! The preachers that are given Prisons as a Ministry, they have a humongous work to do. Because the prisons are one of the institutions, that breed homosexuality and lesbianism.

Proverbs 13:12 Hope deferred maketh the heart sick, but when the desire cometh, it is a tree of life. Jesus our Lord and Savior reminds us that we cannot spear head anything by ourselves. We need Jesus in every fabric of our being. Self-will might gain us the presidency. Self-will might reward us with an Olympic gold medal. Self-will could blow your socks off your feet. Jesus reminds us daily to become humble. It is not about you. It is about Jesus.

We are all born sinners. Only Jesus is perfect. We will continuously be committing sins that we are not fully aware of. These are precisely the things that Jesus is talking about. Sins that god alone sees with his naked eyes. There are a whole lot of people that have passed on in this world that have never realized the hidden monster. It is a torment spirit that rides us everyday of our lives.

One day you would feel that you are perfect. That was the power of the spirit of torment. For those of us, who have family that are drunks, this is the spirit that possesses them. They would never be wrong in whatever they set out to do they would always be happy go lucky people. Without the alcohol they would become the devil. That means that the spirit would remain with them even in the grave. Their drive for Jesus was as far as their eyes could see. They would not go to hell when they die. Jesus knows that they have become afraid of their Lord.

On the other hand, the heroin addict reacts differently. He is always up, sleep evades him. He is a great pretender. This sick man will assume a very positive attitude. He will exhibit no fear. Friends of his will marvel at his energy level. He tires not.

The coke addict displays a very similar attitude. He eats a great deal of food. His clothes size will never increase or decrease. He will be smiling at everything you say. Do not question him! He will be on the defensive. His eyes will be flashing from side to side, because he has to see all moving things around him.

The crack coke addict is referred to as a junky. He sits one place for many hours seemingly oblivious to what is going on all around him. Faces he does not forget. He works for his juice. But you will never be able to find out who supplies him with drugs. That is one reason why the prisons are filled with the wrong culprits. A preponderance of the evidence is not enough for a conviction.

Those of us who are plagued with pill-popping sisters, have a great to learn from Jesus. There is a reason why they will take a pill. Spirits come in different forms and these are the best ways to describe them. These spirits will walk in and out your mouth. Because there are no covering for your mouth. They will sit on top of your head for easy entry and exit purposes. They will make you laugh at anything that passes you by.

Everybody wants to be like Jesus, but nobody wants to do the work of the Lord. From the time the doctors commit their siblings or their children to the mental institution their visits trickle down. They are referred to as "crazy." The mental institution is a Ministry. It is the right hand of Jesus. Come walk with Jesus and Jesus will make you free! This is no time to give up on your sweethearts. This is no time to flee. This is no time to abandon the ship. Jesus is in charge.

If the crucified one was paying you $2500 a minute, you would be on the job all day long. This is exactly what the risen Lord is paying you. But you prefer to leave him at the hospital and lose your fortune. Jesus gives you the visions, but you just cannot interpret them. You sit at the house believing what the psychiatrist telsl you that he will never make it.

Now you believe some false prophet telling you that your family is cursed. Your answer shall at all times be: get behind me Satan! And you shall see him flee. We live in a world of free speech; nobody cares about what they say. The news media play the same thing over and over again. The social media is one for publishing whatever they feel is right. The new fad is tweeting. The journalist writes the way he views it and the lists goes on. It reminds me of the world's crooked street in San Francisco.

When your best friend is mentally ill, do something about it. Take it to the Lord in prayer! Stay on Jesus till he pulls you through! Pay close attention to his promptings! He will lead you to the water. There you will find rest in Him. Pay no attention to the mumblings of your best friend! Do not get angry, as he paces the floor! Do not be dismayed with his loud speaking! This is the devil inside of him trying to scare you away.

Moses was told by Jesus to speak to the rock. Instead he struck the rock and God convicted he and his elder brother Aaron. They both lost entry into the Promise Land. The spirit of torment got them. So will the spirit of torment prevail over us, when we yield to temptation. God in his mercy did not abandon his two sons. He stayed with Moses to the end of his life.

How many 100-year old could climb any mountain to the very top? How many 105-year old could begin to ascend Mt. Everest? How many 110-year old could swim across the English Channel? How many 115-year old could walk 1,000 miles? How many 120-year old could climb Mt. Zion? Only one, his name is Moses. He alone has accomplished this phenomenon.

The spirit of torment trips us up. You are walking down the street as it were minding your own business. Someone crosses the road and threatens you. Your reaction is to become belligerent. God requires you to turn the other cheek. You believe that you are right to start a fight. Dead wrong! You hate to be called a coward. You must not give into the spirit of torment.

Peer pressure walks with an evil eye. They are aware that the Bible teaches that abortion is wrong. Yet they will go along with others. Or go along with the views of technocrats (another group of self-will people). Some people allow the professor or the admissions officer to place them into a lucrative discipline. Did Jesus tell you to pursue that major? If he questions you, you will say that the Pastor told you to pursue that major.

God sees everything, knows everything, even our most secret thoughts. Yet we pretend that Jesus only exists when we kneel in prayer. Nonsense. Jesus wants you to see him as the owner of the whole universe. He chooses you before the foundation of the world. You can sit there and cry all day long. You can hide your one talent. You can disregard his voice. You can lie and say that he never spoke to you. You can say that you do not need him for this or for that. Jesus hears your murmurings.

Jesus sees that you do not want the talent that he has blessed you with. Jesus sees that you do not want tobe called a chosen one. Jesus sees that you do not want him in your everyday life. You only want to use him as you see fit. You shall be able to go precisely where Jesus needs you the most. You shall be able to partake in the will of Jesus. You shall be able to say what Jesus wants you to say in church.

These are the ways of fallen men. These are the ways of men who are too ambitious. These are the ways of people that allow others to rule their path.

Shut-ins fall under the umbrella of the spirit of torment. Some churches do go door-to-door and they would come into contact with afew shut-ins. Visiting the sons and daughters of God that are caught and placed into strongholds are a noble task. You got to be willing to devote a great deal of time to these impoverished soldiers.

Some shut-ins require house repairs. Because poor souls, they have been lost but now are found. Pastors that have deacons who are jack of all trades can pitch in and get a tremendous blessing from the Lord. House repairs could be costly. Most times when these children of God are found, the house is about to fall. The yard has not been cleaned for years. Dumpsters have been stolen. Deprivation is the order of the day.

It is a monumental task. Sometimes the whole church has to get involve. Sometimes the whole neighborhood has to get involve. Sometimes other churches in the immediate tiny town have to get involve. There are no free blessings. Nothing happens by accident. It is very easy to give up. It is very easy to say that nobody will give you a penny to complete this job.

Jesus is solemnly present especially in impossible situations. The greater the risk, the more purposeful you have to become in order to win this great battle. The road to Jesus is narrow, steep and dangerous: this is why few would be tenacious. Most times us Christians would do our utmost best to avoid this walk with the Lord Jesus. As soon as we are aware that we earnestly need Jesus; our walk with Jesus have now begun.

For your goodness: God the Father, God the Son, and God the Holy Spirit will open a new Ministry in the church. Business owners all over the state will come knocking on your door to supply you with everything. You do not have to ask Jesus for a Ministry. Jesus will come upon you and anoint you and add Ministries to the fold. You do not have to force your parishioners to pay there tithes and offerings. You do not have to talk down to your members at the church. You do not have to raise hell in the house of the Lord.

It is all good to say that you are the Pastor of this great Church. But are you taking calls after midnight? Are you keeping a pantry at the church? Are you encouraging your members to bring can goods to the church to give to others that are in need? Are you seeking out the sick in your neighborhood for the congregation to pray for the infirm? And for the members of the church to go visit in a timely fashion.

Are you praying for the dead? Are you lifting them up in prayer every Sunday morning? Are you helping to finance burials not just for church members? Are you feeding the poor? You see that there is a whole lot of work to do. The dead needprayers at the grave site. Their souls have not been risen to go with the Lord.

Some people incarcerate their own selves. You never see them. You never hear from them. They do not telephone anyone. They do not answer the telephone. They just exists. Living the life of a loner is a miserable empty life. Members of the family need to be vigilant. God did not forget them. Jesus did not forget them. Holy Spirit did not forget them.

This is prayer in action. Members of families need to form groups to visit their siblings, sons and daughters, whenever they become absent in mind and in body. Walk with your Bibles! There are some things that you do not need your Pastor for. There are some things that you can do for yourselves. God wants you to love him. God wants to show you the power of prayer. God wants you to see His power as you read His Word.

There is on assumption a blind one in the family. Seek him out! Go clean the house! Go clean the yard! Take a barber with you or a cosmetologist! Get him new clothes! Bring him to church! Jesus knows that he wants to fall asleep. Jesus is not ready to take him away. Jesus wants to show his love.

Genesis 28:14 And thy seed shall be as the dust of the earth, and thou shalt spread abroad to the west, and to the east, and to the north, and to the south; and in thee and in thy seed shall all the families of the earth be blessed.

The family shut-in is a growing anomaly in this 21st Century. They are shut-in because they choose to live apart from their very own. They change their customs and cultural heritage, so as not to be identified with the seed of Jesus. They go not to Holy Spirit Churches. They live in rural tiny towns hidden from the rest of the world. Some of them will change their family surnames.

The expatriates are a perfect example of the family shut-in. they are seen running from country to country to find success in another man's land. Ostracize by their very own as they huddle together trying to make it by the grace of Our Lord Jesus Christ. God does not like ugly; he is full of mercy and abiding in faith and love.

We often say, "take me to the water." In this case the narrative does not apply to baptism. Jesus is mysterious for the three in one is a mystery. Without water we will all grow thirsty. We have to go through great lengths, breath and height to drink from the water gushing out from the side of Jesus. With the hope that we will nourish each other, as we walk with Jesus hand in hand.

We got to learn to seek out each other, and when found open up to one another for Jesus to come in, and heal our hearts. We alone cannot do this great work. It is a job of enormous magnitude. Heaven alone can and will help us. Heaven alone is the only way to the top of this gigantic water peak.

The Word of God does not go void. Jesus says in his word that he will bless his seed. We are his seed. One night, as we roll in our beds to sleep, he suddenly wakes us up and tell us to go visit a remote neighborhood. Success is in the air. We meet a very shy family that is unwilling to bend. A week later the Lord sends us back to the very same family. They apologize and say that, "they have no clothes." Obliging, we return with clothes for the entire family. This is the goodness of Jesus.

You fall asleep at the bus stop and in that moment, you were blessed with a vision that God is going to give you money. You immediately wake up. You did not miss the bus. At this time, God is not saying or giving you a specific reason or command as to how to spend this money. If you are a preacher that means that you will be building a church from the ground up. If you are congregation that means that you will be building a house from the ground up.

Jesus seizes the moment that you can run, but you cannot hide. The stubborn family shut-in cannot escape the mysteries of Jesus. There is something that Jesus will do so that someone will discover the family. A great athlete will emerge from the family. The coach will be determined to meet with the family. The child will become a great one.

Scouts will follow the athlete to his home in order to meet with the family. Dad cannot hold back the tears, because he had dreamt all about this moment a very long time ago. Do not play with Jesus! Journalists will seek you out no matter what. Writers will be up in your face to signature your first book.

The angels of the heavenly hosts will encamp about you. Sleepless nights you will have. Long days and longer still will come over you. Jesus cuts a new road for you to follow. You will see him in the distance beckoning you to come. You will see him at the top of the mountain waiving you on. Jesus will show you himself, as you ascend the mountain high.

The family shut-in will then grow in leaps and bounds, spreading the good news of Our Lord Jesus wherever they go. Jesus will now tend to the sheep. Jesus will now tend to the heaping of the first fruits. Jesus will now tend to widely increasing the number of the family.

Promises by God the Father, God the Son, and God the Holy Spirit will be made. The generations to come will know all about these promises. Because the spoken word will emerge around family tables. The spoken word will emerge at family reunions. The spoken word will emerge at funerals. The spoken word will emerge at visits to the hospitals. Jesus will use the family to bear witness wherever they shall go. They will be a force to be reckon with as the Lord increases the love for each other. We are truly our brother's keeper.

Children strapped in foster-care homes have become shut-ins. Far too often society excludes the Universal Church that is anointed by God to take care of all children needs. Children that are abandoned and left on someone'sdoorstep, should be given to the Pastors of the respective neighborhood, rather than to someone else. The devil is likened to a roaring lion and he will devour anything that is put in his way.

Society does not want to acknowledge God's anointed sons as true sons of the Living God. They take the law into their own hands. They do as they like. Foster-care children need discipline and this means discipline for real. Pastors and their first ladies demonstrate this type of behavior both in the home and at the church. God the Father, God the Son, and God the Holy Spirit transforms his sons and his daughters. This is a miracle at work.

Foster-care children come with all kinds of ill-health. Preachers and their wives will be given a Word from the Lord to deliver and make free a child of Jesus. Sunday mornings they will be at church. The children will be singing in the choir or taught to play a musical instrument of their choice. They also will be in attendance at Sunday school.

Attendance and punctually are virtues. School is a must. Homework shall be done at all times. The children will be taken to the libraries frequently to learn how to read and write. As for those who are athletic, the same attention shall be paid to their respective disciplines. God does not make mistakes. Only mortals make errors. It is all well and good to say that life is too hard. Do not cry about it!

Children are the future. Orphanages are not the best place to raise children. Absolutely no children shall be given to homosexuals, lesbians or handed over to extended family couples. To gain respect we must show respect. Jesus was fostered by his father Joseph. It is plain to see that God the Father does not have any weaknesses whatsoever. Jesus grew in wisdom and knowledge in the house of Joseph.

How is it that we are not following the good example of our earthly parents of Jesus? We are too quick to make changes to God unchanging hands. Things must always go the way that we want them to go. The whole wide world is guilty of changing the decrees of Jesus. This good thing was put in place by Our Heavenly Father because Jesus had already known the outcome and the future of this planet.

Jesus is once again teaching us by his earthly example, that only a husband and wife can truly take care of fostering a child. Not what we choose to call husband and wife. And placing our judgment on our own wisdom, which is foolishness in the sight of God. You better believe it!

Foster-care children need our undivided attention. They need us to be there for them in every possible way. And of course, time shall be put aside for socializing. Sunday evenings, you can take them out to the movies. Or take them out to the parks. Where they can play games, ride their bicycles or play and have fun for the rest of the evening.

Taking care of children that are not yours biologically is not an easy thing to do. This is a gift or a blessing from the Lord. Patience you must possess. Tolerance is a dire need. It would be a greater blessing, if you can get the entire family to be fostered in your care. In this way, everyone is accounted for and they would grow to appreciate and to understand each other.

There are too many rules and regulations that one has to meet in order to qualify or to become the parents of these children that are left behind. Society feeds off each other instead of the table of the Lord Jesus. We put away our Bibles as soon as we get home, and forget Jesus for the rest of the week. We become nonchalant.

Because we are Gentiles found in every corner of the earth, and spread throughout the length and the breadth of this planet, we are the seed of the Patriarch. Divinely blessed wherever we inhabit and call home. Jesus is the sole voice crying in our wilderness that is our body. Seek and you shall find! Jesus commands that you find him.

Firstly, you should follow the voice of Jesus talking to you deep within. Jesus will call his own name to reassure you that he alone can say Jesus and nobody else. The devil cannot say the name Jesus. Beelzebub cannot say the name Jesus. Jesus will constantly call his name Jesus within you for you to understand that you are definitely speaking to Jesus.

Jesus just does not compare his seed as the dust of the earth: we are his seed to bring down the curtains of his resurrection before the closure of the world. We are the ones to stand up and be counted for Jesus. We are the ones chosen to spread His Word, moreso in life and death situations—not relenting to no one. We shall no give up our position. We shall not back down. We shall not runaway.

Yes, he is the answer. We do not need to ask Jesus a question or questions. We have already realized that Jesus shall not be questioned. For the unemployed, Jesus got a whole lot of vacancies. Just apply! Jesus will teach you all about the job and you do not need a resume. Now you are conscious of His Greatness. Jesus is the Almighty. Jesus is the I am who I am sent you.

Countless children shall come out of every generation. Babies everywhere! In the Pentateuch, Moses was mandated by Jesus to number all of Israel's children. In obedience, he did. Moses proved to his people that when given a command by His Lordship—do it. In these end times, we are mandated by Jesus to become much more ferocious than Lucifer, the devil.

We must spread the name of Jesus in every tiny town, in every city, in every parish, in every district, in every capital, in every province, in every state and in every country. That is why Jesus made our seed as the dust of the earth. We got work to do. We can no longer sit idly by and let the devil trample all over us. Satan had already declared war on us from the first day that God the Father and God the Son threw him out of Heaven.

We are presently bearing witness to all of the evil one's threats. There is always something on the news media. There is always something to take our eyes off Jesus. There is always something for us to look the other way—some preconceive notion. Jesus is with you always; do not care how dismal it looks.

And thy seed shall be as the dust of the earth: out of thy seed would breathe nations of people. A peculiar people. A people that no one want to tolerate. A people whose ethnicity breathe violence. People take offence by the way you walk. People take offence by your accent. People take offence by the way you comb your hair. People take offence when they become aware of the town or the city you came from.

Jesus had already told you so. What is the problem? You cannot force anyone to like you. They do not want you around. Take it to Jesus in prayer! Give him the fight! You are in love with someone whom you have never seen. His name is Jesus. You are blessed twice, because you have never seen Jesus in the flesh.

God the Father had blessed you and your seed even before Moses began to write it down. God the Father and his Son had already discussed this even before the foundations of the world. All of this provoked Lucifer, the devil. He hated the name Jesus whilst he lived in Heaven.

Jesus came to make you free. Jesus came to free you from the wiles of the devil. Jesus came to free you and take you out of bondage. Jesus came to deliver you from all evil. Jesus came to anoint you so that no one steals anything from you anymore. Jesus came to baptize you in the name of Jesus. Jesus came to baptize you with water and fire. Jesus came to baptize you with his Holy Spirit. Jesus came to confess of your sins one to each other. Jesus came to baptize you in the precious Blood of Jesus. Jesus came to eat of his body in the form of the Eucharist—the breaking of the bread. Jesus came to drink of his blood in the form of grape juice.

Jesus is taking the dust that you are made up of and sprinkle it all over the land. The planet is harboring too much sickness. God relents for cures to come in. Jesus is lengthening the lives of some preachers who are chosen to clean out the house. The devil is continually disorganizing families. The devil is continually ruining entire generations. The devil is on the rampant. But God is alive.

Jesus keeps us breathing not just by the circulation of the blood, no, no, no, because he gives us hope. His book the "Apocalypse" is to spread hope out, amidst all of the turmoil. Jesus is there. When we acknowledge Jesus as our Lord and Savior, the devil gets mad.

Jesus and his Father are building a new heaven and a new earth. Whether we believe this or not it will come to pass.

Some people are afraid of the book of Revelation. Foolishness. God is not the author of fear. Jesus job is easy. All he asks of you is to follow him. Follow him wherever he leads you! Follow him as he ascends his mountain of love! Follow him through thick and thin! Let him lead and you just follow!

This is our only fear. We humans are frail and fragile. We treat Jesus as our parents. We treat Jesus as our teachers. We have to know where we are going before we make a move. We got to have money for the taxi. We got to have money for breakfast, lunch and dinner. Jesus must first answer all of our questions. We have been brainwashed. We must learn to walk blindly.

When we ask questions, the devil is listening to our every question. And like a whole lot of people, he is taking notes to set us up. Have you ever been lost? Is there anyone around you to question? You got to trust Jesus. We are angry, but we are speaking to Jesus. We are mumbling, but we are speaking to Jesus. We are fearful, but we are speaking to Jesus. Jesus placed you in that situation. Did you see him? No, no, no, you did not. Perfect example!

The next day you are telling the story and smiling. If it happens again, what would you be doing? Trusting in Jesus is tantamount.

Unexpected visitors stopped by the house. You opened the door, come to find out that they are preaching Jesus. You ushered them out, because the football game took precedence over Jesus. You just lost your blessing. Yes Jesus did bless the seed. But which God are you serving now. You cannot use Jesus. Jesus will spit you out. You cannot charm Jesus. Jesus will put your blessings on a back burner. You got to be real.

Jesus wants you to love his book of Revelation. Jesus wants you to read the book of Revelation. Jesus wants you to read to your children the book of Revelation. By doing this, you slam the devil out of your house and its surroundings. Your visions are broaden. Your children will remain bless. Your keys: you will not have to look for. When you return home your house will not be ruined. Jesus is continuously there for you: all you need to do is to follow him.

The book of Revelation is a very serious, truthful, and awesome Word of Jesus. Its substance is pure and divine. It is pointless to believe that you can gain knowledge from this book without the gift of humility. Human beings should pray to Our Lord Jesus to prepare them in the spirit of truthfulness when examining the book of Jesus. The anointed preachers and/or Pastors, who are given this book to elucidate would not be afraid of the devil and his band of angels.

There is a great deal of things to be revealed before the Son of Man returns to the face of the earth. We are blessed to be living in these times to see the goodness of Jesus. To see his greatness. To see his power displayed. Jesus is invariably waiting for you, waiting until the last one goes through the door of forgiveness.

We got to learn to forgive in order to obtain the gift of hope. Without hope we cannot get to love. We cannot see the face of Jesus. We cannot see the crucified one. We cannot see the one who is to come. Jesus wants you to pick up your cross and follow him. Jesus will not turn you away. Jesus will no hide his face from you. Jesus will not allow the devil to devour you. Jesus is the Light of the World.

When you pray Jesus will keep your sons and your daughters safely in his arms.

And thy seed shall be as the dust of the earth, and shall spread to communist Russia, communist China, communist North Korea and communist Cuba. Jesus is the one and only true living Son of God the Father. Jesus demands respect from all countries. None is excluded.

All countries whether they are rich or poor shall not inherit the kingdom of God. Satan, the devil shall devour all flesh. On opening the graves to examine dead bodies, the corpses will not be found. Graves will be rearrange and darkness shall not cease.

3. To Lay Foundation

Genesis 1:1 In the beginning God created the heaven and the earth. Jesus had already known that the day of the millennials will come. The day when 18-year old men and women will be targeted and shot down in the streets of America, because of the color of their skin.

At 17 years old, I remembered going to see a movie that was documented and shown at the Deluxe Cinema in Trinidad. All colleges and all high schools were ordered by the then government to go and see this movie. It was based on Apartheid, in the republic of South Africa, a rigid policy of segregation of the non-white population. This was the year 1968.

School children between the ages of seven to 20 years old were gunned down in the streets, in the day time, because they were black. This is the same thing that will occur on the streets of America, if America continues in denial of present-day happenings. The new adults of today will not tolerate and forebear what their fathers and their mothers endured or forced to endure from present-day congress.

Racial profiling that is done all across America, especially by the State Police must cease. Systemic slavery must be abolished from the East, West, North and South of all America. America needs a renaissance. Far too often, the untouchables try to ignore the signs. Jesus is not going to relent. Jesus hears the cries of his children, who are forbidden to walk the streets at night. Jesus hears the cries of his children, who are told to get out of this neighborhood.

All Christians Churches that refuse to come to the aid of these little ones will be held accountable by the precious blood of Jesus. No man came on the face of the earth with anything in his pockets. No man was given total ownership of anything on the face of the earth. No man has the perfect right to any land on earth. Jesus reigns supreme. Do not shut him out!

Provocation of the millennials will turn your days into nights and your nights into days. Your history books are on the shelves of the libraries all across the country. God has gifted them to read and write and to understand things of the future that you are not equipped to ascertain. Every generation comes to the earth to carry out a job given to them by Jesus. Take heed America! Do not listen to outside influences!

The future of any country is its children. Sometimes you have to sit back and listen to the voice of Jesus, which is the voice of the little ones that you are caring for. Jesus is in control. Jesus does not want your help. Jesus is gently touching you to listen to the voice of innocence. Jesus is gently touching you to open your Bibles and read. Jesus is anointing some of you to bring about change in the future.

Jesus created the heaven and the earth, when we were not formed in our mothers' wombs. Jesus walked the face of the earth praying that his heavenly father will bless the seed of the patriarch even beyond the earth. Jesus sprinkled his blood wherever he went. Jesus will not hide his face no more.

When you are loving on Jesus he is going to take you there. You do not have to be special he is going to take you there. You do not have to be perfect he is going to take you there. You do not have to be scholastic he is going to take you there. You do not have to be rich he is going to take you there. You do not have to be a billionaire he is going to take you there.

The millennials are already having a tuft time with the transgender in the society. The government of America has passed the laws for men to marry men and girls to marry girls. This have further pressured the tears of Christian children across the land. Jesus is saying that America will pay a high price, a very high price for this nasty evil. Preachers and Pastors have long been targeted by technocrats as having no power, but some power. Jesus is saying that he will not forget.

In the beginning god created the heaven and the earth. Jesus and his heavenly Father created the heavens. When a child looks up into the sky, he sees a blue sky, clouds and at night the stars and the moon. He definitely does not see the angels and the saints. The child is amiss when he hears the Bible talks about heavenly creatures and bodies. To explain these phenomena are a mystery to unfold.

Jesus places on the face of the earth preachers and prophets to break down the mysteries of the universe. A formidable task. A steep mountain to climb in order to receive the word from God the Father. So-called pundits, which are called false prophets also inhabit this world. Coupled with all these different denominations scattered to the ends of the earth are a sure sign that one day something will occur.

No one got to be educated to unwind the signs of God. All it takes is Jesus to disclose the mysteries of his heavenly hosts. A gift that is freely given by God just for the asking. Be it as it may, 99.99 per cent of the world is yet to ask for this truly divine gift. Money tops the asking.

Jesus has given us precious children to raise up in the fear of the Lord. We often wonder why Jesus created the heaven because we do not think that we can ever make it. For us it is not a foregone conclusion. Our behavior becomes pathetic. Just remember you ask not; you receive not. Jesus has equipped all of us with a measure of faith.

The heavens are there to show you that Jesus has opened a door for you. Jesus is very much aware that the enemy will do everything to stop you from entering. Be not dismay! Press on! A woman in labor has to push and push and push to give birth to her wonderful son or daughter. A miracle of Jesus. A miracle that everyone takes for granted. This is the time for everyone to start talking about heaven. This is the time for everyone to start thinking about what a wonderful place Jesus is preparing for us as a family.

Satan, the devil, is not preparing a wonderful place for anyone. Only the Father, the Son and the Holy Spirit is preparing a place call home. Sweet Jesus wants you home. Jesus wants you to gather yourselves together and pray. Open up prayer lines from country to country! Write letters to friends overseas!

Jesus is about saving families. The family that prays together stays together. This is real. Create a heaven on earth! Everybody has a lunch break. Everyone could meet at any restaurant in the neighborhood and pray and share. To the beach lovers: arrange a day or a weekend for the entire family to read the Word of God and have fun. To the movie goers: arrange a day to meet and enjoy a good movie together.

It is good to be in the house of the Lord. Make Tuesdays a day for families to pray and share a meal! Make heaven your topic of discussion! Quote stories of Jesus's resurrection and his ascension into heaven! And do not forget to talk about Jesus's return to the earth to stay with his disciples for forty days and forty nights.

The visit of the angel to Abraham and his wife Sarah, who was sterile. The meal of a young sheep, that Abraham prepared for the heavenly angel. The miracle of Sarah's baby Isaac: prophesized by the angel. Sarah giving birth to a child at age 90—a sight to behold.

Jacob falling asleep in the wilderness and using a rock as a pillow, when God the Father awoke him and told him that his seed would be like the dust of the earth and they would be blessed for generations to come. We are presently seeing the reality of this prophecy. It is still being fulfilled to this very day. Elijah the prophet being taken up into heaven by a chariot of fire. One of the few men, who walked the face of the earth that physically did not die on this planet.

The great vision of the king of Egypt, that Joseph one of the younger sons of Jacob, disclosed the meaning of the king's vision. Freed by the Pharaoh, whilst in prison, and made governor of Egypt. Produce enormous food for seven years, thus saving the lives of the Egyptians and his father and brothers' lives—ending a great famine.

Luke 6:48 He is like a man which built an house, and digged deep, and laid the foundation on a rock: and when the flood arose, the stream beat vehemently upon that house, and could not shake it: for it was founded upon a rock.

Luke 6: 49 But he that heareth, and doeth not, is like a man that without a foundation built an house upon the earth; against which the stream did beat vehemently, and immediately it fell; and the ruin of that house was great.

Saturday, August 6, 2016 marked the beginning of the 31st Olympics held in Rio de Janeiro. A house that was built without foundation. Jesus is saying that zealousness is not of God. The Olympics is not of God. God gives gifts that live on forever and ever and ever. Train the child whilst he is young for tomorrow he would not sway. This is a good example of self-will. Yet everyone is perched looking vehemently at a man-made event.

Jesus says I come to give life more abundantly. No preacher that is anointed by Our Lord Jesus Christ to bring his Word can dope himself and still deliver Jesus's Word in spirit and in truth. Doped athletes, if not discovered would set world records. And that is why Russia was banned. A country that suppressed its own people. A country that would do anything to be worshipped and adored. Their impassioned behavior would never end. Yes, some of them were allowed to participate simply because they were dopefree.

Every country that is represented at the games had a flag. Where was God flag? Everybody flag was colored. Where was God colored flag? The games were opened by a torchbearer lighting a fire that would burn till the end of the games. That bears no relationship with God the father, God the Son, and God the Holy Spirit. When you do things without Jesus's anointing then you do it in vain. All countries that are represented at the games should be ashamed of themselves, especially the countries that called themselves Christians.

Jesus is not playing games with the minds of his children. The world would make you believe anything; the world brainwashes you. Everybody at the games was there to steal God's Glory. Jesus says ask and you shall receive, seek and you shall find, knock and the door will open unto you. As soon as you find Jesus, now you would understand the very depth of the life of Jesus. What he had been through.

There is a format. There are guide lines for you to follow. Listen to his voice and come follow him! You wake up in the morning surrounded by an ocean of water. Seek his face! Your baby cries all night. Seek his face! You have a miscarriage. Seek his face! Your baby is born still-birth. Seek his face! You are up all night pacing the floor. Seek his face! Your house is on fire. Seek his face!

Jesus is assembling his people. Did he speak to you?

Invariably, Jesus is in the driving seat. Are you allowing him to do the driving? Must he keep taking away the steering wheel from your hands? Jesus wants you to slow down. Stop the running around! You keep praying the same prayers everyday. Change it! You keep following your lover everyday pretending that you were just in the neighborhood. Cut it out!

Jesus is the same yesterday as he is today. You better believe it! Jesus goes around showing his people their pitfalls. Of course, they doubt Jesus. Jesus goes around showing his people their downfalls. They ignore him. Jesus goes around showing his people their misgivings. They do not believe it. What more must Jesus do?

Jesus is everybody's everything. Jesus knows everybody's everything. Yet everybody tries to hide their everything. Jesus wants to give you his goodness. The whole wide world is lacking in goodness. Won't you come follow Jesus. Jesus is waiting for you. Jesus is standing there waiting for you. Jesus is solemnly standing there waiting for you. Jesus wants you to receive him with the spirit of gladness.

Jesus wants you to have his bouquet of flowers.

Jesus is the man that built his house on solid ground. Jesus is showing you that he is seeing you coming in the distance. It is Jesus's job to build your house on a rock. Jesus is the lifebeater. Jesus is the architect. Jesus is the plumber. Jesus is the mason. Jesus is the cabinetmaker. Jesus is your rivers of water.

Too many times people are seen going the wrong way, calling the psychic hot lines, and expecting Jesus to build their house on a good foundation. Jesus is the apple of your eye. Jesus will wake up your mother and send her over to your house to tell you to stop the gambling. You on the other hand, will tell her a whole bunch of lies. Even swearing that you will never do this on grandmother's grave.

Jesus wants the best for you—the very best. When Jesus blesses husband and wife with eight children, he provides the father with enough land and money for each of them to own their home. Jesus does not want you to go begging for bread. Calling the psychic hot line will eventually cause you to fall and become destitute. You have just dug your own grave. That is what you do when you are lukewarm.

Jesus comes to you in the midnight hour. And like Jacob he will give you a vision surrounding you with beautiful trees, springs, wells and the tallest mountains that you have ever seen. Jesus makes it abundantly clear that he is giving you a beautiful house. Immediately thereafter, Jesus awakes you only to find out that you were hanging out with the Lord. Now you are expecting that beautiful house. Every time you tell someone about your vision they do not believe you. So you stop talking. Years later here comes the house.

Jesus is teaching you so that you could teach others his ways. But when you keep procrastinating then you would have lost the treasure which the Lord has built deep within you. Jesus is immaculate. The good Lord is showing me that a whole lot of people keep tripping and falling. There is nothing to grasp; nothing to hold on too.

Looking at the news one day in August, 2016, the state of California was in flames, 1,000's of acres of land were burning rapidly. Homes were destroyed. Families were dislocated. The point was whether or not the state or the government would reimburse the homeowners was not the point. Jesus is saying Enough is Enough.

Jesus is about troubled minds. Fear steps in. There is an answer for everything under heaven. Are you listening? Seek you first the kingdom of heaven and his righteousness and everything will be added unto you. You are definitely the downfall of your own shortcomings. Stay awake and pray with Jesus!

Jesus is about laying his foundation on the earth as it is in heaven. Jesus is continually showing his hands to you in order that you turn away from all evil. Jesus is reassuring you by your pitfalls that he is the one true Son of the Most High. Your steps are guided by the light of Jesus. Jesus orders your steps. Jesus opens your eyes for you to see wondrous things. Jesus opens your mouths to speak words of wisdom.

The house that Jesus is building for you will be built on good soil. The house will have no wrinkles. There will be no debt owed on the house. No second mortgages will be put on this house. Satan, the devil, cannot set fire to this house. Satan, the devil, cannot ruin this house by floods. Satan, the devil, can never make you homeless. Satan, the devil, cannot put this house up for sale.

Jesus is your knight in shining armor. Jesus is going to make you free. Jesus is going to clean the whole house out. The furniture you always wanted, Jesus would give it to you. The new car you see in the show window would one day show up at your door step. The hats, handbags, dresses and shoes would one day be in your bedroom closet. Jesus gives you everything.

The tears running down your cheeks would one day be dried up. The wrinkles in your face would one day be smoothed out. The belligerent neighbors would one day cease. The children that brought you tears because of unforgiveness would one day bring you great joy. Jesus remembers.

Jesus knows that you are bearing the pains of suffering for righteousness sake. This is not evil. This is good.

We take pride in slandering each other on *Facebook*. We take pride in showing our nakedness on *facebook*. We have made *facebook* our god. We have made *facebook* our knight in shining armor. We have made *facebook* our heaven on earth. The owner of *facebook* is just as evil, evil, evil.

Ephesians 1: 4 According as he hath chosen us in him before the foundation of the world, that we should be holy and without blame before him in love:

God is an on time God. The arrival of Jesus, which had already been spoken and prophesied by so many prophets as it is written in the book of the Old Testament is a perfect tool for His Holiness. Be ye holy as I am holy! This testimony lived by Jesus on a day-to-day basis created hemorrhage in the minds and hearts of unbelievers. They did everything to destroy his teachings. They showed him maps to prove that there word came from god.

In other words, human beings must nail god down as to how many ingredients the sesame seeds contain. Printing it up nd laying out all the calories and sticking it on the backs or sides of all manufacturing goods on the market shelves. God is Holy. Discontinue that practice! It is not for you to know God's business. It is not for you to question him as you do in your classrooms. God is not a human being. Think strongly and clearly about it!

Jesus is not in the gymnasium. Jesus is not in the boxing. Jesus is not in the track and field. Jesus is not in the wrestling. Jesus is not in the hoopla. Examine your minds!

Take a step forward! Yes Jesus is conscious of the fact that you will be beaten on that vey leg. It is okay. It is good to suffer for Jesus. Yes there are some churches that believe that the good Lord Jesus Christ had already paid the price for your suffering. Then why are you suffering? In this case your suffering is a fruit of the spirit. It is called long suffering. Everybody wants to build the house without foundation.

Jesus hath chosen us in him before the foundation of the world. Jesus creates more value as to why he came and rose again and is to come. Our purpose is to edify Jesus in every aspect of our being. We bless our breakfastevery morning. We bless our lunch every midday. We bless our dinner every night. Jesus never came to bless that food anyhow because your hands are dirty. The family will continually be sick until your hands become clean.

The truths of life will be easier for you now since Jesus has given you sweet favor. There is a people that need to taste the favor of the Lord. They want his favor but do not know how to achieve this blessing. They are all shattered and frenzied. They are all puzzled. They are all perplexed.

Jesus is in his tent. Jesus is continuously working in heaven to bring about new change on the earth.

Jesus is not to be held under a mirror for you to read and see his every move. The astronauts that God has blessed with his gift in physics should not allow outside influences to use and abuse Jesus's gifts to carry out their motives of spying on heavenly beings. The earth is full of rubbish. Do not add to it! Turn around and let God use you for something more beautiful and more effective!

There was a period, in ancient times, that angels would leave heaven and pay a visit to humankind. These times were recorded in history books world over. Since then man has continued to ignore Jesus as the Son of God on the face of the earth and has broken his bond of trust with Jesus. Ultimately, God the Father has stopped the angels from visiting the earth.

It is not a race to find truth. It is not the use of human wisdom to penetrate the wisdom of God. If God the Father really wants you there, he will give you a vision. Taking directives from groups of people because they are funding all your other operations, are not an answer to become a byproduct.

Jesus is not tricked even by the genius of earthly creatures. Jesus is not fooled even by the craftiness of satan, the devil. Jesus is not manipulated by mankind. Jesus is not driven by the threats of the tongues of earthly creatures speaking on behalf of satan.

Jesus is the whirlwind. When Jesus returns to the earth, he will return in the form of the very same whirlwind that he returned to his apostles. His entry will be magnanimous. Earth will be asleep as Jesus touches down. A wave of light will only be seen by the chosen children of God.

2 Timothy 2:19 Nevertheless the foundation of God standeth sure, having this seal, The Lord knoweth them that are his. And, Let every one that nameth the name of Christ depart from iniquity.

Where is the book that satan, the devil, has written. Yet we follow him. Jesus is creative. Satan is not creative. Jesus is innovative. Satan is not innovative. Jesus is the genius of all geniuses. Satan is not a genius. Jesus is the Lamb of God. Satan is a fallen angel. Jesus is the king of kings and lords of lords. Satan is the devil. Jesus is all truth. Satan is a bunch of lies. Jesus is the morning star. Satan is a fallen star.

Nevertheless the foundation of God standeth sure, having this seal. Which seal are you bearing? The seal of satan is borne in your hands. Whatever you touch would be dirty. The seal of the devil is mean spirited. The seal of Lucifer is wickedness in high places. The seal of the one that brings fear and makes you afraid, even so afraid of Jesus the Lord. The seal of the fictitious one will continually be trying to win you over.

On the day that you were baptized in the water, you were sealed by Jesus. On the day that you were given his Holy spirit and you received him and embodied his fire, you were double-sealed by Jesus. When you were called to preach his Word, you were triple-sealed by Jesus. Then his anointing start to flow on you, now you are becoming his very own. You have entered his transformation process. This process is likening you to Jesus. You will walk like Jesus. You will talk like Jesus. You will be fashioned like Jesus.

Every one who cometh in the name of Jesus is strengthened by his mercy and is given his grace to help them to depart from all evil. Sunday morning worshipers like me must adhere to these principles of God the Father, God the Son, and God the Holy Spirit. "the Truth is not spoken on the pulpit." These prophetic words the Lord Jesus allowed me to speak in a church, one Sunday morning, in the City of Valdosta, Georgia. The year was 2001.

Jesus is coming to destroy. Jesus is all about his truthful book called the "Bible." Jesus encourages you to speak the truth. You do not have to lie to the congregation to obtain more money fromtheir pockets. You do not have to run cake sales and raffles to help you pay the expenditures of the church. You do not have to economize to run the affairs of the church. You do not have to go begging Wal-Mart and other companies for money to aid you in your Ministry. God provides.

Jesus is not about you helping him out. Jesus does not need your help. Jesus does not need your sympathy. It is sinful to tempt Jesus. This is exactly what you are doing. It is sinful to tempt God the Father. It is sinful to tempt God the Holy Spirit.

It is utterly sinful and an abomination in the sight of God to produce a movie about Jesus's intimacy with Mary Magdalene. Blasphemy! The City and County of San Francisco are not to be blamed for this production. The LGBT group is responsible for this propaganda. Jesus is saying only a very few of you will enter the kingdom of heaven. And for those of you who have tried in vain to stop this vulgarity and temerity, yours is the kingdom of heaven.

Jesus is cleaning the house out. Jesus is reminding the faithful families, who are praying for their homosexual sons and daughters that their hour are at hand. One day before the close of this century your sons, daughters, siblings and best friends will receive a whirlwind of deliverances. The decapitation of the head of satan.

Jesus is calling you to bear witness to the truth, the whole truth and nothing but the truth so help you God. Jesus is fully aware that some of you have no knowledge of these deep wounds that Jesus must bear. These atrocities of life. The people that have given their souls to the devil. They do not care what they say or do. The devil takes care of them. They will go to the cemetery and spit on their mothers' and fathers' graves. They blame them for their once abject poverty.

And, Letevery one that nameth the name of Christ depart from iniquity. Jesus is saying that at the closure of the Olympics at Rio de Janeiro the people of Brazil assembled in the form of a picture of Our Lord Jesus Christ. Being devoted or diligent do not make you Christ like. Jesus sat at the bar and they, the population, judged him as a drunk. Pastor and the first lady and their deaconess stopped at the restaurant and bar to have lunch. They ordered lamb chops, red beans and rice, one coke, one pepsi and one glass of orange juice. The usher passed by and saw them. Within a few minutes a picture was taken and placed on *facebook*. this is the *status quo* of a whole western world.

Invariably, every Christian church should depart from iniquity for theirs the kingdom of heaven. To many times the flock is not listening to their pastor. Too many times the flock wants to tell their pastor what to do. People are very much afraid of peer pressure so they roll over and die to their nakedness. Too many times the one they love must consistently reward them even when they maliciously do wrong.

Jesus is angry. He is angry with his body the church. Isaiah, the father of all prophets, prophesied the life, death and resurrection of Jesus. Jesus one day reads this reading before the congregation. Word got around and they stoned him. Jesus does not care when people call you names as you go around doing the Lord's business. Jesus does not care when they call you a pedophile, simply because you love them children. Jesus does not care when as a preacher you wear the same black dress every time you go door-to-door. All Jesus cares about is that you do his will.

Jesus is exceedingly upset. He wakes you up every morning. Did you take notice of that? Jesus gave you a wife who irons your clothes everyday. Did you ever thank her? You go to work regularly. Did you buy your wife a birthday card? As soon as you get to the house, the tub is filled up. A clean towel is placed on a rack and your slippers are in its rightful place. Did you remember your anniversary? Valentine Day is here. Did you buy your wife a bouquet of lilies? Yet you say that you loving on Jesus.

Jesus is everywhere. The whole Christian population wants to be a winner. The Olympics is not a place to be showy. Track and field athletes are called for football or rugby. Swimmers are designated for the Navy or Air Force. Gymnastics will make very fine army officers. Boxers can open gyms. Wrestlers can become great explorers if only they give themselves to Jesus.

We are very quick to lay blame on the Mexicans. Jesus is holding the answer for everything. We are very quick to lay blame on the El Salvadorans. Jesus is holding the answer for everything. We are very quick to lay blame on the Ecuadorans. Jesus is holding the answer for everything. We are very quick to lay blame on the Hondurans. Jesus is holding the answer for everything. We are very quick to lay blame on the Guatemalans. Jesus is holding the answer for everything.

It is easy to call a snake, a snake, because you know it. It is easy to call a pig, a pig, because you know it. It is easy to call a rabbit, a rabbit, because you know it. It is easy to call a giraffe, a giraffe, because you know it. The Bible says love thy neighbor as thy self. The Bible says do not throw stones at glass windows. The Bible says not to remove the mote from the man's eye if you cannot remove the mote from your very own. Americans cannot play God. Prophets are anointed with the gift of discernment. Technocrats are not. Scholars are not. Professors are not. Presidents are not. Governors are not. Prime Ministers are not. Kings are not.

The gold medals given to the recipients at the Olympic Games belong to Jesus. The silver medals given to the recipients at the Olympic Games belong to Jesus. The bronze medals given to the recipients at the Olympic Games belong to Jesus. God is not happy when you take his gold to try to make a fool of him. God is not happy when you take his silver to try to make a fool of him. God is not happy when you take his bronze to try to make a fool of him

Jesus is at the house. Where are we on Sunday mornings? Flooding everywhere. Where are we on Sunday mornings? Fire everywhere. Where are we on Sunday mornings? The night clubs are full every Saturday night. Where are we on Sunday mornings?

And, Let every one that nameth the name of Christ depart from iniquity. There ae times that the road gets rough; we got to hold on. Jesus robed like Solomon as he walked through the crowds of people. Jesus had already healed the man born blind. The multitude kept pressing on Jesus. We got to abide by the statutes of God. We got to learn to respect each other. Keep still the tongue!

In America we have whitewashed some of the statutes of God the Father. We have created a void between Jesus and ourselves. We have dug a massive hole 1000s of feet deep into the earth's crust. In other words, we have once again wounded Our Lord and Savior Jesus. Jesus had been beaten with a cat-o-nine tail. This law still stands in the state of Louisiana. A state that God made my home. Jesus is saying Enough is Enough. The earth has grown in some wisdom. These Old Testament laws must cease.

Jesus is preaching his Apocalypse. We want Jesus to wait on us. On the earth there are end time preachers duly informed with the Word of God. God waits on no man. We have to align ourselves with God the Father, God the Son, and God the Holy Spirit. God has to teach us on a daily basis. Jesus has to prepare us for his home coming. God has already anointed his Sons and Daughters of the House to preach his Word.

This is not a fashion show like the Olympics held in Rio de Janeiro, whereall the athletes parade with their respective flags of all nations.

And all the performers' suits are tailored to their cultural colors of their homelands. The world is sick. Jesus is the only doctor who is qualified to heal every broken mind. Jesus is the only doctor who is qualified to perform every failed operation. Jesus is the only qualified doctor to mend every split nerve. Jesus is the only qualified doctor to save every soul.

When people of Jesus go out to another country, to display their bodies in a way offensive to Jesus, in order to earn a better job and to be held in very high esteem—this is a wound in the very heart of Jesus. Jesus did not walk to the cross and got beaten, stoned and whipped for you to go do what you want to do. There is no man on the face of the earth that can say that, Jesus did not speak to him. There is no man on the face of the earth that did not hear the voice of Jesus. There is no man on the face of the earth that Jesus shall repent for.

Families have lost beloved ones that never return home after a plane crash. Pray for them. Families have gone out into the woods to have fun time and have lost their dearly beloved ones. Pray for them. Families have lost their best friends whilst swimming. Pray for them. Families have lost their loved ones at the World Trade Center. Pray for them. Families have lost loved ones during wars all around the world. Pray for them. Families have lost loved ones that were beheaded in other countries. Pray for them.

Jesus never gave up on anyone. Please do not forget. You cannot allow your shattered dreams to separate you from the love of Jesus. You cannot allow your deceased spouse to separate you from the love of Jesus. You cannot allow a bad marriage to prevent you from seeking th face of Jesus. You cannot burn your Bible because Jesus die not meet your demands. Jesus just do not want you to try him. Jesus died. You in turn must die for your very best friends.

The Olympics Games at Rio de Janeiro were glitz and splendor. Jesus has something for everyone to do for him if only he will ask and accept. Many a time we look to see what our neighbor has. Many a time we want something that we see someone else is enjoying.

Many a time we want to go somewhere to have fun. Jesus is building a new heaven and a new earth. It is not this earth.

Jesus and his heavenly Father is indeed building a new heaven and a new earth. Can Jesus give you a preview? Yes he can. When you attend the Olympic Games, you sought another god. You have already lost your preview. You cannot blame your pastor for your impassioned behavior. You cannot blame your government. You cannot blame your mother. And finally you cannot blame your father. You will have to blame yourself.

When you leave your house to go anywhere, did Jesus ask you? This is very, very, very important. You must receive the Word from Jesus. You just do not pick yourself up and get on an aircraft to vacation somewhere or anywhere. Did you ever taught that they were dead wrong like you? It is imperative that you first consult Jesus

4. To Cherish Your Love Ones

Matthew 12:46 While he yet talked to the people, behold, his mother and his brethren stood without, desiring to speak with him.

> 47 Then one said unto him, Behold, thy mother and thy brethren stand without, desiring to speak with thee.
>
> 48 But he answered and said unto him that told him, Who is my mother? And who are my brethren?
>
> 49 And he stretched forth his hand toward his disciples, and said, Behold my mother and my brethren?
>
> 50 For whosoever shall do the will of my Father which is in heaven, the same is my brother, and sister, and mother.

Jesus is screaming out loudly as he stands atop the Arctic mountain peak in weather no human being on this planet can stand, no matter what they eat or drink. There is a reason why Jesus and his angels can resist the wear and tear of below zero degree temperatures. Jesus is speaking clearly, for even the children, who attend kindergartner schools to understand precisely what he is definitely saying. Jesus wants parents and teachers notto speak above their comprehension.

Train a child whilst he or she is young for tomorrow when they come into contact with the evil of this world, they would stop and turn around and go back to the basics. Jesus is taking you through this thought process. It is not what you say. It is not what you were going to say. It is what you do, because saying does not get the job done. When a teacher stands before her children of innocenceand breathes in that fresh air of purity that teacher becomes a mentor in the eyes of the children.

There are teachers that make it their duty to go to the supermarkets to purchase wines and beer. This is ridiculous. This is derision. This is preposterous. This is laughable. Jesus is a Teacher. Jesus will not stand before his children or babies with a breath strong of alcohol. Jesus will not make an excuse and say today is my birthday and I must have a drink.

Jesus is not taking "no" for an answer. Jesus is even looking at the school's curriculum and is saying repeatedly Enough is Enough. Teaching is a Ministry. One cannot and should not become a designated teacher simply because they choose to be one. Teaching is Jesus and Jesus is teaching. Jesus taught his disciples. He taught them Theology. Did Jesus call you to be a teacher? Everybody is given a talent at birth that needs to be explored. You just do not go and steal one.

Jesus is not playing with any teacher who overseers his little ones. Jesus will show you up. Jesus will reveal all of your weaknesses. Jesus will allow the spirit of torment to overcome you whilst you teach. You will consistently be conjecturing; seemingly trying to do right.

Teaching defines the Word my burden is light and my yoke is easy. Teaching is found in the mountain of love. Children are virgins. They need your undivided attention. They need your patience. They need your forgiveness. They need your stewardship. They need your understanding. They need you to take them one by one to the mountain top. Do not play with Jesus?

The children of the entire world belong to Jesus whether you agree with him or not. There innocence is Jesus innocence. They are free of wrong doing. These children need your guidance and your supervision. As soon as you enter the classroom, the ones that love you will always come running to you. The ones that are afraid of you need you more than you think.

Sunday mornings at church, where are the teachers? Are they taking time off from attending the service or services at the local church? If this is true, then the teachers need to talk to their Pastor. A Pastor's job is never done. He is as busy as a bee. Teachers must go to church often to show these little ones that they too are Christians. On Monday mornings, it is the right of the teacher to ask her little ones if their parents took them to church. It is also the right of the teacher to write a letter to the parents in support of her Pastor. It is these little things you do that mean so much to Jesus.

The children that attend Middle school require a teacher who is like omnipresent. This teacher must be Holy Spirit filled. No question about it! There are no substitutes in the absolute for God the Father, God the Son and God the Holy Spirit. Equally, there are no substitutes for Holy Spirit teachers than another Holy Spirit teacher or a Holy Spirit Pastor. Jesus is fair, very fair.

Jesus is Holy. Teachers in general take on the persona of holiness, as they conduct themselves in front of the students in the classroom. Middle school students need that attribute to take home with them. Parents take their children to school so that the teachers become the surrogate parents.

It is easy to say and to think that to be a teacher is as easy as 1, 2, 3. The Phoenicians, whose hands were guided by Jesus as they formed the letters of the alphabet from claydid not mold these individual letters in one day. When a people are disobedient, Jesus stops the job. Jesus will go and inspire another mortal being and continue the work of the Lord. God is in no hurry to complete any good work for nobody. Jesus goes about his business sweetly, slowly. There is no clock on the wall.

Middle school students are fast becoming the adolescents of tomorrow. During this time, the child eats more food than usual and drinks more fluids. His understanding is developing rapidly. He or she asks a whole lot of questions. The teacher has to be fully equipped with the answers so as not to derail the child. Jesus remembers.

It is indeed a dangerous period for the child. The parents might be hooked on drugs and are always quarreling in front of the children. Language is not of the best. Attire is not of the best. So the children go to bed hungry. When children truly love their teachers they would be the first ones to know about the situation. Teachers must pray before they confront the parents. And they should do it in love.

When Satan, the devil, is in the house a lot more work needs to be done. This is a failure among American peoples. This is not a job for the psychiatrist. This is not a job for a social worker. This is not a job for the family to come over to the house and choose sides. This is a deliverance. The teacher shall work with the Pastor and not the other way around.

You do not have to eat the fruit when it is green. It is better to eat the fruit when it is ripe. As an islander you get to know this adage real quick. Patience is a virtue. Most times teachers blame the parents before blaming themselves. They look at their astute position. Jesus does not care about your pride. Pride is the devil. Satan is full of pride. Jesus's children are at war with the devil. This war will not end until Jesus comes.

Teachers must pray by forming circles in their lunchrooms. Select a leader! Read a passage from the Bible! Time is not of the essence. The world will continue to do what it is already doing. We must stay vigilant. Always. Yes, Jesus is coming again. The time and the hour no man knows. Not even Jesus.

Children born to heroin addicts that are attending Middle School are prone to violence. They will do anything and everything to draw attention. Their focuses are very small and run like water flowing down steep steps or like a chimney giving off soot in the air. Their eating habits are enormous and will do anything to get food. Children in this age group are apt to get rape or become sexually molested by adults. This is our society today. Something we pay very little attention to. Jesus is looking.

Everybody feels satisfied to take their children to the doctors. Where is Jesus? Jesus is looking. Looking to see exactly what you are going to do. You do not need a degree to pick up a Bible and pray. Of course when there is a preacher around simply turn and go get him. God always know where to put his Sons of God. Jesus is looking.

We fail the test miserably on a day-to-day basis. Jesus is allowing us to realize that everything is a test. Then we blame God the Father, God the Son, and God the Holy Spirit. Jesus is looking.

The Bible clearly states that we live in hazardous times. The world does not agree with God's Word. That too is another reason that things go the way they do. Our child is not the baby of a heroin addict. Why shall I care? My father became a heroin addict after my birth, I am lucky. My father is an adult he can take care of himself. We can somehow get a whole lot of people to agree with us and that make it right. Jesus is looking.

Heroin is a dangerous drug. Building a wall in Massachusetts will not stop the flow of heroin. Building a wall in New Mexico will not stop the flow of heroin. Building a wall in Arizona will not stop the flow of heroin. Building a wall on the boundaries of Canada will stop the flow of heroin.

Teachers, who are called by God the Father, God the Son and God the Holy Spirit have and will have a formidable task. For those who are not call by God must leave. Jesus is not going to use anyone who is not call to this Ministry in these times especially, these perilous times.

It is true that some mothers of these children will entertain adults to pay for intimacy with their own children. This too is something that society turns a blind eye to. Jesus is here waiting to fix broken hearts, windows, doors, ministries, families, neighbors and neighborhoods. Where is everybody? Jesus is looking.

Some Pastors have a deliverance service at their church once a week. Few people attend. Some Pastors pay a preacher whose ministry is healing to do a week of Revival. Attendance is poor.

Jesus would have Pastors whose Ministry is Evangelical, to go from city to city or state to state keeping services in the open air. Some people of all faiths will attend. These Ministers are gifted to heal the sick. They pitch a tent and they have services nightly. Some neighborhoods do attend in good numbers. Jesus is looking.

In these risky times, you need to pray for wisdom and understanding. God the Father, God the Son and God the Holy Spirit is still waiting for you to pray this prayer. The gift is freely given. You need wisdom and understanding to create a menu for the entire family. You need wisdom and understanding to manage your affairs. You need wisdom and understanding for Jesus in the form of Holy Spirit to inhabit you and take you wherever he wants you to go. Jesus is looking.

When one is endowed with this gift of treasure as a middle school teacher, one is able to correct the wrong in another by looking him or her straight in the eyes whilst he is speaking to the student. The gifted teacher can summon the child's parent to come to the classroom instantaneously to view the child's behavior. The gifted teacher does not need a crystal ball. The gifted teacher will leave the classroom and on his return can discover the plot of evil. Jesus is looking.

To cherish your love ones is not a difficult task. Jesus is viewing you the parent looking away from the evil that you are imparting to these kids as the day goes by. Popping pills in front of your children is a very serious and deadly thing in the sight of God.

To earn respect one ought to display respect. It is easy to say that you are an adult and that you can do whatever you want whenever you want to do it. It is not about consequences. It is about Jesus. Jesus is not going to pop pills in front of his little ones. No sir. Jesus is not going to Pop pills in front of His Heavenly Father. No sir. Jesus is not going to pop pills in front of his angels. No Sir. Jesus is not going to pop pills in front of his saints. No Sir. Jesus is looking.

Telling lies to the children to make them believe that you are sick and that you have to take these pills to get you well will work only for a very short time. The kids at the school are already popping pills. Some teachers at the school are already popping pills. The custodians at the school are your biggest perpetrators.

When a kid takes a pill that takes him or her to another dimension he performs the same way the drug will want him to perform. After having a desirable experience, he goes out to become the seller rather than the employee. He begins to cherish his new job. He sees his reward. He also sees big business.

It is easy for us to say that this will not happen to our well-bred children. It is easy for us to say that I am a Pastor and this will never happen to my son or my daughter. It is easy for us to say that I am an educator and I have taught my children everything and they would not disappoint me. Do not lie to yourself! God have begun the book of revelation. Jesus is looking.

Parents are the largest and sometimes dumbest of secular evil. It is a paradigm. The children have a field day as they celebrate their birthday or birthdays together. Pills are everywhere. Parents are behaving more childish than their own children. They are too busy talking on the telephone or cell phone. They are too busy playing or gambling on their cell phones. They are too busy ignoring what they see even before their very eyes. They are too busy worrying about tomorrow.

The teacher sends a report card at the house, nobody responds. The child is forever playing—no homework is done. A junkie is on the horizon. Where is the ten year old child? He is out all night. He is out all night with his elder cousins selling drugs and popping pills. He is wearing designer shoes. The kid is wearing designer slacks. The once ambitious child is replacing his natural teeth with gold teeth. Jesus is looking.

God the Father, God the Son and God the Holy Spirit is saying loud and clear that the mind is under attack when someone keeps popping pills into their bodies. The mind, which is the mind of God, belongs to Jesus. Satan, the devil, came to destroy the mind. The trinity has made us to think and reason for ourselves. This is part of the mind process.

Signs are placed on the sidewalks of schools which read, "no drugs or no to drugs." Are these really the signs that Jesus wants posted on the sidewalks. Jesus is saying remove the signs and carryJesus in your heart. The signs do nothing. The signs just take up space on the sidewalks. The mind of a child is deeply rooted in the mind of Jesus. We do not know the height, depth and width of the universe.

The mind has to think clearly. In a cell phone there is a chip. It cannot go to the height, depth and width of Jesus' mind. The chip cannot tell you anything about Jesus' universe. But your mind could become another Jesus. Keep focus on Jesus and you will have the mind of God! Keep focus on Jesus and you will have the mind of Jesus! Keep focus on Jesus and you will have the mind of the Holy Spirit!

Popping pills knock the antennas out. They are like the television set. They need the antennas for the television set to work. These pills destroy the sensory nerves behind the eyes. The eyes are near to the temples. The temples are the ones to process the information.

So you are looking at a whole lot of damage that popping pills do, when you become vulnerable to this practice. Jesus is just using me to point out the misperceptions in this secular world. The drug dealers do not care about you.

The drug traffickers do not care about you. The pharmaceutical companies do not care about you. It might be too late for you. Jesus is looking.

When the children get to High School there is a graduation from one drug to another. And this ascension take them to Coke--short for cocaine a bitter crystalline alkaloid. A stimulant that quickens the vital process of the body. A teenager hook on coke does not care about tomorrow. And tomorrow will not care about him.

There is no city in America that is not plague with coke. There is no town that is not plague with coke. Jesus is saying that there is still hope for this pandemic. Everything begin with the teenager. Incarceration is not the answer. In the Bible there is 150 Psalms. Each one is distinctly linked to an evil. Anointed preachers of God will be led to the appropriate psalm to be prayed and administered to the afflicted ones.

Coke beginners need this food to crush the head of Satan, the devil. A clean hand and a pure heart shall see God. Parents of teenagers shall remove their eyes from the Ouija board and their tongues and ears from the psychic hot lines. Jesus wants to work but flesh is always in God's way. It may appear that the devil is winning; that is for fools like you. Scraping the pot at the bottom will not help either.

An adolescent using coke is his first step to the graveyard. An adolescent born from the seed of a coke addict will forever be impoverished. An adolescent coming from generations of coke addicts will ultimately be a walking zombie. There is no stone that cannot be overturned by God the Father. There is no spring that cannot be well-up cause it is dry. There is no river that does not have a beginning and an end. Jesus is looking.

We give up on our little ones far too quickly. We give up on ourselves in the blink of an eye. We may say that we will never give up, but the mountain stands before us. We will make promises to each other that will not last. Our children see through our transparency. We often try to ignore the truth.

As soon as people of importance come over to the house, everyone get to cleaning, scrubbing, washing and baking. Immediately thereafter everything return to normal. Jesus is treated much the same way. Jesus gives the family a windfall. Sunday morning the whole family go to church. The windfall have come to an end. The whole family stop going to church.

We cannot be in and out of the house of the Lord. Jesus is not going to accept your abuse. Stop using him! Stop making New Year's resolutions! Until you stop your children will not prosper.

America take a good look at the people in Italy. The month is August,2016, an earthquake with a seismic reading of 5.6 killed over 300 people. Bodies are still being dug out of the rubble left behind. We take our blessings for granted. Jesus is saying that when much is given much more shall be given back. We want Jesus to heal our teenage-coke addicts. Then, what are we going to give in return? Are they empty promises? Are we going to love our neighbors as we love ourselves? Jesus is looking.

God the Father, God the Son and God the Holy Spirit is no respecter of persons. Had Italy done something wrong to deserve this traumatic aftermath? Oh no!. Jesus gives life and Jesus takes life. Jesus is the beginning and Jesus is the end.

Our teenage children are who they are, because the adults do everything before their eyes. Yes our children are fragile and vulnerable. They are in dire need for Jesus tobell the cat. Treat Jesus with dignity! Do not be two-faced at the house! Let integrity be a watch word! Speak the truth at all times! Jesus is looking.

It is all well and good to spend your money on the military. The school children need it. It is all well and good to spend your money building up your infrastructure. The school children need it. It is all well and good to spend more money on the veterans. The school children need it. It is all well and good to go and rebuild the city of Detroit. The school children need it. It is all well and good to spend more money on space programs. The school children need it. It is all well and good to give aid to foreign countries. The school children need it.

America is playing with yet another inferno, marijuana, a cannabis, a hemp. I remembered as a child smelling the use of marijuana, the scent of the burning leaves irritated me. Jesus is saying to America to cherish your love ones. Cherish your children, because they are the onesto get hurt more than anyone else. Jesus is looking.

In 1965, I was thirteen going on fourteen and was allowed to go party with my two older brothers. Though we were all teenagers, we encountered marijuana being sold on the streets of the island of Trinidad. The scent was so rank that I could not bear it in my nostrils. It never dawn on me that marijuana would have become a world-wide feat.

Elementary school children suffer from this addiction at an early age. This plant can grow anywhere. It can grow in shrubs on the side walk. It can grow in pots in attics. It can grow on any or on many vacant abandoned houses premises. In other words it can grow anywhere. Jesus is speaking to all 50 states. Jesus is saying that a time is coming for children to see his heavenly glory stretching from earth straight to heaven.

The constant use of this drug will disrupt their sight of Jesus. Could Satan, the devil step in? Of course he can. Your sight was made for Jesus and not for the devil. How are you going to write books when your sight is in the reverse? You mess with the drug you mess with Jesus. There is a reason why the drug grows rapidly. There is a reason why the devil sits and stands in you after you have smoked the plant. There is a reason why it is called "pot".

Jesus is not found in any pot. Jesus blows with the wind and goes anywhere and everywhere standing with the wind beneath his feet. Jesus walks on water. Moses parted the sea and walk on the ground. Jesus is a consuming fire. Jesus is never, never, never, ever, ever going to come before his children smoking. We live in hazardous times. Jesus says so.

Please do not take Jesus for granted! You walk the streets everyday; there is a shoot out. Don't just look at Chicago! This is happening in all 50 states. There are fables everywhere. Speak the truth! It is easy to grow and live in a pretensive town or city. It is easy to look away when something is happening. It is easy to say that this is none of my business. It is easy to ignore what has already become a paradigm. Jesus is looking.

Jesus is saying that marijuana is prodigious. One can use it for medicine. Boil the leaves and mix them up with spinach and okras. This is good for ulcers in the stomach. Boil the leaves with the stem and mix them up with cauliflower. This is good for sprain ankles and knees. Boil the roots and mix them up with cabbage. This is good for rheumatism. Boil the leaves and mix them up with egg plant. This is good for running ears.

When you use marijuana in this way and many other ways that wisdom shall take you along then and only then Jesus will bless you.

Marijuana is useful in the construction industry. It acts as an adhesive when mix with cement and lime stone and iron. It prevents the cracking in walls and sidewalks.

The Bible says to cherish your love ones making sure that the children do not follow their parents into alcoholism. Drunk drivers are a visible sight. At least two out of every four adults checking out at the grocery stores are buying beer or strong drink.

Children are very curious. They watch you daily. They see exactly where the beers and the strong drink go. As soon as you are not in their eyesight they will steal both the beer and the strong drink. We adults have to be more vigilant than we think. Especially, when they are at the house first, before we get home in the evenings. The youth does not take long to begin a party. The youth knows how to clean up quickly. We adults underestimate our children.

The children take the alcohol to school. They walk with the bottle of wine in their book bags. They carry the can of beer in their lunch boxes. They put the flask of whiskey in their slacks. They pour the bottle of brandy in their juice bottles. They are very notorious in the use of alcohol. Jesus is looking.

The youth is not waiting to become a license driver. From the age of 12 he or she can be seen driving someone's car. Could you imagine them drunk at that age? Causing accidents that were never reported. Fleeing from hit and run accidents! Taking lives on the streets and not turning themselves in. Some of these accidents are so mysterious, one wonders who did it. The fines do not change anything. Jesus is looking.

After graduation our children go to colleges/universities. Hallucination begins. Its definition is a sensory experience of something that does not exist outside the mind, caused by various physical and mental disorders or by reaction to certain toxic substances, and usually manifested as visual or auditory images. Jesus is saying that this is preposterous. This is a fine example of stupidity from a school of scholars. When everybody wants to be first, there go the evil.

No one in the absolute plays with the mind of man. Taking God's children to make footstools are a habit for Professors at very distinguished universities. God the Father, God the Son and God the Holy Spirit does not care about accolades. Jesus shows his phenomena in the form of prodigies.

When a prodigy is born, earth bows its head to the heavens. The cherubims and the seraphimspay a visit to earth's new born king. He reads extensively. His power to retain is tremendous. The prodigy sleeps but few hours. Most times he eats one meal a day. He is very, very shy. At school he seldom plays. He is like eccentric.

The parents of a prodigy are very wise. Their child is never out of their sight. The angels in heaven comes at night and plays with him. They do not disturb him when he is in company with anybody. He is very seldom at the library. Before age 13 he already is a scholar.

God puts his prodigy on the planet to show the psychiatrist not to play with the mind of human beings. It is about time that America closes the faculty of psychology. It is not of God the Father. It is not of God the Son. It is not of God the Holy Spirit. America shall not bend its knees to Satan, the devil. Jesus is looking.

There are Preachers, Teachers, Evangelists, Prophets and Ministers of Music, who can or are able to cast off any demonic spirits that trespass against us. Societies world over want to distance themselves from Jesus that they will go and worship their respective gods and place them in their offices. They have been doing this long before Jesus came to the earth.

When you cannot remove the evil that cohabits or inhabits your fellowmen, turn and have a seat. Don't allow Satan, the devil, to take you to his mountain top. Jesus is your only hope to paradise. Jesus is your only hope to creating heaven on earth. Jesus is your only hope for betterment. Jesus is looking.

To cherish your love ones is not as tedious as one shall think or belief. The drug amphetamine is a racemic drug. It stimulates the central nervous system used chiefly to lift the mood in depressive states and to control the appetite in cases of obesity. This drug is for adults only.

When children are left unattended by the parent or parents, a whole different world falls upon them. They are apt to interfere with anything. Their inquisitiveness get them in mayhem much more than you think. Their thoughts are not the same. Their learning are tremendously, rapidly, swiftly, aggressively, flashing before your vision can seize the moment. They do not share the upbringing you had.

Drug addicts that gave birth to children in the 1990s, are now giving birth to children in these times of great risk. Most of these drug users added amphetamines to any or every other drug that they have taken in the past. The results are children behaving in a way that is so different from the norm. We try to circumvent the problem. We try to research the situation in our minds. We try to bleach with detergent the enigma that is steering down atus from heaven. You cannot get rid of Jesus. Jesus is looking.

The doctors are researching the fundamental principles of this puzzle, with the hope that they find an answer. The light is Jesus. As a child growing up in the church, I rarely saw a doctor at any service. Doctors believe that they are the greatest among human beings. Doctors in their philosophical minds believe that God the Father, God the Son and God the Holy Spirit make them to walk on water. It is a false belief. They need to humble themselves the same as all of creation. Until their knees hit the ground, Jesus will consistently pass them by.

They are of the opinion that self-will is going to help them in the solving of this particular dilemma. This is not an isolated case. This is pandemic. Children are Jesus first choice. Children are Jesus purest cherubs. Children are Jesus' children. Children are the seraphs children. Children are the delight of heaven. Jesus is not going to answer your prayer until you become like one of these children. Jesus is looking.

God the Father, God the Son and God the Holy Spirit is not going to take directives from no earthly creature. Jesus alone can fix it. 75 per cent of doctors have given their souls to the devil. Jesus alone can fix it. Ethics among doctors are liken unto Jesus when the people shouted out, "crucify him, crucify him, crucify him."

Jesus is saying before the first quarter of this century and after the last quarter of this century, heaven will raise up a new breathe of doctors in all of America.

Sleepwalking is the act or state of walking, eating, or performing other motor acts while asleep, of which one is unaware upon awakening somnambulism. This is chronic in children between two years old to eight years old. This age is dearest to Jesus, because it is a very dangerous time for both the parent/s and the child. It is a sign of a ruthless period in the history of the world.

Coke addicts are the mothers and fathers of these children. The coke addict is up all day and night due to the constant or continuous use of the drug--cocaine. While on the other hand their offspring become sleepwalkers. It is like one is mocking God.

These children cannot go to school. Supervision is of the utmost. Parents cry night and day and day and night. It is easy to point fingers. Jesus has sent prophets and evangelistto bring the good news to the poor. On their journeys many of them were beheaded. On their journeys some of them were thrown into deep pits of about 100 ft. Food given, one loaf of bread daily.

Others were thrown into prisons and beaten with a cat-o-nine tail. Yet the world want to forget the onslaught of innocent blood, that men of God the Father, God the Son and God the Holy Spirit, shed by the children of God. They want heaven to relent since they did not dwell in those days. They want heaven to withhold its arm from the wantonnessand greed of coming generations. They want heaven to turn a blind eye on the sinfulness of societies. Jesus is looking.

Earthly laws will change to benefit a few, but the laws of Jesus are unchanging. The prophet Moses suffered tremendously on the mountain of God as he wrote the laws that were ascribed to him by Jesus. On Mount Sinai, the statutes and the ten commandments, which were written by the hand of Jesus, weregiven to Moses, the man of God.

Jesus paints a very fluid picture that somehow has been thrown into the abyss of hell. The Word that was given to Moses did not come to an end because the planet has gone the other way. The Word of God is still revealing itself even to this day.

The Word spoken to Moses on Mount Sanai is the same thing that is happening in the schools of our cherish ones. We live in a land of milk and honey. Who has the milk and the honey? Jesus is saying that when much is given much more must be given back. Jesus is looking.

The parents have to go to specific stores to purchase clothes for their children. Why? These stores have tailored clothes with specific designs on them to meet the aspirations of the schools' Principals.

The Bible says come as you are and worship me. Jesus is at the top of the mountain speaking to you but you put cotton in your ears. You play that you did not hear him. You ignore his footsteps coming after you. You ignore the cries in the morning dew. You ignore the little drawings on the walls. You ignore the tiny footprints in the sand. You ignore the childlike voices in the sky. Jesus is looking.

Jesus is coming. Yes he is. Before he comes, the birds would have given the children songs to sing. Their lyrics will be of things to come. The seas will grow deeper. The sun will be catching you as you journey through the streets. The moon will eclipse at least a dozen times a year. The stars will get brighter, but the nights will grow shorter. The mountains will grow taller and taller and taller.

It is about time that the instructors at our schools take a good look at themselves. Are they pleased with their tutoring? Jesus is not happy with their performance. The good book keeps reminding us that we must come as we are. Whether some nonsensical fool took prayer out of school, Jesus does not care and he will annihilate that person along with her cohorts.

If we will only open our eyes and gaze upon the morning dew, Jesus would have left heaven to nourish our sight with the falling rain. Moses eyes were brighter than the eyes of a new born baby at age 120. How many people in the world can see anything without glasses after age 60? Jesus is looking.

Human beings have been living in doubt for more than 3,000 years. They are still hoping that God the Father, God the son and God the Holy Spirit will one day sin. Disobedience in a ruthless world has brought us all this pain. Jesus walked to Calvary with the pain of love in his heart as he carried the cross of all our sins. Love is a pain. And until you are willing to bear this pain of love as a teacher of these little ones, you will not enter the kingdom of heaven.

You can run but you cannot hide. You can lie to a whole world and profess to be born again. You can continue to play the national lottery. You can continue to play bingo. You can continue to play box four. You can continue to play scratch. You can continue to go to the race coast and gamble. Jesus is looking.

Providence is the Holy Trinity watching over humankind. It means Jesus sees all things. Every creature under heaven knows the voice of the true living god. Intimacy in the wilderness of the earth is a refreshing sight to behold—the birth of a calf.

His omniscience is the pain that God the Father bore in heaven when his Son was pierced with the lance. His turning of the sod is a sign given to us by His Throne. Jesus is showing that his journey on the earth represents His Father's journey too.

We burn candles every night with the hope that we would one day see our love ones in heaven. We burn candles at the grave side all day long with the hope that our love ones will make it to heaven. We burn candles in our yard all day and all night with the names of our love ones written on them; with the hope that our love ones will make it to heaven. We burn candles in the corners of our business places with the hope that our business will make it to heaven. Jesus is looking.

Jesus is saying that when you stop burning them candles. I will take care of you.

It is easy for us to lay blame on children when they have overdose themselves with drugs. We are driving down the street at night all alone minding our own business. Suddenly, we ran into a parked car and never stopped. Our children sitting in the back seat saw everything. We observe all of this, but convince ourselves that nobody got hurt. Are we really seeing through those eyes of our children?

We kid ourselves because we believe that God the Father, God the Son and God the Holy Spirit never saw us. We convince ourselves in the absolute and honestly declaring that Jesus was not there. We make a telephone call to our good friend Grace, who further convinces us that ain't no way Jesus saw that accident. We believe that we have the **most**arduous job in the world. We further believe that these children are our children and not Jesus' children. But, as soon as something happens, who are we calling on. Jesus is looking.

I remembered one night in Brunswick, Georgia, sitting on a chair with my bag on the table that I used as a pillow. It was a supermarket and the outside lights were not on. The time was April, 2001. Jesus always put me to sleep. Jesus shuts out everything from around me in a snapshot. The fear of the night, he takes away. The sound of the trucks at night, he takes away. The siren of the police cars, he takes away. The ambulances with all that noise, he takes away. The gun shots at night, he takes away.

We say that we are loving on Jesus. The Holy Spirit, who is Jesus, stops by to test you. God the Father, who also is Holy Spirit, because of the mystery of God interchanges quickly in roles faster than the light can shine. They, all three are testing you but you cannot see the mystery of God unfolding as the dew on the leaf.

We give birth to a handicap child. This is what the doctor says. Jesus is saying the birth is one coming out of the seed of a drug addict. The woman must in no way be blamed for this birth which is considered not normal. Faith in Jesus which is as small as a mustard seed will move the mountain that absorbed the child. Never give up!

This is a time for every member of the family to get together in prayer unceasingly. Continuous prayer means that the Holy Spirit must dwell in you. Without you having the Holy Spirit no one can move the mountain. When you fall asleep Jesus who is the Holy Spirit is still praying in you.

The time shall be shut out. The days of the week shall not be counted. The months of the year must not be chronicled. It is imperative for us to lose ourselves in Jesus. It is the epic of surrender. No stone unturned. No blood painted on the walls of the house. No sugar-coated Gospel. No feeding of the spirits. Jesus is looking.

We all want Jesus to massage our jaws as we eat His Word. We all want Jesus to massage our throats for the food which is His Word to go down smoothly and enter our stomachs. We all want Jesus to act as glucose and take his word throughout our bodies. This is the thinking of the flesh. This is thinking of the doctor. This is the thinking of the president. This is the thinking of the prime minister. Jesus is in command. Jesus is looking.

His Word goes beyond human understanding. When we eat his Word and drink his Blood we become new creatures. Now we begin a new walk in the Spirit and not in the flesh. It is called a process of healing. Jesus will take his sweet, sweet, sweet time to finish the job. Patience is now a virtue.

5. To Break the Walls of Religion

Isis andJihad are both the same. They are all fundamentalists. Their job is to bring the whole wide world into subjection to the faith of the Muslim. A monotheistic group: the belief that there is only one god and not three persons in God.

One day in August, 2016, I was walking along North Market Street, in Shreveport, Louisiana. It was evening time. And, as I looked to the right of me, I behold a great, great, great, sea of Fire. Jesus is still talking. We keep on taking Jesus for granted. We keep on playing with the Word of God the Father, God the Son, and God the Holy Spirit. We keep on doubting the very Word of Jesus. We keep on believing that nothing is going to happen. We keep on being brainwashed by social media. We keep on playing with *Facebook*— an arm of Satan, the devil.

Understanding is a cancer in our minds. It is eating out our whole thought process. When the Trinity is bringing about an invention on the face of the earth, Jesus sends his prophets a long time ago to broadcast the good news that Truth is about to happen. Where is the Truth of all that is happening? Wake up! Don't be caught by sight and the so-called niceties of life! Stay away from the window!

The cells of the fundamentlist groups are in all nations. They are in France, Sweden, Norway, Belgium Austria, India, Pakistan, Turkey, Switzerland, Argentina, Brazil, Spain, Australia, England, Wales and the entire frontier of the Atlantic Ocean. They use the internet as their footstool. They roll the dice at Casinos. They chauffeur very important peoples of the world. They live on the tops of very tall buildings. They work in shipbuilding yards. They advertise in language not their own. They use pigeons in groups of hundreds to take messages over a whole world.

This sea of Fire encompasses the beginning of a world war with China. China though not a cell, is too ambitious in the world standing. They do not love the idea that America is the Super Power; followed by Russia. They too must conquer the world. They too must become a Super Power. They too lust for Power. Jesus is looking.

When it is not given from above, that means thatyou have stolen Jesus's Fame. Isis and Jihad will send their sons and their daughters to dwell on the frontiers of all developing countries. They all will not be wealthy or rich in disguise. They will come as small business owners; some as brick layers;others as industrial apprentices in large corporations. They will be students in computer science and communications with a specialty in Physics.

The children will not be carrying the same last name or any similarity with the first name. Their dress on the streets will be consistent with the going trends. They will always be walking and not driving. Their demeanor will be happy go lucky.

On weekends, they will travel to learn the entrances and egresses of the towns or cities or provinces or parishes that they occupy. They will participate in horse racing. And use the tickets and its number as a code name. Their motives are to spread the wickedness of a radical regime throughout the world and recruit others to do so.

This picture is painted by Jesus to send a message to the wise in espionage and not the wise in foolishness. The sea of Fire will show you the light upon the heads of the people who you will detain for further questioning. These people will not give up at any cost. Others will have encryptions tattooed in their arms and under their feet. Babies will come into the country with encryptions tattooed between the thigh and the buttock. Girl children will carry their encryptions in the middle of their foreheads. Fingers will be amputated and send by mail with a chip sewn in the flesh.

The war on Radical Islam is indeed an ongoing war. This war has been planned out since the beginning of the 20th Century. Their goal is to become the Super Power of the Free World before the close of the 21st Century. This is their number one tiptop priority. Their number two priority is to have as many children as possible with their wives. Their number three priority is to have the highest quality education. They must be the envy of the free world.

Hindu: one of the largest religions in the entire world which originated in Northern India. It is estimated to be about one billion people. They believe in many gods. The vision of the Sea of Fire is allowing India to have one last warning from God the Father, God the Son and God the Holy Spirit. Serving many gods cripple the economy of any country. No one can survive on only one dollar a day. This is in fact utterly horrendous. Jesus is looking.

There is a caste system that has existed for well over 2,000 years. There is the wealthy; there is the poor. And the poor means one dollar a day. The poor man is given a name "coolie"--a derogatory name. Yet America allows the practice of this religion under the First Amendment of Freedom of Religion. What hypocrisy!

Hinduismis another form of slavery. It is easy to call yourself a Christian because you have been baptized. It is easy to tell everyone that you have been born again. It is easy to study your Bible to have knowledge and foreknowledge of the Universe. But, as soon as Jesus embraces you, and tells you what you have to do for him you become like the rats and the scavengers of the city of Detroit. Who are you to tell me what to do? Jesus is looking.

We do not want to bell the cat. Do not say the word slavery—just do it! You must do what your master tells you to do. The Bible says that you cannot serve two masters you will love one and hate the other. Jesus does not force you to do anything. Jesus does not want you to spend the rest of your lives on food stamps. Jesus does not want you to be always accepting something for nothing. Jesus keeps showing the butterfly in its cocoon.

When people invite you to their worship service, it is absolutely necessary to find out whether the Pastor is Holy Spirit. You just do not walk into somebody's house, because he wears a priestly garment and has a chant of a priest. Then after the conclusion of the service, serves you lunch. He has already overtaken you with the evil at the entrance of the door. The evil spreads rapidly.

Shaking handswith people serving all these gods; being in their company going anywhere is catastrophic. They will teach you how to feed the spirit. Their Jesus is the cow. Jesus is not going to tell you to wake up every morning and feed him rice. Jesus is not going to tell you to put food under a statute with all these hands and worship her. Jesus is not going to tell you that his cow you must not eat. Jesus is not going to tell you to memorize all these so-called sacred prayers that never came from the Triune God.

God the Father, God the Son and God the Holy Spirit has blessed India with the Indian Elephant whose ears are smaller than the African Elephant. Its tusks are exclusively given to males. Its tusks have become the biggest bread basket in all of India. Jesus is not pleased with the cruelty given to his most adorable creature. Hinduism will pay for everything under the sun. Jesus is looking.

Heretofore, Jesus is showing me that he is drawing lines, not straight lines, alongside the bricks of the wall that stands tall. The evil must go no matter what. There are Christians in India working feverishly with the disbelievers of their people. There are Christians getting into fights with all kinds of peoples that are trapped in the walls of India. There are Pastors whose lives were threatened and beaten up by the warmongers of South Asia.

Out of India came another widespread evil Buddhism. Its founder Indian religious leader Buddha, who brings enlightenment and wisdom. This evil has spread to China, Burma, Japan and parts of Southeast Asia and has gone around the world. It is easy to say that you are a Christian. It is easy to say that you are a real Christian. It is easy to say that Jesus is your Savior. Are you reading your Bibles? Jesus is looking.

The meaning of enlightenment in its philosophical sense is belief in the power of human reason and so on.

Solomon, the second king to succeed his father David was already prophesied to be the wisest man to have ever lived. It is impossible for God to tell lies. Jesus is, will always be is, is always is no matter what. Because of our human nature in our local schools we would be told to use the words was in its past tense. But when God calls you he instructs you that Jesus is also God the Father and the Son and the Holy Spirit. In other words this is God's business. It is a mystery of faith.

Jesus proves to you that when you are called, Jesus anoints you. The Triune God is omnipotent. Jesus anoints people with the gift of wisdom which is the ability to reveal or uncover imposters.

Buddha was just a man like any other man. He could not say the name Jesus. His hands were not anointed with the gift of the Holy Spirit that others could truly come to Jesus. And Jesus is saying that Buddha was evil, evil, evil. And because of all their blood-stained hands from the killings of Jesus' Prophets and Prophetesses and Pastors and Missionaries and Mens and Womens of God, the wall of buddhism will now tumble down.

There is an adage out of evil cometh good. Jesus is saying this is wrong, wrong, wrong. Good begets good. Evil will come out of the seed of evil.

Hare Krishna: a religious sect base on Vedic scriptures, whose followers engage in joyful congregational chanting of Krishna's name founded in the U.S. in 1966. Jesus is pounding the table with a hammer and taking a saw out to divide the table in two separate pieces. Jesus is shouting that Vedic scriptures were not about knowledge; it is about evil, evil, evil.

They claimed that it originated in the 1400 BC. This is rubbish. All these religious cults did not originated from the Caucasian, so-called Indo-European mixed people. These people originated from the twelve of tribes of Ishmael. Hagar fleeing from Sarah was stopped in the wilderness by God and told that out of her son will come twelve sons.

God the Father always keeps his promises. History has proven time and time again that when a people want to go off into the wilderness to change the order of prayer to suit the echelons of society, Satan the devil, would devour you. This fallen angel has knowledge of God the Father, God the Son, and God the Holy Spirit.

The Sea of Fire for the followers of the Hare Krishna forms of worship, which they tried to spread throughout the West Indies and other surrounding islands means that Jesus will not relent on those who are utterly disobedient. Jesus is looking.

Look at yourself all dressed up for church and the moment you step outside of the building, Satan, the devil is waiting to steal the Word of God from you, before Jesus sews it in your heart. You go to church to eat the Word that the Pastor is feeding you.

The Sea of Fire is Rastafarianism: a religious cult, originally of Jamaica, that records Africa as the Promised Land to which all true believers will someday return and the late Haile Selassie, former emperor of Ethiopia, as the messiah. Beware of sheep in wolves clothing! Remove the scales from your eyes! There is subversive literature. There is only one True Messiah, and his name is Jesus.

Jesus is the last king of prophecy coming out of the seed of David. Jesus is the 42nd. Providence will not bow its head to earth. Disobedience to theCreator will be your downfall. The Bible says that many will come in my name. My name is Jesus. It is not Selassie.

The Sea of Fire will stretch itself all across Jamaica, where every knee shall bow and every heart shall confess that Jesus is Lord to the Glory of God the Father. Far too often, provocation by the people of Jamaica, whose god is the drinking of blood seen at ceremonies scattered throughout Jamaica. Sacrificing of chickens, goats, cows, pigs and the like, have to be eradicated for Jesus to come home.

Utter disregard for the Word of God, and total allegiance and loyalty to a religious cult, which is spreading rapidly to other foreign countries, is a no, no, with Jesus. The Jamaican people need Jesus. Kingston, the capital of Jamaica, needs Jesus. All surrounding towns and cities need Jesus. The children of Jamaica need Jesus. The seniors of the sunshine Island need Jesus. The poor people of the largest West Indian Island need Jesus.

The Sea of Fire will hover over Jamaica. It will stay there for a while as a sign that Jesus is coming. The love of money is the root of all evil. Many Jamaicans have chosen this part and as a result, has afflicted their loves ones, who have to bear the pain of the fiery arrows.

Children will be faced with pandemics. Diseases will be widespread. Hurricanes will come and go and come again. Water will be everywhere. A vast increase in rats, roaches, centipedes, mosquitoes, and snakes.

Before the plague of Rastafarianism came to Jamaica, all was well. The plague of this religious cult brought a division between the haves and the haves not. Poverty became widespread. Medicine for the poor became scarce. The economy was shipwrecked.

The Sea of Fire will rage and increase an awareness that Christians all over the island must be born again for they to enter the kingdom of heaven. The Christian churches will now be filled up with believers throughout the very land. Then, the Triune God will be able to perform the many miracles that Jesus had already prophesied.

Rosicrucian Order is a very active secret society of devils. Founded in the 17th and 18th century in the heart of the city of Rameses, Egypt. Pharaoh's cult. a religious sect, possessing esoteric principles of religion. Its membership is composed of the higher echelons of the society. These men who are your city officials: doctors, lawyers and professors that form the very backbone of the country.

They deal with the supernatural spirits of the underworld. They believe in the power of the dead. They teach you how to harness the power of the dead and use that power for your glory. The Sea of Fire which beholds my very eyes on North Market Street will engulf you. Jesus is showing me that you will do anything to own Real Property in affluent societies.

The people of the Rosicrucian Order would always have a say in the Middle East. They will become voices of Isis and Jihad in present-day warring factions. They will become the boots of the infantry men. They will become the spies of the future kings of the entire western world. America's might should be overturned. Egypt without exception wanted to be the Super Power, not of the ancient world, but of the entire world.

And so their war began with Moses and the twelve tribes of Israel. The Sea of Fire is the same fire that the Rosicrucians saw that inhibited them from crushing the tribes of Israel. Israel was not as armed as the Egyptians soldiers. Moses the anointed one was blessed to carry the Word of God.

Joshua his successor was so honored to champion the twelve tribes of Israel to the Promise land. No one is good but the Lord and there is none beside me. Jesus foretold all that is happening today. His disciples took the message to the ends of the earth. Theyhadspreaded the Good News to the length and width and breath of the world. The Muslims of Egypt will one day see the Sea of Fire in the form of a dried coconut split in two halves.

Each half will represent the top and the bottom of the river Nile. The river Nile is the longest river in the whole wide world. It begins from Victoria Fallsand empties in the Mediterranean Sea. Its bounteous land has given food to all of Egypt Its bounteous land has given minerals to all of Egypt. Its bounteous land has given shelter and buildings to all of Egypt. Jesus is saying no more, no more, no more, no more. Jesus is looking.

Karl Heinrich Marx was born on May 5, 1818, in West Germany. The son of rabbis, Jewish descendants of one of the twelve tribes of

Israel, who at 17 had begun to study law at the University of Bonn. The next year he transferred to the University of Berlin and majored in Philosophy. Years later he founded Communism, another form of religion. Karl Marx became the anti-Christ.

Communism which means common or belonging to all. Plato proposed that a ruling class should own everything in common and put the welfare of the state above all. This philosophy became the reason and argument in seeking truth and knowledge of reality.

Karl Marx, idealistic views, was to promote himself as the true son of the Most High. I am a genius. I alone can make you proud. I will put money into your pockets. I will have a revolution. I will replace one ruling class over another. The workers shall be in control--down with the hierarchy.

He taught his religious politics that capitalism must go. An economic system in which the chief means of production isprivately owned.

In 1991, MikhailSergeyevich Gorbachev did everything to put an end to Communist Rule and signed a treaty to eliminate all the intermediate range nuclear missiles of the two countries. USSR was dissolved. 13 of the 15 Soviet republics had declared independence.

The Vision of the Sea of Fire is a tremendous warning to Russia, whose president Vladimir Vladimirovich Putin also is an anti-Christ. The baton of Karl Marx has been passed on to President Putin. Jesus laments that God the Father and God the Son, and God the Holy Spirit will hardened the heart against Russia, who has vowed to Satan, the devil, to spread this yoke of evil around the world.

The officials of China have been to Russia secretly meeting with thepolitburo of the communist party. Their job is to spread the religion of communism World Wide. Their mission is to become watch dogs of the entire universe with North Korea as their pivot. Their center causes distractions by shooting rockets in the sky so that our focus would be interrupted. Jesus is looking.

North Korea leader Kim Jong-un is bespectacled. Its official name is the DemocraticPeople's Republic of Korea. Jesus is spreading the Sea of Fire all along its borders to show young Kim that the power which he possesses will one day come to an end. Its mining of copper, zinc, magnesite, silver, tungsten, iron ore, lead and limestone is given from above. Wasteful spending and the manufacturing of weapons and weaponry and machineryare grossly dumbfounded.

The peninsula of Korea split into two in 1948. The division became North Korea and South Korea, a country in East Asia. Japan the main culprit in this split came about for one reason and one main reason--iron and steel. The Sea of Fire also falls on Japan, for forcing and abusing the People of Korea in forbidding their spoken language. Its appalling, when force is used by another country to subject the people of the other country to their dogmas.

In the 1780's Christians missionaries came from China to Korea, where the Korean authorities persecuted the missionaries and killed thousands of Koreans who had become Christians. God the Father, God the Son and God the Holy Spirit does not forget His Sons of God that were beheaded.

Jesus is saying this Sea of Fire is on the heads of all Buddhist monks world over. Everywhere Jesus feet pressed and his darling apostles feet pressed became wealthy. Gold, iron ore, tin, copper, limestone, tungsten, diamonds and silver to name a few. Jesus is not playing church. Quit the games!

Moses the deliverer came to free the Israelites from Egypt. The evil one came after him. Anytime Jesus puts you on the job to bring about a brand new work Lucifer becomes jealous. He puts on his masks. He tweets all his brethren in that province, city or town. They go on the internet and email everyone giving their respective localities. They Instagram or redefine their respective positions.

The Sea of Fire is reminiscent to Moses and thousands of people walking over high mountains, deep valleys and rolling hills.

The Berlin Wall, a guarded concrete wall, with minefields and controlled checkpoints, erected across Berlin by East Germany in 1961 and dismantled in 1989. The religion of Communism fell in Germany in the year 1989—a great feat for Jesus.

Germany one of the most beloved countries in all of Europe had seen many a dictator, but none like the nefarious Adolf Hitler. After 16 years of freedom here came the erecting of the Berlin Wall. Jesus is saying the Sea of Fire came and melted the hearts of the Germans on both sides of the wall.

The fallen wall is Jesus falling three times as he makes his way to the Cross. His life, death, and resurrection is a sign that this unification of brothers and sisters be taken seriously in these perilous times. Jesus is looking.

The Sea of Fire is burning into the minds, hearts and souls of the children, because they see a future of milk and honey. Jesus shows his love to all and sundry.

The Mormon Church came into being in the U.S. in 1830 by Joseph Smith and based on the teachings of the Book of Mormon. The Bible is not the Book of Mormon. The Bible is the King James Version of 1611. It's authentic. It's real. It consists of 66 Books.

Joseph Smith, a prophet, was misguided on his way from earth to heaven. This means that he was shipwrecked and did not wait for a full comprehensive translation from God the Father, God the Son, and God the Holy Spirit. Where is their Holy Spirit? Before the service is concluded do they say that the Doors of the Church is Open.

We live in the End Times and Jesus is raising up preachers for these times. Is there any in the Mormon Church? These are a list of things that Jesus is angry with:

1. There are no preachers in the church that is anointed by Jesus.

2. There are no Revelation Preachers for these times.
3. Jesus is not in their breaking of the bread which they call communion.
4. Tithing is a must.

The Sea of Fire is burning on the heads of all their pastors around the world. Because the Truth is not spoken on the Pulpit. Their tongues are not anointed to speak the Word. Their hands are not anointed to release the Holy Spirit in the belly of anyone. They are not blessed with the gift of wisdom and understanding to guide the church through the valleys of the shadow of death. They cannot raise the dead from the grave and put a new suit of clothes on his body to go preach the Word. Numbers does not count in the sight of God. Your opinion does not count either.

Jesus is showing me that the Sea of Fire is the burning of churches all over the world that misrepresents the Savior of the world. All work and no play make Jack a dull boy. Jesus is very angry with the Mormon Church, because they go door to door to win souls for Jesus. Rubbish, Rubbish, Rubbish, Rubbish, Rubbish!

The great wealth of the Mormon Church comes from the few billionaires that join the church. They believe that the giving of large amounts of money to the church will allow them to enter the kingdom of god. They believe that feeding the poor through donations to the Red Cross, the Salvation Army, and other Charitable Organizations will get them into heaven. They believe that giving their literature freely will allow them into the house of the Lord.

The members of the Mormon Church who are Congressmen and Senators and sit on the Board of Directors believe that Jesus was just a farm boy. There is no lawyer that will allow Jesus to rule over him. There is no doctor that will allow Jesus to rule over him. There is no professor that will allow Jesus to rule over him. There is no architect that will allow Jesus to rule over him. Jesus is looking.

Homosexuality and lesbianism are very high in the practices of the Mormon. The children are not scolded at school or at their homes for this practice. The people go about their business as if God the father, God the Son and God the Holy Spirit owe them something. Jesus owes nobody anything. Jesus is the same yesterday, today and tomorrow. Jesus is the Light of the World. Jesus is the Great I am who sent you.

The psychic hot line in all America has become a billion-dollar industry. How do you break the wall of this religion? Easy. Jesus says I am the Way, the Truth, and the Life. You call yourself a Christian, yet as soon as Our Lord Jesus Christ does not come right away, you turn and call the psychic hot line for a price. What are you doing? You are paying the devil to do his evil work. Jesus is looking.

The Sea of Fire is lingering over marked houses owned by Aristocrats who did the evil to become successful. These aristocrats live in great big mansions. They are dapper, well-mannered and drive very lucrative cars. Many of them were soldiers; technocrats; owners of golf courses; owners of chains of supermarkets. God knows everybody's heart.

Psychic people are seers. Satan, the devil, sits in them to tell you what's happening. The devil has a limit as was shown in the Book of Exodus when the sorcerers encountered Moses. God the Father, God the Son, and God the Holy Spirit knows no limit. In the Book of Job: it reads fear not the one who can kill the body, but fear the one who can kill both body and soul. Why are you running from Jesus?

The vision of the Sea of Fire is Jesus taking the carpet from under the feet of psychics that go around messing with the Sons of God. Psalm 105:15 reads Touch not the anointed do my prophets no harm. Jesus is looking at me straight into my big brown beautiful eyes and saying you are heal.

Psychics cannot heal you in the absolute. Like the doctors that you visit and take their medicine daily, they too cannot heal you in the absolute. Jesus is saying, "Love me, Love me, Love me, Love me, Love me". Turn from your wicked ways. Don't speak falsely of others! This is your own downfall.

Sin is only sin only when you feed sin. Sin is only sin only when you stoke sin. Visiting any psychic person is sin. Whatever the psychic person tells you to do and you go do you have become another psychic. You have become another cheater. You have become another very mean person. Your friends do not trust you np more. Your hands have become dirty.

Remember clean hands and a pure heart shall see God the Father, God the Son, and God the Holy Spirit. We are all sinners born and shape in iniquity. This is our frail identity. When we go and do other things outside of our calling, then we become sinful. Calling the psychic hot line is adding to our sinfulness. The psychic people who were baptized in their youth or adult life will not enter the kingdom of Heaven. Jesus is looking.

You want to go gamble and you call the psychic hot line and is told the number or numbers to play. That's on you. Don't blame Jesus! And please, do not put the blood--ten per cent in your tithing. Whatever you purchase with blood money will determine the level of hell that your soul will dwell.

You want to own 1000s of acre of land and you call the psychic hot line they will tell you what to do. Jesus is not handicap. Your soul is worth more than money can buy. Your soul is priceless. Being able to purchase expensive cars is not the true sign of Jesus. You must know where your money is coming from. Is it clean hands that belong to Jesus? Or, is it dirty hands that belong to Lucifer? Take your pick! Jesus is looking.

The Sea of Fire is also a flame burning in hell and Jesus is raising the flames real tall, so that your annihilation will take place quickly and rapidly. His omnipotence is his keeping his eyes on you daily. Jesus has already paid the price for you. Jesus has already shed his blood for you. Jesus has already died for you.

If what you have just read did not stop you from seeking the psychic hot line then you are mad with God. The question is not why. You have blamed God the Father, God the Son and God the Holy Spirit for everything. Seek ye first the kingdom of God and His righteousness and everything will be given unto you. Are you seeking him?

Psychology is the scientific study of mental processes and behavior. Another wall of religion that makes Jesus angry on earth as it is in heaven. They consistently refer to Jesus as the carpenter's son. The Bible says, that Jesus is the King of Kings and the Lord of Lord.

Psyche is the mind of God; also the mind of Jesus. The miscreants of the scholastic world penetrated Jesus as he made his way to do the will of his heavenly father. God the Father dwells in the belly of Jesus. The Sea of Fire is Jesus who they would like to put on his knees and begged them to stop the sufferings of their love ones trapped in hell. Disobedience, disobedience, disobedience. God does not change.

Lucifer, the devil, a proud rebellious angel fell from heaven on earth for his disobedience. He wanted the seat of Jesus. He wanted the name only begotten son. He wanted to be on the right side of God the Father. He wanted to sit next to God the Father. Jesus is the only one true living begotten son of the Almighty God.

The Sea of Fire is purging the world of the misnomer that there is a field called psychology. Absolutely misleading! Jesus does not need any help. His heavenly father does not need any help. The Bible talks about Lazarus eating the crumbs that fell from the table of the rich man. The well-to-do man died and went to hell. The man of wealth could not bear the fire in hell. He called on God the Father to send someone to talk to his other brothers of the family so that they would no tend up in hell.

The Sea of Fire is Jesus striking the heads of universities in their heads for they to end the department of Psychology. Jesus does not want nobody to play with the precious minds of his people. We shall not forget that we are made into the image and likeness of God. Jesus is still in the healing business.

Too many people are placed in this discipline just for the love of money. Look at the curricula! Jesus is not looking through any window. Jesus is not standing at the front door steering at you. Jesus is not writing every little thing that you do on the face of the earth. Jesus is coming, coming, coming.

The Sea of Fire is Jesus tearing down the curtains from the walls of your eyes so that you will not suffer as your predecessors did. Jesus is the answer to all of the foolishness that surrounds the planet that nobody cares about. No one knows how long it takes to produce the mind of man. No one sees the long hours of Jesus in creating one mind. Every human being is unique. Jesus is looking.

Earth manufactures cars on the assembly line. There is no assembly line in heaven. Every single leaf on any tree is unique. They may look alike, but they are not the same. In real estate no two pieces of land is the same. Every single human creature is individually put together by the loving hands of the Triune God.

There is no nap time in heaven. There is no sleeping time in heaven. There is no TV time in heaven. There is no psychology class in heaven. There is no athletic class in heaven. There is no bingo played in heaven. There is no gymnastic class in heaven. There is no boxing in heaven. There is no wrestling in heaven. There is no motor car racing in heaven. Jesus is looking.

How many courses must include the study of psychology? Jesus is very angry with a world that plays games with the minds of his people. Stop producing mind games! Please stop playing games with each other's mind.

The Catholic Church boasts of their dogmas. This religious church began as it were after the death of Our Lord Jesus Christ. They claim to have the bones of the Apostle Peter buried in one of their tombs fully guarded by the soldiers of Vatican City.

They believe that they have the Holy Spirit and can stir the spirit up in your body. During communion, they will carefully take their time with the Lord's Supper. Their blood at Holy Communion is real wine made in Vatican City and sold to all their churches respectively. The priest, who is an alcoholic must drink grape juice. A splendid change, that should become a permanent rule for all priests. It is a disgrace to drink real wine on Jesus's pulpit.

They burn candles all day and night. They believe in praying to the angels and the saints and offering up prayers in the form of novenas. Candles are sold in the church daily. Services that they call Masses are done daily. It is one of few churches that opens its doors to the public daily.

Confession is held every Saturday in the church. The Priest sits in his confessional box to hear your confession. Then he gives you one our father and three hail marys to recite for the forgiveness of your sins. At the end of the Mass the priest does not say that the doors of the church is open. No priest carries the distinction of Evangelist, Minister of Music or Prophet. Their so-called highest title is Pope which is not mentioned in the Bible. Their Bible is a translation of the King James version with other books added. They exceed 66 books.

The Vision of the Sea of Fire is to remind the Catholic church of its vows given to the first pope who wrote it down yet nobody follows the order.

Since him the church has become political. Priests no longer get married. And they live under the conditions of the church. This means that they have vowed to live a single life.

As I am penning this page the Lord Jesus Christ is showing me people falling, falling, falling. These are risky times and people are hearing the voice of Jesus speaking to them within themselves and directing their path to other churches.

People in these hazardous times need to hear from the Book of Revelation. They need a Word from Jesus. They need to walk in the spirit. They need to be in proper perspective. They need to walk the walk and talk the talk. They need to stop sugar coating the Word of God.

The Catholic Church is a denominational church. The feet of the priests need cleaning. The hands of the priests need washing. The name denominational has to be changed to non-denominational. The walls have to come tumbling down. Evil has to find a new hiding place.

The priests need to change their attire. Leave the robes out! Wear shirts and slack! Or wear conventional suits and ties. They need to stop stealing their own monies and then cry wolf. They need to stop blaming the world for their own wrong doings and misfortunes. They need to remove Mary the mother of Jesus as co-mediator. There is only one mediator and his nameis Jesus.

It is about time for the Catholic Church to begin ordaining women to preach on their altars. It is about time to make deacons of the church. It is about time to remove the statutes from the hall ways. It is about time that they stop kneeling on one knee when they enter the church. It is about time that they preach the Word and stop looking at the clock. It is about time that they stop fasting rigorously and just skip one meal.

This day must be a new day for the church. The bye-laws of the church should be changed and updated. The statutes of anyone sitting outside on the lawn should be torn down.

Rivers of Water shall flow through all the churches. Jesus is cleaning out the house. Jesus is cutting a new road for the priest to finish the job. Jesus is looking.

The Catholic Church teaches that when you have committed a venial sin or a mortal sin or both, you are expected to go to confession. The priest sits in a confessional to hear the sins of its members of the church. This is totally disgraceful. The Bible says, "confess your sins ye one to another". There is no need to have a show. We can all sit with someone that we love and trusts and disclose all our frailties or misgivings one to another.

Confession is good for the soul. We say that we love Jesus. Stop hiding your sins! You do not have to go to a psychiatrist to disclose all of your shortcomings. Jesus is the Light of the World. When we hide our sins, we put ourselves in utmost darkness. This is exactly where the Catholic Church sits. The priest does as he likes. He believes that he is above the law.

The Presbyterian Church is another denomination that conflicts with Jesus. They believe in the doctrine of John Calvin, who was a dropout of the Catholic Church. He brought to the church two things that Jesus wants to talk about. There is no such thing as politics in the church. Presbyterian congregations are governed by boards. Jesus is the Head of all Christian Churches worldwide. Jesus is not about to let anyone run his house.

Jesus is the Presiding Officer. Jesus anoints a Pastor for the job as overseer of his house. The Pastor does not need anyone to tell him what to do. The Pastor comes and brings with him a Vision of the church. This plan is not to be taken lightly. The church is not to be run as a political market place.

Secondly, predestination is a doctrinewhich states that God determines the eternal destiny of humanity. Scholars have a tendency of speaking down to its followers. They believe that they have arrived. Jesus fulfills. Where are your humility? What are you afraid of? There are two fruits of the Spirit that make humankind tremble. They are humility and love.

The vision of the Sea of Fire in respect to the Presbyterian Church is by no means an encouragingone. Jesus is always showing and teaching the church that the battle is not ours, it is the Lord. The Church is not to be run as a conglomerate. The Church is the house of the Lord. Board meetings are not to be conducted in the house of the Lord. Everybody must be held accountable for their stewardship.

The success of the church will not be determined by its wealth. The success of the church will not be determined by its membership. The success of the church will not be determined by its standing in the community. The success of the church will not be determined by its great outreach programs. Jesus is looking.

Everybody wants to be like Jesus. He lives. Jesus is the only perfect one. Jesus is the bright morning star. Jesus is the apple of your eye. Jesus is our redeemer. Jesus is our Lord and Saviour. The walls of the Presbyterian denominational church have to come tumbling down for Jesus to rebuild.

The Sea of Fire will one day swirl around the head of the hierarchy, who will bend those knees and listen for the first time to the voice of our Lord and Savior Jesus Christ. Then the church will have a new simple doctrine. The choir will resonate and pivot in a whole new direction. The angels from heaven will give to the church a real Minister of Music to take charge of the choir. Jesus is looking.

The church will now have real anointed Holy Spirit preachers. The Holy Spirit will be hot, hot, hot in the house, when the doors of the church are opened. The people will be stamping their feet. Holy Communion will be done in the right and proper manner. The choir will be touring and singing a new song that Jesus will put in their hearts.

Now the church will be known for its giving. Ministers will be fulfilling their Ministries. Prophets will be prophesying. The yoke of evil that beset the church will return no more thus saith the Lord.

Greek Mythology rethree goddesses: Clotho; Lachesis; Atropos. The Holy Ghost is a jealous Gpd. The Triune God speaks with one voice. When people travel around the world and visit priest and priestess that see God the Father in a totally different way than one will assume that this is cute. Did Jesus send you there? Your opinion does not count. So is fate and predestination. God the Father sends his prophet to the home of someone to do his heavenly purpose. The Father of the child will have the confirmation of the Word from the prophet. Then the man of God goes into action and he becomes Jesus and the Holy Spirit.

6. To Teach the Differences between God the Father, God the Son, and God the Holy Spirit

My first experience with God the Father came in the year 2001. Sent to Valdosta, Georgia, in the sizzling heat of summer! Though naked, I came upon a woman Pastor, who purchased the house next door and used it as a Church. Sunday morning as I entered into the Sanctuary, she the Pastor, told me, "that the Spirit of the Lord told her that I have to bring the Word".

Immediately thereafter, God the Father spoke to me and said, "turn to the book of Mathew 5:1-12--the Sermon of the Mount, the Beatitudes verses 1-8. Then suddenly, the Lord Jesus inhabited me and he took the driver's seat. It was indeed the first time that Jesus overpowered me. In attendance were the Pastor and her husband the prophet. I preached the Word as never before and the only thing I heard was the heavy downfall of the rain beating the roof of the church.

Out of my mouth flowed Rivers of Waters, a thesis without a topic, Word resounding left, right, and center, as Jesus kept pounding His Word. Jesus is the Redeemer. Jesus is he only one that can save your soul or any soul. Are you trusting in the name Jesus? Your Bible is put away: polish and shine. Your pages are brand new and untouched. Sunday mornings or Christmas time you take your Bible out of the glass ceiled library and off to church. Your Bible is five years old and still looks brand new.

PROPHET ALLYSON MICHAEL D'ESPYNE

Where is your confidence? As soon as you land a great job you forget to pay your tithes and offerings. When the Bible is discussed on the job, you become low-keyed as if the cat cut your tongue out of your mouth. You move out of your neighborhood, because you do not want to associate with them people no more. You promised to help your mother pay off the mortgage on the house, the day your father died. You put your mother's business all over *Facebook*.

Sunday afternoon, you were at the Mall shopping, and you ran into your Pastor. Happy to see you Pastor! The First Lady invited you to church on the coming Sunday. You obliged. You never turned up for church. Your soul is very important to God the Father. Jesus our Savior is right at the side of you waiting. But, of course, you did not see Him. You just answered your very own question. You are blind.

Jesus, most famous miracle, is the healing of the man born blind. Jesus is now prominent. Jesus is continuously working. One day Jesus is taking a walk in his garden, and sees the man, who was born blind. He makes his way to the sight-filled man and says who he is, "my name is Jesus". Invariably, Jesus never withheld his name from anyone.

We love to throw stones at glass windows. Jesus is the glass window. Jesus is nice and clean and we must dirty the window. Whatever your enemy threw at you, Jesus gets a hundred fold in return. Jesus is the King of Kings. They laughed at Jesus, because he is wearing the same clothes daily. Jesus is at the café having a drink of coffee. Jesus is still up three days straight. Yet they say, "that Jesus is a drunk." Jesus is having a cold drink of lemonade. They say that, "Jesus is having a cold beer."

Before Jesus hour is come, his mother Mary told the people at the bridal ceremony, "to do whatever he tells you to do." Jesus does whatever he says that he is going to do. It is not do what I tell you to do and then turn around and go do something else.

The whole world is full of hypocrisy. Jesus is real. Jesus is the truth, the whole truth and npthing but the truth so help you God. Jesus is the Rock of all Ages. Jesus is our everything. Jesus is the standard bearer. Jesus is the silver lining. Jesus is the only hope for us in the Book of Revelation. Where were you, when God the Father and His darling Son begins creation? Jesus is creation. Jesus is innovations. Jesus is the only One who is to come. There are no games in heaven.

We do not need anything earthly to take with us to heaven. We do not need to take any baggage with us. We do not need to take our best clothes to heaven. Jesus is making our custom-made suits in heaven. Jesus is making our diamond-tip golden shoes in heaven.

Where is your belief that when God the Father tells you what to do, you know in the absolutethat everything will be alright? Abraham the first Patriarch and progenitor of the Hebrew people was given a wife Sarah. She was childless. Abraham interceded for his wife to bear him a child. God the Father promises Abraham that one day he will give him a son from his own loins that will inherit everything that God the Father had given to him.

Did God the Father brought about the miracle right away? Yes he did. Everything with God begins with a seed. Then His Royal Highness comes along and manures the seed. Rain falls from heaven in the form of dew and absorbs the seed. The morning sun rises on the seed to give it nourishment and the seed grows into a tree.

The story of Abraham resembles some of us in this day and time. God the Father will speak to us directly. A week later we will call our Pastor to find out what God is saying to him about us. Well our Pastor did not give us a very favorable answer. So we call our sister the Prophetess and ask her a rhetorical question.

Months later we meet a stranger at the supermarket. The stranger says, "that I am a prophet and the Lord says to get on with the business of the day." We return home only to find out that even the dog is aware that we have something to do for God the Father. Yet we still procrastinate.

PROPHET ALLYSON MICHAEL D'ESPYNE

The year has come to an end and we have not begun. to do anything. Where is our faith? Jesus comes along in the form of the Holy Ghost in the Old Testament and as Jesus in the New Testament. Jesus is the High Priest.

Abraham persevered to the point that God the Father had to remind him that he heard his prayer and his son is on the way. It took Abraham forty years and forty-forty nights to see the birth of his son Isaac. Once again, where is your faith?

In today's world our faith is playing scratch. We line up everyday to play the lotto or the lottery. At night, we go clubbing. Or we gamble at the casino.

On the other hand, the preachers will have a cake sale. Churches get together and have a clothes sale. Instead of giving away their used clothing, they are on the roadside as vendors. After the service food is for sale. Then someone comes around selling raffle tickets.

God the father does not make mistakes. He sees you in the distance coming. He knows your every move. He prepares you for the future. Will you make it to the top of the mountain? That's on you! Therefore you shall maintain your focus. Do not sway from left to right. Keep it real! When Jesus commands you to stay at the house! You better not move.

The story of Abraham is more alive than we think. We want instant children. We want the brand new car now. We want the scholarship that Jesus promises us rightaway. We want to be an inventor instantaneously. We want to be a prolific writer, who never wrote a book. We want to be the greatest painter that ever lived but, cannot be taught. Abraham's faith moved the mountain for his wife Sarah to conceive and bear their son.

There are too many women that go childless. What you need to do, pray. There are too many women that go husbandless, pray. There are too many women that do not want to have children, pray. There are too many men that do not want to take care of them children, pray. There are too many women aborting children, pray. There are too many women abandoning their children on the streets, pray.

Prayer moves mountains. Prayer resolves matters. Prayer heals the wound and straightens the tree. Prayer lifts up the soul. Prayer sings out a loud song to the Lord. Prayer puts food on the table. Prayer blesses the family.

Abraham the founder of Judaism was given a son Isaac, the promise. Isaac's wife Rebecca also was childless. Isaac prayed for his wife to have a son, but out came twins--Jacob and Esau. The promise of a multitude of children as the grain of sands at the seaside became apparent. Jacob's 12 sons became the progenitors of the 12 tribes of Israel. And out of them came thousands and tens of thousands of children that scattered a whole globe.

There is no place on earth that is not represented by one of the seeds of Israel. God the father promises the Patriarch that out of his seed as far as your eyes can see will inhabit the earth.

Since 1948, God the Father fulfills his promise to the Jews that one day he will stop their wonderings. Now Israel is a nation in the Middle East. They have taken dry arid land and made it into luscious, agricultural and rolling hills. They have performed a miracle with 8,522 square miles inclusive of Jerusalem.

God the Father gives the whole world the sign of "We Are Lifebeaters". God the Father will not fail you. His Omnipotence will always be on time. There is absolutely nothing that He will withhold from you. God gives Israel bromine, copper, clay, gypsum, magnesium, phosphates, potash, salt. The Jews are the only people on the face of the earth, whose hands are blessed to cut and polish finished diamonds.

The Jews are a sign of a suffering people, who God the Father admonishes. Jesus coming from a line of Kings to the 42nd Generation. Coming to finish the work of Moses and preparing His 12 Disciples. for spiritual warfare. Also laying out a picture of eyes have not seen and ears have not heard the Glory of God.

Jesus's life on the face of the earth was one of tremendous travel. His noteworthy line is I am the way, the truth, and the life had hardened the hearts of his enemies, especiallythose who preach and teach monotheistic theology. No man cometh unto the Father except through me bleeds the hearts of men and women. These words make men tremble.

Jesus life on the planet is only 33 years. His wealth of knowledge shows that Jesus read every book at the library. The genius of geniuses never left anything unread. His sleeping time is but few hours. His work ethic is superbly excellent. His work load is enormously tedious. He will be chanting verses of scripture as he goes about His Father's business.

For transport Jesus will be riding horses and camels across the desert. When Jesus stops by, he will be anointing the sick and delivering his children from all evil. Jesus does not need a telescope. Jesus does not need an x-ray machine. Jesus does not need a computer. Jesus does not need an iphone.

Parents have an obligation to take their children to the library and registered them. The library is a place of knowledge. You want your kids to become an intellectual teach him/her how to read. Make sure that when they choose books, they would have chosen a spelling book!. Make sure that one of those books is illustrative! It is imperative that you have one of the largest dictionaries at the house.

When a child can read at least seven books in one week, you have to replenish the supply. Rereading books are not the best method of teaching children. It would be a splendid idea to take the household to book sales that meet the family's budget. Join book clubs!

Jesus reads from the book of Isaiah where he will be beaten up, scourge, and put to death. This is not predestination. Jesus is. Lives in heaven with his heavenly Father long before any human being knew his name. This is not reincarnation, which is obsolete. This is not a séance. Jesus is God too.

In the Book of Genesis Jesus asks a rhetorical question. Where were you, when God the Father and God the Son created Heaven and Earth before the foundations of the world? Jesus is the truth, the whole truth and nothing but the truth.

Jesus comes home one day to find a letter in his post box. Mary writes and says, "that her brother Lazarus is dead." Jesus is on his way to the house. Mary greets him sadly, and let him know that her brother is now stinking. Jesus under the anointing ignores her narrative. Jesus is led to the graveside of his beloved brother Lazarus, whose sister is Mary. The Holy Ghost, who is God the Father, dwells in the belly of his only begotten Son Jesus.

As soon as Jesus pronounces the Word that his Father regurgitates to him a miracle is unfolding and out comes Lazarus from the grave. Jesus says to the gathering, "unbind him". Proof that God the Father is alive. Jesus embraces his beloved brother Lazarus, whom he weeps for, whilst reading the letter.

The planet will like to receive the feat of Jesus. The first man in the history of the Universe, to raise a man from the dead. The awesomeness of Jesus is watered down by the very churches that he destroyed, when he lived here on the face of the earth, because Jesus allows it. The good and the evil will live side by side, because Jesus allows it. The animals will die every single day unmercifully by the hands of poachers, because Jesus allows it. The wretchedness of societies that created global warming will pay for it, because Jesus does not allow this.

Climatologists have produced evidence re global warming: standardized measurements; growth rings in trees; cores of ice drilled from the Antarctica and Greenland; cores of sediment from ocean or lake beds. Jesus is the only evidence that one shall seek before drawing conclusions of any kind. Noah was just one man. Abraham was just one man. Moses was just one man.

God who is Jesus is still waiting for one of the scientists to bend his or her knees and thank him for a special gift to unravel one of Jesus's mysteries. It is common knowledge that the scientists want

PROPHET ALLYSON MICHAEL D'ESPYNE

Jesus to bend his two knees and give them the glory. Where were you when God the Father and his darling Son were standing on a cloud creating a whole new universe?

Anthropology: the science that deals with the origins, physical and cultural development, biological characteristics and social customs and beliefs of humankind have long been the subject of compromise by European societies that border along the Atlantic Ocean.

They stole animals of every specie and used them as a laboratory of breeding in countries that they believed would enhance and fatten their wallets. In disobedience to Jesus they created a blasphemous crime by mating the horse and donkey to produce a mule. Two animals that are not of the same kind. Jesus is extremely angry, because God does not like ugly. And God does not need your curse.

When people begin to use self-will as a crutch, then Satan, the devil, inhabits them to go and do his dirty work which includes global warming. In the Book of Daniel 12:7 And I heard the man clothed in Linen, which was upon the waters of the river, when he held up his right hand and his left hand unto heaven, and swear by him that liveth forever that it shall be for a time, times and an half; and when he shall have accomplished to scatter the power of the holy people, all there things shall be finished.

Jesus is continuously showing America that they alone are the Super Power of this planet. Yet Presidents after presidents still engage in the evil world to sit in the chair and then become mean to a watchful world. God the Father, God the Son and God the Holy Spirit will not become one with you until you become one, which is fair and just to a whole wide world.

That is why all of God's people are suffering, because we keep bombarding new elements that are not numbered in the 92 elements that Jesus created. These so-called impure elements are not real. The results are: Cancer, Diabetes, Heart, Eyes, Nose, Mouth, Throat and other neurology diseases. It is now that time: that the whole wide world must bend their knees in prayer with their eyes to the heavens any one day for forgiveness to the TRIUNE GOD.

The Prophet Daniel was seeing the hand of God the Father writing on the wall as he laid motionless in his stupor. Jesus came along to give him the answer to the writing on the wall. In these times of risk, preachers and teachers of the Word have told their congregations that the coming of prophets has ended. So prophets as me, who are stoned by the tongues of humankind have no alternative, but to do the will of Jesus no matter what. The road to heaven is never easy that is why few take it. Jesus teaches me that daily. The road to hell is like the river Nile multiplied by 1000 times. Many will take it to damnation.

The Word of God says that in these hazardous times many will come in my name. Jesus already knows all the imposters. Jesus gifts his prophets and prophetess with the eye of discernment. We see the evil one first before he sees us. We rescue children first before we go chasing evil spirits. We adore Jesus, who is Savior and Redeemer of the earth. We praise his holy name. Jesus anoints us deeply, because he sees way ahead of us. His anointing is our strength as we pursue the valley of the shadow of death.

I remembered one day in Florida, more precisely Miami. The year 2000, just coming out of the City of Manhattan, New York. The Lord Jesus told me, let's go to Washington, Seattle. Being a vagrant, we wended our way to Greyhound station, which was walking distance. The fare I had. We purchased the ticket, five days and five nights on the bus. I Slept all day, because everything looked the same. I ate less so that I could keep more money in my pocket. I Lived an austere life. Dressed in black beret, sweaters, slacks, socks and boots.

Daniel a true prophet, whose word never fell to the ground needed Jesus to take him through the deep precipice of a mountainous journey. Steep hills and very steep mountain peaks, no handles or rails to hold on to. No biking roads cut out of the sides of the mountain. No playing fields in sight. Just rough and very rough terrain.

It is all well and good to say that you want to be a Christian but where is your heart of forgiveness and forgetfulness. The world of human beings is consistent in saying I'm sorry. I apologize. It will not ever happen again. The question is did Jesus tell you to say that? Or did you hear it so often that it has now become a paradigm? The answer is Jesus, because he came to lift you up.

Quit running and hiding from Jesus! Jesus wants you to get on with the business of the day, and he will see you through. Quit tempting Jesus! Don't make a mock of His Word! When you need a friend go to the Bible and read your favorite passage with great intensity. Read it with your mind! Read it with you heart! Read it with your soul!

The writing on the wall is presently what you see passing before your eyes on a daily basis. Tattooed and painted bodieshavebecome the status quo. Narcissism has become the order of the day. The now President Barack Obama has passed gay and lesbian marriages into law. Though some states are putting up a fight. Jesus is not going to sugar coatanything. This is Blasphemy and Blasphemy is Hell.

Alighting from the bus in the City of Seattle was like a Saturday like any other Saturday. It was 12 noon but dark and damp with a dry cold breeze. The wind blowing was kind and gentle to my body as I took my time to locate a McDonalds. I entered and walked right up to the cashier whose gender could go either way and paid $1.00 tax included for a hot cup of black coffee. No milk. No sugar. I took my seat on a long-leather cushioned chair. Back pack sitting against the partition, as I leaned on it. My Bible opened on the given Word of the Lord with the smell of fresh coffee in my nostrils. It was not long after, I went into a siesta.

Daniel's vision is stretching all across South America into the Andes of Western South America where the halling of timber and the clearing of 1000s and tens of 1000s of land will create further floods throughout the Western Hemisphere. Affecting animal husbandry, thus creating a void in global distributionof much needed natural resources.

The beginning of World War II in 1939 was all about gold, iron, lead, mercury, platinum, silver and tin. Precisely what the Andes Mountains possessed. The word anta came from the natives that worked in the copper fields of the great mountains. When a country is blessed by Jesus to have a gigantic amount of copper there will always be a war. Because people are hateful. The war stretched out all the way to 1945 for lust of power.

Jesus is constantly showing leaders what to do. But they are hiding behind the fence throwing stones. And as soon as they fall into a predicament, they cry wolf. Then everybody comes running to their aide, without realizing, that they have become another Adolf Hitler. Now the world keeps stumbling, stumbling, stumbling trying to get a grip on a ledge. Jesus is a doer of the Word and not a talker.

Jesus is the Word that became flesh and dwelt among us. America did not start the war, they were drawn into the war thus saith the Lord. Jesus stands on his Word. Are there any other wars forthcoming? Yes there are. Is America prepared or fully prepared for oncoming world wars? America has everything to annihilate any foe or foes. Is there anything lacking in Americans? A sincere belief in Jesus.

We won World War II by using uranium the fuel for nuclear weapons. But is America the only country in the world that produces uranium? No. Kazakhstan is the largest producer followed by Canada, Australia, Niger, Namibia, Russia to name a few. God the Father, God the son and God the Holy Spirit does not play. There will be a place or places unreachable by the hands of shenanigans, that come to rob, steal, kill andplunder.

Leaving McDonalds about midnight, I roamed the streets with Jesus speaking to me. I saw signs for the university which I followed tenaciously. Crossing the street as I would usually step off the curb as though I am on the island of Trinidad brought the state police officer to a screeching halt. The white officer about six foot six towered over me. Stoned face, legs wide apart, eyes unblinking, stared at me in my large big brown eyes. "I can tell that you're not from here". I replied in the affirmative. "This is your first and final warning!"

Jesus does not allow his sons and daughters to walk the streets at night all alone. His speaking to me is 24/7. Even in my sleep Jesus is still speaking. There are no guarantees of life or death. Jesus is no respecter of persons. Obedience is everything. Jesus tells you what to do, you just do it. You cannot second guess Jesus. You cannot stop to think. And most importantly, you cannot question him.

I entered the study area of the university about 1 a.m. There were about 20 students burning the midnight oil. I discovered a book lying around, which I began to read. Before you knew it, I was fast asleep. I heard a constant pounding on the table. The University black police officer woke me up. He said with a firm harsh voice, "this is no place to sleep, the next time I find you sleeping, you got to go!" The next time the chair was pulled from under me. I survived three days.

I vividly recalled my beloved grandfather first black Superintendent of Police and his adorable wife Carmine. His name was Etienne Felix D'Espyne, a man of divine integrity. He taught us in the form of humor. There would always be laughter during our short two-months of summer vacation at their home, at the corner of Freeling and Wells Streets, Tunapuna, Trinidad. He would proudly hold up two fingers in the form of a peace sign, but in this case the sign meant that he took two people to prison in his entire police career. How many police officers could make this gesture? In their first three months, they already have 100 hundred cases in the court house. Grand Dad made it to the top.

In 1991, Argentina, Brazil, Paraguay, and Uruguay formed the Mercosur Southern Common Market. One of the biggest evils that had come out of South America. Another arm of the Prophet Daniel's writing on the wall. The United States of America goes to Argentina and spends billions of dollars in commodities. Jesus is saying that America owes nobody anything. We question God too much and that is one of the world's greatest evils.

Isn't it ironical that in the very said year the Union of Soviet Socialist Republics(U.S.S.R.) fragmented. Whose existence stemmed from 1922 to 1991. A demise of the other Super Power Communist Countries, that were broken up into Independent States. In Jesus there is no irony. God the Father, God the Son, and God the Holy

Spirit allows everything. The Evil of Communism is like the Fall of the Roman Empire. You just do not go do your own thing.

On the streets each day looks the same except Sundays. No traffic. Longer waiting time, standing in line to catch the bus; church buses rolling out between the hours of 9 a.m. to 10 a.m. picking up their parishioners to take them to their designated churches. Most church services begins 11 a.m. to 1 p.m. Some serve a lunch. All churches will pass and pick up the homeless for any service.

In the City of Seattle, there is a free zone, where you can ride the bus for free. The bus takes you from the backdrop of the Majestic Alaskan Mountains and showcase you in front of Macy's a surrogate of the Largest Men Department Store in the World—Macy's Manhattan. A booming and very lucrative shopping area, where the rich and famous spend their money frequently day and night. A metro very similar to the one seen arriving and departing in the Cpunty of the City of Northern California, San Francisco.

London is a producer of coal, natural gas and petroleum. Another hand of the Prophet Daniel's writing on the wall. What is England doing for all its deprived citizens all around the globe? Absolutely nothing! A Queen going out and one coming in. Absolutely nothing! Prime Minister going out and one coming in. Absolutely nothing!

Now England is lying to all of Europe of their shortage of coal, when the queen is the head of state of Australia that has large deposits of coal. As a matter of fact Australia is the fourth leading coal-producing country in the world. Jesus is saying that the writing on the wall is liken to the writing on a head stone of a grave. The aborigines are descendants of Australia's first settlers and to this day have not been given whatever was promised.

The Prophet Daniel took this prophecy with him sewn in his heart when he entered heaven. Jesus Word will not go void. The aborigines were hunted down massacred and killed for what God the Father, God the Son and God the Holy Spirit has blessed them with. They were not just led to the continent. Not because you cannot read and write means that you are stupid. God teaches his people everything.

They are a people humbled by Jesus. They will give you what you ask them for. They will take you to their homes and feed you and watch over you. They are very much aware of their surroundings; they will keep you warm.

Jesus is showing me a fallen soldier fleeing to that part of the world: lost in the wilderness. Who came to his rescue? The aborigines. They did good to him.

It did not take me long to get the tone of the city—a few hours. Thousands and thousands of Ethiopians flooded a certain section of Seattle, which was about a mile from the University of Washington that housed a law degree faculty. In the distance, I saw a restaurant; it was the first Ethiopian restaurant that I ever saw. As I pushed the door open, the chef, small in stature like all his counterparts, greeted me with a familiar greeting of brotherly love. He was very proud of his seasonings. Both the outside and the inside of the restaurant smelled robustly strongly of some seasonings that I have never nostril before. I took my seat and had to slap my face three times before I left. Unbelievable!

Sanctions: authoritative permission or approval that makes a course of action valid. The Prophet Daniel's writing on the wall has put a choked hold on smaller nations and yet still smaller, smaller countries. The small fish or fishes are grossly afraid of NATO. The small fish or fishes are flagrantly afraid of OPEC. The conglomerates shall rule no matter what. The merging of companiesare an evil.

Everything that God has created is unique. Every leaf, though of the same tree is unparalleled. Every piece of real estate, though look the same is not. Every human being coming out of the same parents will have different characteristics. Jesus is magnificent so is his works. Only a few will be gifted with the gift of creativity.

The plan of Jesus is not the plan of the earth. Human creatures be aware, that your heavenly Father took his son Moses up Mount Sanai to write all these laws and statutes for everyone to live by. Jesus sets his boundaries by using springs, water falls, rivers, lakes, seas and oceans. But what we find today, chaos in the world. Whose doing? Your doing. Who cares? Only Jesus. Why? Because it is his world.

We are tested in our tithing. The book of the Prophet Malachi speaks on giving a tenth of gross earnings to Jesus. Jesus does not care if everyone agrees with him or not. John 3: 16 says For God so loved the world that he gave his only begotten son that whosoever believeth in him shall not perish, but shall have everlasting life. In disobedience we tempt Jesus. In disobedience we tempt God the Father. In disobedience we tempt God the Holy Spirit.

Before all this chaos, end times Preachers, Prophets/ Prophetesshave surfaced up. Prophecy. Jesus pre-empts. The Word says touch not my anointed do my prophets no harm. An adage: A still tongue keeps a wise head. David the second King after Saul had to go in hiding, because his father-in-law received the word from God that none of his seed will get the kingship.

Jesus sets the tone. God the Father, God the Son, and God the Holy Spirit went into operation. Heaven prepares for earth to receive. David had many opportunities to rout Saul. He remembered the Word touch not.... It is an example for us to follow.

It took David another twenty years to assume the throne. Secular people like the millennials have no patience whatsoever. The race is not for the swiftest, but for the one who can endure it to the very end. Many battles and wars David had to fight, but his son Solomon, who succeeded him had none. God gave his Son Solomon peace at all fronts. Take a look at it!

There are professional athletes world over making hundreds of millions of dollars a year that Jesus have put a touch of greatness in their lives. Where is your one-tenth? The church in your neighborhood is falling down. You know exactly what Jesus is talking about. Well, go fix it. Or give it to someone, who will leave your name out when she gives the money. Or open a foundation. Jesus loves a cheerful giver.

The Moon shines at night and lights up the whole highway for you to see clearly. Did you see Jesus? You are too busy running the streets and cannot be still not even for a moment. Are you listening to Jesus? As I sojourned through the streets of downtown, Seattle, Washington, wheretechnology is second to none.

Abraham gave his tithing to Jesus whose name is also Melchizedek. King of Kings and Lords of Lords. It is amazing, how people seek to rob Jesus. It issurprising, that they will still try to rob Jesus, though they know that, they cannot take anything with them when they leave this planet. It is astonishing, how people solemnly believe that they can rob Jesus. Who do you think you are?

I was walking up the hill behind the downtown library, heading in the direction of a supermarket. It was about 12 noon. As I was nearing the top of the hill, I felt the pavement moved under my feet. The houses to my right were moving. The street moved up and down like a sea saw. To my left the buildings were dancing. Suddenly I realized, that this is indeed an earthquake. The good Lord Jesus started speaking to me and in that moment Jesus relaxed me.

After the tremor which lasted for about 15 minutes, Jesus brought me to a halt. Then Jesus spoke to me and said let's turn around and go view the seismic damage. After a storm there is a calm. Walking downhill everything looked the same, when I passed by. The sidewalk was the same, because I alone went up the hill and I alone came back down.

As I walked down the main road I could see buildings being taped around with yellow tape. One church was taped around. A few buildings had some cracks in their structure and the steps were sealed off from the general public. The reading on the seismic scale was about 6.9 on that day. But the damage done was not enormous.

After spending about two months in Seattle, Jesus allowed me to receive a gift of a passage by a good Samaritan to ride the grey hound bus to Brunswick, Georgia.

The grey hound bus was packed out to its maximum. If the trip is six schedule stops to your destination, add six more stops because that's the way the bus line works. Excuses! Excuses! Excuses!

I reminisced pushing back my seat all the way back in a lying position. I lived in Philadelphia, Pennsylvania. One night Jesus woke me up and commanded me to leave Philadelphia, the city of brotherly love, for Georgia. Jesus said to me, "I got a church for you in Georgia." I got out of bed and started packing. Thirty suits some three-piece and the others two-piece along with forty pairs of shoes. I placed everything in the trunk of my brand new 1997 Sedan de Ville. The two-piece suits were 10 in number.

The time I left Philadelphia was midnight one day in September, 1998. I took the I95S to Georgia. Driving in cruise, I pulled off the road and filled up the tank. The journey took 12 hours non-stop. I passed about a ton of gas stations; hotels: motels; restaurants; fast food; very few rest stops. Business places of all types displaying their signs with their respective telephone numbers on bill boards standing tall like giraffes clothed in steel. This is America Man. Unbelievable!

Meanwhile the bus pulled off the road after 16 hours of driving. Everybody had to come off the bus and overnight at that station, so that the bus could be cleaned and ready for the next day. This stop was the second stop or so I thought. And after that I stopped counting.

For dinner I had a ham sandwich with pickles and a large cup of Pepsi cola drink. Afterwards, I took my seat and placed my feet on my bag pack and went to sleep. At 5 a.m. in the morning, all the lights were turned on and everyone was awakened by the bus conductor. He spoke over the mike and told everybody to have their boarding pass ready in hand to ride the bus.

Leaning back in the seat I started to recall my entry into Brunswick, Georgia. I pulled off the highway and parked my car in front of Wal-Mart. It was the perfect spot because the conglomerate opened 24/7. Virtually all Wal-Mart Stores open all day and all night. I fell asleep with my Bible on my lap. It was 12 noon. A few days later, perambulating on the pavement of the store, I ran into a Pastor, who told me that when he saw me Jesus showed him green and green means to go. He was expecting me and I became a Minister of his Church. A month later, I became a licensed preacher of the St. Andrews Church of God in Christ, St. Simons Island, Georgia.

The greyhound bus arrived in Brunswick, Georgia about 10 p.m. that Saturday. It took two days. My last visit to this part of the town was in 1998. The year of my return was in the spring of 2001. I made my way to the nearest Super Market, which was a fifteen minute walk. I purchased a sandwich loaf and walked away into the wilderness to sit and eat.

The temperature was excellent. I headed out in the direction of the mall which is downtown Brunswick. It was about that time of night. Walking down lonely streets and sidewalks on opposite sides of the road with Jesus as company means that when you get into trouble that is good trouble. This takes the fear away. Then too, I was in familiar territory. Very relaxed I and Jesus is having a wonderful time.

The next day Jesus is waking me up at the mall with instructions for my former pastor. After delivering the word to me, I proceeded in the direction that I had just come from. As soon as I got to his house, he came outside to talk to me. He enquired about the car and I was about to give him the story. But I had to tell him why Jesus allowed me to stop by his house first. I said, "Pastor Jesus is telling me to say to you to continue your ministry." Yes brother even though you are right, I am not making any money. I immediately remembered my high priest, Bishop Collins, churched at Bread of Life, Savannah, Georgia.

In that moment, I felt and before I could say another word the Lord Jesus shut my real tight mouth and turned me around and headed me into the direction of the mall. It was now about one in the afternoon. Then a big black SUV pulled up at the side of me, I opened the door and got in, a familiar face, money was given to me and I put it in my pocket. I told him exactly what Jesus put in my mouth to say to him. The brother blessed the man of god and so Jesus returns the favor.

Before he let me off, he tip me ten dollars and said, "have lunch on me." I thank him then and I thank him now.

At the super market Jesus is taking me to purchase a bag of yellow raw onions;bananas on sale $1.00 for a ten-pound bag of very ripe bananas; a loaf of bread. After paying for the before-mentioned items, I sat on the outside to have a meal. Jesus says to me to reach in to the bag and take out the biggest onion and eat this one first. I took it out and began to peel off the brown skin. My first bite of the onion had me wondering for a while but I knew that Jesus is with me. It took me about two hours to finish the onion. For a moment I thought that I would have regurgitated it all but the good Lord Jesus keeps it for me. Is Jesus real, is Jesus really real, is Jesus really really real? Yes, Jesus is real.

As the evening sun started losing its way in the wilderness, Jesus says to me that we got to go shopping. Jesus literally grab me by the hand and off to those double doors. He took my gaze from those colored suits that I once wore and reminded me of the times that we window-shopped in the dead of night broke without a penny. This is what I want you to wear. I took down the three-piece black suit and it fitted to precision. Black and white shoes and a black bow-tie with shirt to match. Did I knew that I had all that money in my pocket? No, I did not. But Jesus did.

7. To Go Through The Iceberg

Psalm 150: PRAISE ye the Lord. Praise God in his sanctuary: praise him in the firmament of his power.

> 2. Praise him for his mighty act: praisehim according to his excellent greatness.

> 3. Praise him with the sound of thetrumpet: praise him with the psaltery and harp.

> 4. Praise him with the timbrel and dance: praise him with stringed instruments and organs.

> 5. Praise him upon the loud cymbals: praise him upon the high sounding cymbals.

> 6. Let every thing that hath breath praise the Lord. Praise ye the Lord.

One night in Seattle, Washington, Jesus kept saying to me that he got something to show me. We left about midnight with Jesus leading the way. There was no moonlight. As we traversed uphill and downhill, looking for a Cathedral that I never saw. The places that I am passing I cannot remember ever going there before. As we turned about the twentieth corner and got around a building there stood that huge Cathedral that I would not have seen even during daylight in the distance. Hidden as ifbuilt below sea level.

The Cathedral stood motionless like the huge iceberg that I loved to look at out on the ocean floor in front of the Majestic Alaskan Mountains. Jesus opened my already big brown eyes. Though most times always red. We climbed those steep steps in the front of the church and when I got to the top then I could see to read the Church;s Menu. Then Jesus speaking to me deep within my belly is now laughing and simultaneously talking. We will be here first thing in the morning. I recalled being christened at the St. Patrick's Catholic Church, New town, Port-of-Spain, Trinidad.

Jesus woke me up in an instant. It took some strength to push those very tall solid doors. The eight o'clock mass began in ten minutes. The presiding bishop read the gospel, though his thesis had nothing to do with the gospel reading. At the end of the service, the priest invited everyone to join him for breakfast. Jesus and I were very happy to fellowship. The very bishop preached all the morning masses, and after the final morning mass, we left.

It is strikingly amazing, when you have to cut off a dominant church namely: the Catholic Church that ruled over the family for a very long time. Because it is truly all about doctrine. The adage once a catholic always a catholic is a tenet. What is a tenet? An opinion. Jesus who is Holy Spirit does not care about anyone's opinion. You got to walk in the spirit, so that you can talk precisely what Jesus is putting on your tongue from the inside out. It is a transformation. Oldthings have passed away, and you have become a new creature. It is all about Jesus.

During World War I, July 28, 1914 through November, 11, 1918, in Europe and the Middle East, between the Central powers and the Allies. Germany and Austria-Hungary with their allies turkey and Bulgaria following an assassination in Bosnia-Herzegovina, a system of military alliances plunged the main European powers into a war. The Roman Catholic Church hid a great number of refugees in their sanctuaries all over South EuropeSome of these refugees were Scholars, Doctors, Scientist, Kings and Queens an people of like manner.

Because of their great kindness and goodness many countries throughout the whole wide world gave the Vatican lands, enormous. Then of course, they sent their young missionaries to these countries to build schools and orphanages and churches to carry on their work. And so the elementary school system was borne out of priest and nuns who settled in some of these far off countries.

And so the missionaries started to infiltrate these and open up new ground. They will take children of any age and start to teach them how to read and write. Out of their hard work, people of privilege would send books, pens, pencils, tapes, television sets and technology to help these students come up to par with the rest of the progressive world. Thus enabling them to move on with their lives and make themselves better citizens of the world.

The catholic church is losing their grip in this 21st Century due to the fact that the Holy Spirit is not active in the church. Jesus, who has become Holy Spirit in these turbulent times, is not using the power of the church to quell the fire of the fiery darts of Lucifer.

When praises go up blessings come down. These churches think too highly of themselves. They believe that God owes them something. A position that is called a stronghold. A position that Satan, the devil, loves to subdue you... A position taken by Satan to regurgitate and vomitup his vermin all over you. Jesus is consistently speaking to church leaders to humble themselves, so that Jesus can one day bring them a blessing.

One of the prayers that the church left with me is the Lord's prayer. As a child when you wake up first thing in the morning you knelt and prayed the Our Father. In the Bible the disciples that Jesus love ask their Lord and master. Lord teach us how to pray. And Jesus taught them the Our Father.

A truly magnificent prayer that Jesus created on spot; not just for his twelve disciples, but for everyone. Look in the mirror and tell me, what do you see? A Church without wrinkles, that is God the Father—a holy man without wrinkles. The church in heaven is ageless.

The infantile earth is mindless. The war on drugs is something that the catholic church ought to put on their list of top priorities. They occupy a peninsula that sits on the Mediterranean Sea. One of the major highways of the sea. A corridor that many a cartel sailedl to get to the ocean to distribute their drugs. That reminds me of the City of New York at 3 p.m. Holland Tunnel—gridlock.

Vatican City, an independent state within the city of Rome on the rightbank of the Tiber. Established in 1929. It is the earth's smallest nation 109 acres. It is the pope's residence and also houses St. Peter's Church. In 1976, Jesus blessed me with a windfall of $12,000. One night as I laid down to sleep, a vision engulfed me. Go to France! Did I question God. No I did not. Did I tell anyone? Yes I did, my parents.

In 1982, armed with visas for France and America, Jesus and I fell asleep on an American Airline direct flight to Kennedy Airport, New York. The plane taxied on time. Mr. punctuality. Going through customs was like a breeze in a bottle. Before you knew it, I was on a taxi to 1256, Bergen Street, Brooklyn, New York. The residence of my beloved aunt Zena Williams, my father last sister, both are presently now deceased.

In New York, I could not stay still. I got to get out and see everything. I must walk Allyson it's dangerous. I must walk. Allyson you are not in Trinidad. Take the bus! I must walk. It took me a while before I took the bus. I must walk. What people failed to realize is that on the bus there is a thousand stops. And there is always something. Conversation that you do not want to hear. There is a cultural difference. So before you miss your stop—walk.

On June 10, I boarded the aircraft from Kennedy Airport to Paris, France. The most famous city in the whole wide world. The aircraft's altitude was enormous. The pilot took the plane perpendicular through clouds and more sky and more clouds and more sky. There was a ringing in my ears throughout the ascension. Then, as soon as, the pilot got to his height he put the aircraft in cruise control. I immediately, placed my seat all the way back and fell asleep. The only time I woke up is when the airhostess gently touch me to ask me what am I having for dinner. This or that. I took the curry chicken and rice, over the other choice, because I did not like the way it look.

Everytime the plane enters an airpocket. It felt as though you have just fell off a cliff. You wake up only to find out that you are not even half way there. Then it's daylight. Then it's night. Then it's daylight. Too many intercontinental zones.

It was 12 noon when the aircraft taxied on the Paris runway. The packed plane applauded the pilots. One suitcase was picked up off the ramp. Passport stamped and off to catch a train to Lourdes, France. The veneration of Our Lady of Lourdes, Mediatrix of Graces—one of France most famous pilgrimages. People came from all over the world.

Waiting time for the train was three hours. I paid for the seating area that I can just laid back and sleep. The conductor realizing that communication was not at its best reassured me that everything would be fine once I listened to himEvery six to eight hours the conductor would come to me to find out if I needed anything. Then about midnight he came to me and slowly explained the big why. Half of the train was going to another country and at the appointed time that half would automatically split. The one that I am in will take me to my destination. Already 24 hours had passed.

It was six o'clock Monday morning, when the train had arrived in Lourdes. As I stepped off the train the conductor was very happy to see me off. A cool breeze enwrapped me; my suit jacket that my brother Gene gave to me from his collection of suits was too thin for that 50 degree temperature. A few hours Jesus came to get me and take me to a hotel that nobody spoke English and I slept till ten o'clock the next day.

After showering, I took my seat for lunch, which I ordered. It was rice and red beans with chicken and a bunch of other stuff that was fresh from the garden. Filled to the brim, I got up to leave and the chef ran out from the kitchen to let me know that he has not finished serving me yet. He was totally upset. I did not expect all that food for 10 francs. A whole lot of green leafy vegetables to fill two plates.

Followed by a large slice of cake and a over-filled glass of ice cream. He hugged me and wished me well in French and off I went to go through the iceberg. Jesus will reiterate and soliloquy to me that I did not know what I am doing by following him.

As I entered the first church on site the word peace was heard from the voice of Jesus. Only a few people beside myself was in the church at that hour. I knelt and prayed the Lord's Prayer. Consequently, I left. Roaming the site I came upon one of the largest cathedral's that I have ever behold. It was one cathedral on another cathedral on another cathedral. Two nuns knelt in the front row on either side of the middle aisle. They prayed on their knees for twelve hours. The whole altar was adorned with gold.

The Lord Jesus on reflection is allowing me to speak out in a grandiose manner because these end times would not be as rosy as the honey is sweet in the honey comb. God the Father and God the Son, and God the Holy Spirit is not pleased with the world as it stands. He has shown his displeasure by not responding to the secular world. The only perfect one is Jesus. For all have sinned and fall short of the glory of god. There pope is infallible whether you believe it or not. Their priests walked tall in certain countries. They would not be shackled or brought to justice as happened in all America. They are above the law in a whole lot of countries abroad.

Jesus has prepared me for this journey. The Truth is not spoken on the Pulpit. It does not matter what you think Jesus already gave his life for you and for me. One of the catholic church tenets is a condition of the church. The priest cannot get married. In its formative years he did. They do everything to kill their frailties by beating themselves with whips and the cat-o-nine tails. Self-will no good. The only perfect one is Jesus. Follow him!

Jesus put us here to multiply. The nuns do not get married also. Self-will is Satan. God does not like ugly. This is what the convent has become. Ugly! Ugly! Ugly! Ugly! The sin of narcissism is splattered all over these institutions. But we blind fold ourselves as some of the lawyers do in the justice system. All work and no play makes jack a dull boy. Marriage is Jesus Ministry. Marriage is God the Father Ministry. Marriage is the Holy Spirit Ministry.

It's ludicrous in this time and age for men and women of the cloth to keep on believing that God is sleeping, whilst the whole wide world has gone chaotic. For the few that is doing the will of Jesus. He is blessing you and strengthening you at this very hour. He is presently building a new heaven and a new earth.

Jesus, it is impossible for Jesus to lie. Jesus needs a witness. Jesus needs women for him to put stamina in their bellies. For those who have to travel, he will put them in pairs. He is building Ministries to house women for counseling. He is building Ministries to put women at the forefront. He is building Ministries as battle ground for the angels. Just take a look out on the horizon and you will see what Jesus means by his name.

In retrospect, I reminisced walking from San Francisco to Victorville. The year was March, 2008. It was springtime and I had on a beautiful light spring jacket. About 30 miles well into my walk stood the great Stanford University. Another iceberg that sat on land that stretched so wide and deep. Walls as thick as Cathedrals surrounded with black irongates sewn into brick-walled fences.

When there is a thirst for scholarliness. There also is a thirst for big-game evil. Secular people who want to become leaders in the society will flock to this school of taught. So when you do not wait for Jesus to direct your steps then your feet will dig deeper into the scholarliness of evil. Jesus says that the Word of God is a lamp to my feet and a light to my path. Jesus also says ask, and you shall receive seek, and you shall find knock, and it shall be open unto you.

It's about time that the technology and physics department at Standford University stopped the evil of bombardment of elements thus creating a new element to put to use on the face of the earth. As a result of this, there would be an increase in global warming.

Already the entire Western Hemisphere and parts of Asia, the Middle East, arid mountainous territory in Africa has been saturated with immense heat that has claimed many lives inclusive of plants and animals. Everybody blames everybody and starts pointing fingers at each other when they already know who the culprits are.

Jesus together with his heavenly father delivers his Word from his firmament and here comes 91 elements that are sufficient for all mankind. What do we do? War! Greed! Fame! Then we say that we are loving on Jesus. I Corinthians 23 For I have received of the Lord that which also I delivered unto you. That the Lord Jesus the same night in which he was betrayed took bread: And when he had given thanks, he brake it, and said, take, eat: this is my body, which is broken for you: this do in remembrance of me. After the same manner also he took the cup, when he had supped, saying, this cup is the new testament in my blood: this do ye, as oft as ye drink it, in remembrance of me. For as often as ye eat this bread, and drink this cup, ye do shew the Lord/s death till he come.

After walking, some 400 miles I ascended the mountain of lions a 60-mile walk uphill. I started my climb at six in the morning. The weather was beautiful. On completion of 20 miles a police officer stopped his car and told me that "this mountain has real lions so I am urging you not to continue your journey." I heard him, but Jesus is speaking to me and literally taking me through the iceberg of his firmament.

Jesus says to praise him with a trumpet. How many churches employ or have someone that is able to play the trumpet? Small wonder why so many churches are not being blessed by God the father, God the Son, and God the Holy Spirit.

Too many churches are spiritually dead. On the church's Menu Service starts at 10 a.m. Nobody arrives on time. Jesus insists on punctuality. The church doors must be open half an hour before any service at the church. You need to lift Jesus up.

Holy Communion is served on the first Sunday of the month. On that day very few people showed up to receive the precious body and blood of Jesus. Where is the Jesus that dwells in them? Holy

Communion is the reason why, we attend church. Holy Communion is the reason why we are still waiting. Holy Communion is the reason why wait and wait again till Jesus comes.

The harp is not the easiest of instruments to play. The harp, Jesus commands from his firmament to teach someone or anyone willing or anointed to play this vital instrument. For the angels come out from heaven, praising God to the sound of the harp. Almost 100 per cent of churches do not have a harp. Yet they want Jesus to lift them up.

Let everything that hath breath praise the Lord. But everything that hath breath does not praise the Lord. I paid a visit to Mississippi in June, 2016. As soon as my feet came out of the vehicle to hit the ground Jesus is saying. Evil! Evil! Evil! I was in the town of Woodville, Mississippi. It was Saturday, the most quiet town, which I have ever been. I stopped by the small, but shaggy restaurant, to have a cup of black coffee. It was six o'clock in the morning. The sun was still rising as I pierced through the little rectangular glass window panes to see if anyone would come to the door to let me in. Realizing that there were no footsteps coming to the door, I read the menu on the door that before seemed so obsolete.

The time read eight o'clock, so I sat in a chair on the porch whilst I waited for the restauranteur. Obliquely opposite me was the court house. The main road looked like a side street. One car now and twenty minutes afterwards here comes another one. No town buses perambulating the streets. No human being in sight going anywhere on foot. The town was as dead as a door nail.

Suddenly, a gray car appeared out of nowhere, the city captain, mid-fifty black man, driving in an unmarked car. He waived at me whilst he mumbled under his breath which I took to believe was good morning and enjoy my city. I returned the greeting with a hand gesture as I exchange words with Jesus, the best company on the planet.

Let every thing that hath breath praise the Lord. In 2004, the Lord Jesus sent me to a town called Vivian equal in size to San Francisco. In this town that practically nobody knows about, there are no public transport. Sidewalks are mostly grass and not pavements. At night street lights, that hang off of lamp post, are dim or not erected in that particular side of town. The people are all American beautiful people. The children were kind and respectful and they would continuously refer to me as "Prophet". This I found unique to most other towns and cities.

Wherever I go sometimes I would just turn around even in stride for as not to have forgone unnoticed footsteps running after me. They would find me just to know their future, and sometimes when Jesus starts to speak through me they would be disappointed in what Jesus wants them to be. Jesus is the truth and those of us who carries the truth children would find you and they would tie you to a liein years to come.

We would stand on the street debating what Jesus says, to what they carry in their heart. They would remember what I said about each one of them and for self no remembrance. Some of them would show up more than once to see if I would change my story. Is innocence worth anything? Yes, innocence is Jesus and Jesus is innocence. They would ask me, "why do you wear black in all this heat". My answer is always the same. "Jesus put me in black". "But, doesn't you feel it". Smile.

In the dead of night, Jesus will take me through the town, teaching me all about the shenanigans, as well as the map of the town. Some areas were exclusively all white Americans. In these neighborhoods the houses were more modern and the yards were frequently cut. Acreage per house was about three to four acres or much more. Sometimes, one house stood in the background sitting on about 1,000 acres of land. In this case, the house would be surrounded by a white-wooden fence, with the smell of horses in the midnight dew. His neighbor would have more acreage and a big barn behind the mansion flooded with cattle by the hundreds and thousands too many to count.

Jesus is your knight in shining armor knows everything, sees everything, makes you aware that he is constantly there and will not go away. Jesus uses you as an instrument of his love and he strengthens you in a gentle way as he blesses you. Taking you to higher heights, and deeper depths, as Jesus swirls you around, the steps of earthly heaven to a heavenly heaven.

Leaving the town of Vivian was not an easy thing to do but when a people became nonchalant and not interested in pressing to its fullness then they became food for the evil one. The prophet has to leave when people wants to do their own thing. The prophet has to leave when people do not carry out instructions. Obedience is greater than sacrifice thus saith the Lord!

Let every thing that hath breath praise the Lord. Jesus is speaking to me about the disparities of wealth in this country. Jesus is angry about the economy. Jesus is angry about the distribution of houses in this super pack era. The living wage of every child in each community is definitely not the same. The fare to go anywhere is not equal in proportion to the GDP of that said town. It is not about equal pay across the board. It is about the integrity of the work place. It is about the integrity of the city. It is about the integrity of the parish. It is about the integrity of the province. It is about the integrity of the municipalities. It is about the integrity of the precincts.

The whole world is watching and waiting for hope. There is a whole lot of work to do. The few that are doing something are running out of gas. Namely shell: a huge iceberg on the face of the earth and is doing nothing. It is about time that this iceberg moves out of the way for Jesus to come and blessthe land of this nation. Holistically speaking heaven cares about the entire patient and not the sum of its parts.

It is high time that Shell fall on their knees in prayer. Jesus knows how to bend every arrow and shoot a star out of the sky. Jesus is not playing. This is no movie theater. This is no big screen television. This is no mere drama with the movement of every part of the body synchronizing with the soul. My name is Jesus. Jesus will be respected at all times in mine universe.

No man shall come into my presence except I send and call his name. No man shall walk into my house and command my sons and daughters and subject them to his will. No man shall put them beneath their feet. No man shall rule over my anointed fold. I, Jesus takes care of my own. I, King of Kings and Lords of Lords takes care of my house and my home. I, Jesus will not give way to anyone that is not seal on the inside of the chest.

Jesus is the high priest and there is no other. Stop rolling the dice! Stop calling Jesus name when you roll the dice! Stop mocking Jesus!

Let every thing that hath breath praise the Lord. Jesus is the Lord of our times and without him we are nothing. Just take a deep breath and look around. Tell me, what you see! There is nothing here, which is made by human hands. There is nothing here that Satan, the devil, can lay claim to. There is nothing here that those spirits you seek after daily can lay claim to. What are you doing with your lives? Come follow Jesus!

Take a look at the majestic Alaskan Mountains and the Colorado Mountain Cliffs! No human hands created that excellence in beauty, in architect, in grace, in charm, in wanting to go and touch and feel that it's alive. Join hikers and learn something from everything you see and walk through as you climb magnificent mountains in the future. There is a peace in those hills and deep valleys. Jesus is alive.

Jesus canoes you through canyons, rivers and lakes, while passing under waterfalls, which touch the center of your head at 12 noon, giving you that sense of purpose. Dive off rocks and cliffs and shoot up in the middle of the lake! Now tell me, how you feel? Jesus has built this grandiose world from the ground up and you call him a liar. God the Father and God the Son has built this whole universe. Where is your faith?

Jesus has given everyone a measure of faith. It is as small as a mustard seed. All we have to do is to plant that mustard seed anywhere there is earth. Then we kneel in prayer. At night the dew will come and form a rainbow on your seed and bless it with a kiss of love. Then one day you will be taking a stroll around in your garden and see a miracle. Gosh! It's leafing. Jesus wants you to leave everything for him to do for you.

Trust him! Trust in the name of Jesus!

Let every thing that hath breath praise the Lord. Walking along Greenwood Road, this morning Thursday, October 6, 2016, the Lord Jesus, the Great High Priest, takes my gaze to the dew forming on the plain behind a business place. The dew about three feet high above the ground, stood there motionless waiting for the sun to rise and shine on the misty floor. The time is 7:30 a.m.

Jesus speaks to each one of us daily. Are we hearing him? Really! Are we listening in that moment for instruction? Or are we too busy trying to get ahead of the vehicle in front of us, to cause us to miss the moment, and in essence miss Jesus. The morning sun is shining in our eyes to slow us down, so that we can communicate with the voice of Our Lord Jesus Christ. We pray before we leave the house; we must learn to wait for an answer.

We already write up an agenda for the day. Whose handwriting is it? Or are the angels prescribing to you the direction that you shall go? We believe that we shall give ourselves direction and use our mind to follow through on our thoughts. Can Satan be in our thoughts? Yes he can. Do we really, really want him in our thoughts?

We try to run a race without Jesus. Even though we know that the race is not for the swiftest but for the one who can endure it. Then we realize as we race around heaven that God the Father, God the Son, and God the Holy Spirit is not competing with us. Because, we made our mind to use our free will. We do not need Jesus to teach us what to do.

Little do we know that we need Jesus in every single thing that we do. We often think that we only need Jesus when something happen to us. This is a fallacy. Our first meal is breakfast. We need Jesus to tell us, what to eat. Why? Every single day is different. Every single day, the weather can change two or three times that day. Owing to these constant changes the body does not have time to adjust to all these different temperatures. The result is sickness.

Jesus expects us to communicate with him more than we do presently. We need answers to our questions. We do not need to question him. Jesus reads our minds and hearts daily. He acts on what he thinks comes first. It is imperative that we allow Jesus to have his way with us. Jesus alone can fix it. We must remove flesh first to allow Jesus to come in and break every branch that is evil.

Jesus wants to help us to forgive our debtors and now he can free us so that we can breathe again. It is easy to say that you are sorry. It is easy to ask for forgiveness. Do you have a forgiving heart? And now can you let it all go. Will you ever bring it up again? Jesus alone can fix it.

God the Father, God the Son, and God the Holy Spirit has to breathe His Holy Spirit in his children. Jesus has to teach them how to love:

1. Honor your mother and your father.
2. Have respect for everyone and have more for your elders.
3. Always find something to do at the church.
4. Visit any sick either at their home or the hospital.
5. Pay attention to the needs of the church.
6. Remember to give to the poor and the homeless.
7. Never take No for an answer and persevere through Jesus.
8. Give thanks to Jesus for his everything.
9. Be continually praying for someone until Jesus shows up.
10. Be punctual and regular in attendance at church.

For we are lifebeaters marching on to victory in Jesus.

Let every thing that hath breath praise the Lord. Jesus keeps me up all night long to see and bear witness of the happenings of the day. The whole East Coast is being ravished by the storm that they called "Matthew". Jesus is saying that the reasons given for the storm is not real. People must bear in mind that Jesus is alive and is doing every thing to get the world's attention. What we call a storm is not a storm it is a whirlwind and Jesus is in his whirlwind. What we call an eye is not an eye it is Jesus surrounded by his angels in the form of the wind and is pointing out the atrocities of his world.

If only we will listen and use the God-given talents that he has put in our souls then and only then will we see him in his glory. Jesus is truly His Majesty the King and there is none beside him. Jesus will not leave heaven alone to go ride the wind all by himself. The Cherubims and Seraphims will be with him wherever he goes. The whirlwind is his office whilst his subjects are the most beautiful of angel.

When Jesus parades the sky with speeds of 200 mph Jesus is allowing those countries to know that heaven is not a place for triers. Heaven is a place for doers. Heaven is a place for all children. Heaven is a place for all lovers. Heaven is a place for losers who became successors. Because the losers seek the Lord Jesus with all their might, that's power.

But the world will constantly be hyper by looking at the meteorologist as he goes through the moment of the day and the night. Little do we know, how it felt, when Jesus was pierced with a lance. Some of us live our lives as though it never ever happen. Many of us blame white folks for rewriting the Bible and claiming that it belongs to them. The bible began with the Hebrews—the twelve tribes of Israel. The rest is history.

Jesus is constantly sending his prophets door-to-door in every Christian nation under heaven. Their job is to speak the truth and to do precisely what heaven dictates to them. Prophets come in all shapes and sizes. Prophets receive messages from God the Father, God the Son and God the Holy Spirit. Their purpose is to deliver the Word in spirit and in truth. Their mission is to sew the seed of Jesus into your heart and allow Jesus to do the rest.

The coming of Jesus means time for action. Jesus is saying repeatedly that his coming will not be ever be picked up by the media. His coming will not be known by any newspaper company. His coming will not be seen on TV. His coming His coming will not be seen on social media. His coming will not be anything that was put in the movie "Armageddon". Jesus wants the world to know that his coming is already taking place.

Let every thing that hath breath praise the Lord. Jesus is wondrous. Jesus is remarkable. When Jesus gives you a directive, he expects you to carry it out. Jesus transfiguration is a wonder of the world. Here it is all his clothes turned white. I have never heard of this phenomenonbefore Jesus or after the risen Lord. A whole world is taking Jesus for granted. A whole world is going about their business as usual. A whole world believes that Jesus owes them something.

In as much as Jesus and his Father owns the entire universe then life should be nice and easy. Everybody should be able to do what they want to do. Life is already hard and difficult. The rich gets richer and the poor gets poorer. The work week should be short and everybody should be paid for staying home. Jesus does not make it easy for anybody. God the father did not make it easy for His Son.

It is easy to be given gifts and we sit around all day long and do nothing with the precious gifts that Jesus has bestowed upon us. Time is precious. Time waits on no one. Time is Jesus and Jesus is time. As a child when I open a door for someone, that person will say, "thank you very much." Now it's a surprise when someone says, "thank you very much."

The world has not really change. The people no longer care. Yes, they love everybody. That's lip service. You ask a man for ten cents, 911 is on the way.

Let every thing that hath breath praise the Lord. Jesus is praying with eyes lifted up looking into heaven whilst the planet is praying with eyes downcast. Jesus is standing in line and waiting his turn in the line. Jesus is saying that the world rushes to judgment. Jesus is saying that members of the family want to know from Jesus if everyone will be in heaven eternally. Jesus takes his sweet, sweet, sweet, sweet time to answer, and the family slams the door in disgust and goes their way.

Jesus is saying to everyone that each person stands on their own two feet. There are higher heights and deeper depths. Jesus is reminding each one that no one comes to the Father but by me. Jesus is saying that everyone sees the rising sun but how many of us will not see the setting sun. Jesus is working constantly with the stars way up in heaven.

The sun which is a star Jesus is shifting and bringing it closer to the earth. In this way, the earth will have longer winters; shorter falls; longer springs; shorter summers. The sun will give the food more vitamin A: thus enabling man to live much longer for him to see what eyes have not seen and ears have not heard what Jesus is taking you through.

Jesus wants mankind to have the best the very best. All Jesus asks in return is that you praise him. Praise him as you get out of bed first thing in the morning. Lift your hands up high and praise him. Praise him and dance! Jesus calls everyone citizens of the earth.

Jesus wants us to tolerate each other and be respectful to our neighbors. Jesus wants us to learn to accept each other and bear each other's pain. Jesus wants us to support each other and show kindness for one another. Jesus wants us to take a good look at the world as it is today and look deep into our heart and find a place in our heart for Jesus.

The world will still be here when we are long gone. The hills and the plains and the valleys will be here too. The fishes in the rivers and lakes and the seas all around also will be here. The animals that we pass and see daily also will be here. It is easy to turn your back and look the other way. It is tougher to do right and be resolute.

Let every thing that hath breath praise the Lord. There are quite a large number of runaways all across America. Especially young people seen as it were in train stations hugging their bag packs as they fall asleep sitting in the open air. Parents wondering where there virgin daughters are right now.

Grandparents searching everywhere asking questions be it friend or stranger at every bus stop; at every mall; at every large library in the daytime. As one can see them always in a hurry to leave as they disappear in the crowd. Children looking for answers in the wrong places, as they hitch hike over bridges and dangerous highways running from Jesus who truly cares.

Some will turn up at shelters looking grown as real adults and escape the watchful eyes of people who are doing every thing to locate loss children. They are armed with a fake ID that looks like them as they go through homeland security who patrol the borders both day and night.

Teenagers feel that they are grown and totally invincible. They believe that they can outrun any adult. Jump over any fence and the police will never catch them. They are street smart but not Jesus smart. They will not relent even when caught. They will distant themselves as far as East is to west and as far as North is to South. They made an oath that they will never everreturn home for what has happened to them in the middle of the night.

They trust no one not even themselves. They easily become tearful, when they have no money for food. They will absolutely do anything to survive. These are the pains of a wounded America.

Let every thing that hath breath praise the Lord. Saturday, October 8, 2016. When the Lord Jesus permits or allows a vision to distract you early in the morning it just demonstrates the failures in America. I remembered as if it is actually taking place at this very moment the word "xenophobia." It isa word thatonly foreigners or strangers or Jews can profoundly relate to. It is a word coined to put fear in your soul.

Whatever was promised to me was never given. I took every test in my profession namely: proofreading. They would always say, "that I did excellent," but where is the job. As a result, I decided to attend St. John's University, New York, and do Real Estate. I must get to the bottom of this. It's either racist or prejudice or both.

After two attempts at the state examination I passed. Not satisfied with my no-sales performance in New York. I again decided to take the New Jersey Real Estate examination. Already living in East Orange, New Jersey, I enrolled at a business school in Bloomfield. The state examination was much longer and ambiguous. At least 25 per cent of the questions had nothing to do with real estate. Anyhow I passed.

Let every thing that hath breath praise the Lord. Foreigners are not rapist. Foreigners are carefully vetted and it costs a whole lot of money. This test. That test. This test. That test. This test.

Jesus is extremely angry as is demonstrated along the waters of the Southern States of the Bible Belt. Jesus is saying that it is all well to kneel and pray, because you see with your eyes what is happening. Really. Jesus wants you to know that Jesus does not bring a spirit of fear but of love. Where is your love? Where is your gift or personal gift? Too much rhetoric!

Let every thing that hath breath praise the Lord. Jesus is showing me the future into the future. The whole world is cringing and trying to avoid despotism. Can Jesus give a man an island? Can Jesus give a man all England? Can Jesus give a man all of Europe? Yes, Jesus can.

There was a time when Noah owned the whole world. God the Father, God the Son, and God the Holy Spirit speaks to his son daily. He took Noah everywhere to prove to him that he alone lived on the planet. Jesus is the instrument of proof. Jesus says prove me. Not try to make a fool out of me. Jesus owns the whole Universe. Indeed, this is a mystery of faith.

Alaska is a state of the United States in NW. It is 1,519, 000 sq. km. once owned by one man. When people want to doubt God the Father, God the Son and God the Holy Spirit, they are starting a fight with the Triune. This goes for all fundamentalists. Radical Islamic movements are all the same; they try to be like the three in one. They are one and the same.

Jesus is attributing the alphabet to the Levites, who assisted the High Priest Aaron, when his brother Moses was doing battle with the enemies of Jesus. The gift of the Levites flowed through the Phoenicians. We live in a world where anything goes; we do our earthly best to stop or try to eradicate the foolishness. Where is Jesus?

Let every thing that hath breath praise the Lord. Jesus is saying that we despise him personally, when we have to go to the bathroom. On earth as it is in heaven. Rich folks look down on nurses whose daily job is to clean patients. They do not want those dirty hands to touch them accidently or otherwise. They will report them instantaneously. They will be fired on the spot.

The hospitals work closely with private nursing units. So that when a nursing assistant is fired, here comes another one from another agency to fill the spot or patch the wheel in the tire. The private nurse makes more money. Is there a serious problem in America?

There is always a problem when Jesus is not lifted up.

Let every thing that hath breath praise the Lord. Jesus is sayingthat there are a whole lot of surreptitious people in high places that should not have been there in the first place. Jesus is saying that God the Father, God the Son and God the Holy Spirit already knows the outcome of the general elections. Jesus also is saying that he will be helping in the house-cleaning of Washington.

A people call to law is a people call to justice and a people call to carry out the functions of such high an office must be beholden to Jesus, when he or she breaks the law. Height is might. Jesus has two big piercing eyes too. Jesus does not need anybody's help. Jesus blesses the one that goes out into the world and do the will of his heavenly father, no matter what. A directive given from above returns with love. A directive given from above returns with self-control. A directive given from above returns with humility. A directive given from above returns with longsuffering. A directive given from above returns with goodness. A directive given from above returns with faithfulness. A directive given from above returns with kindness. A directive given from above returns with peace. A directive given from above returns with joy.

Let every thing that hath breath praise the Lord. Jesus is saying that the seniors are still not treated as somebody in the society. The question comes up as to how old are you? Jesus is older than everyone on the planet. Jesus is older than all the angels in heaven. Jesus is older than the heaven and the earth. Everybody wants what God has created on the face of the earth;forgetting that every thing on the earth is old.

How often must Jesus object to polarization? How often must Jesus reject discrimination? How often must Jesus tell you guys what to do, and what not to do? Are you listening to Jesus? Jesus already knows the answer. When much is given much more is expected of you.

Jesus is showing how people react to places. Where is he from? China town. The answer is polarization. Where is she from? Russian Hill. The answer is polarization. Where are they from? The Ghetto. The answer is polarization. The fall of the Roman Empire was built on polarization. The fall of Greece was built on polarization. Polarization is just another word to replace systemic slavery.

Let every thing that hath breath praise the Lord. Jesus is saying that all Americans must learn to love their neighbors as themselves. When we give, we give it all to Jesus. When we share, we share it all in Jesus. When we return from war, we give it all to Jesus. When we tell our bedtime stories we release the pain of war. When we hug and kiss each other, we show love beyond compare. When we walk hand in hand along the side streets, we show great communion amongst our friends and strangers.

Jesus is looking for volunteers to enlighten. It does not mean the philosophical definition given in the 18th century. This is not acceptable; for in no way reason is above every other thing. Jesus is building a movement into a spirit of light. Jesus is the light of the world. There is none beside him. It is a transformation. Jesus is building a garrison on the face of the earth. In this garrison, will be housed his soldiers who have passed the test of discipline, tolerance, patience and self-control.

It is exclusive non-gender. The readings will be exclusively from the book of revelation. A leader will be appointed by a given word from above. The word will be confirmed by one person, because Jesus does not cause confusion. Parents of anyone could come and attend in utmost obedience. It is not an earthly enterprise. When others have refused God's ministry, then Jesus is going to do something to electrify the planet.

The earth shall know who God is. The earth shall know who Jesus is. The earth shall know who Holy Spirit is. The earth shall choose between light and darkness. The earth shall choose between brother and sister. The earth shall choose between right and wrong. The earth shall choose between heaven and hell.

This is not my story. This is the story of Jesus. This is not my opinion. This is the story of Jesus. This was not foretold to me. This is the story of Jesus. This is prophecy.

Let every thing that hath breath praise the Lord. Praise ye the Lord. When they shackled Our Lord Jesus Christ and take him to prison. Jesus already was tried, convicted, and sentenced on spot. The same applies in this secular world that we call change, progressive and has grown beyond the *status quo*. No, no, no. When you stand for Jesus--the same thing that happen to him--will ultimately happen to you.

8. To Confess To One Another

Time waits on no one. One day journeying to Alaska by Greyhound, the bus pulled up at the Canadian Border. And from where I sat, I could see the roots of the Majestic Alaskan Mountains. What a sight to behold! Jesus in his humor puts a smile on my face in moments of despair. The Canadian border police officers were much more relaxed than I thought they would have been. When I showed them how much cash I had in hand they told me that it is not enough for one night.

Trusting in Jesus is an enormous task. When Jesus says let's go. Jesus means right away. You cannot stop to think. You cannot stop to see what you got. You just got to keep on moving. As I sat waiting for the next bus to come, I recalled vividly my trip from Seattle to this juncture. I remembered that in my bag pack I had two packs of underwear;five black cotton long sleeve shirts;two slacks and five pairs of socks.

Was this adequate or suitable for Alaskan temperature? No. Jesus wants his sons and daughters to trust in him at all times. As I cross my legs. I noticed that my black boots though comfortable, was not steel-toed. The snow on the ground in the far-off distance was as rugged as the sides of the cliffs. The mountain peak from where I sat, I could not see. Too high to see through clouds so thick as if Jesus is speaking to me both inside and outside of my being. Invariably. Is Jesus really here? Yes he is.

My Bible was safely placed in the front compartment of my bag pack. My Bible is the Holy Bible (authorized King James Version) Thomas

Nelson since 1790--Sixty-six Books. The only time that I would read is when Jesus is speaking to me and he will literally take my hands and turn the pages to the scriptures that he wants me to reminisce. Then Jesus will begin to break down the word for me in the present time that the world is at and of course the big why.

Nothing escapes the genius of geniuses. I recall this morning Tuesday, October 11, 2016, sitting up in my bed listening to the news on Fox channel at about four in the morning. My hands as it were in shackles, but like my right hand there is still freedom. My eyes are wide open as Jesus is taking me through this vision in this moment. At this time, Jesus is speaking to me through the eyes of the shackles.

Many a time we believe that Jesus forgets just as we try our utmost to forget. Many a time we think that Jesus will not forgive us simply because we cannot ever forgive ourselves. Many a time Jesus forgives us and we will still be asking him to forgive us. In Jesus eyes there are no venial sin and mortal sin. Sin is sin. There is no big sin or small sin. When you sin, you ask for forgiveness immediately.

The Catholic Church believes that there is nothing wrong in playing the game Bingo. What is Bingo? Bingo is a game of chance in which each player has one or more cards printed with differently numbered squares on which to place markers when the respective numbers are drawn and announced by a caller. A winner is determined and money is given as a prize. The catholic church is wrong and has wronged their people in believing a myth of catholic philosophy. This must end if the church wants Jesus to come in to the hearts of the fallen children of God.

It is easy for staunch catholic people to brush off the notion that the priests cannot be held accountable for this grave wrong doing. The Holy Spirit has charged the catholic church for the sin of depravation. Bingo is morally wrong. There is no other way to describe it. Chance is gambling. And gambling is chance.

Then there is the Derby: Any of various annual horseraces, especially for three-year olds. Horse racing is a contest in which horses ridden by jockeys are raced against each other. People gamble by placing money on the horse that they have selected to bring home a prize at the end of the race. The catholic church as well as the offspring of the catholic church flock these Derbies to gamble under the heading of "having fun."

Matthew 5:32 But I say unto you, That whosoever shall put away his wife saying for the cause of fornication, causeth her to commit adultery and whosoever shall marry her that is divorced committeth adultery. One of the dogmas of the Roman Catholic church is no divorce. Indeed this was the problem with the first pope. He who was married had a problem with his wife. And so other cardinals, archbishops, bishops, priests and laity found themselves in uncompromising situations. These marriages could not stand the test of time.

So here came another tenet: political. The catholic church then formed themselves into a political body. The majority of priest voted against marriage to avoid the stigma of divorce. Shame! Jesus has given his sons and daughters divorced ministries all across the world. Jesus is saying that the truth is not preached on the altar of the catholic church. The church today still holds on to their self-opinionated dogmas.

To confess to one another is something that we need to do every day. When we wake up in the morning to see another day, it is common knowledge that we will sin at least six times this day. That is why we must slow down and examine our conscious during break time. We quickly sin in our thoughts at a moment's notice. Jesus is saying that some of us already have been wounded in our temples by Satan, who now lives in them.

As soon as someone enters our space our thoughts begin to conceive evil things. And that is why we pause in that moment and say, "thank you Jesus". Jesus will be with us quicker than we think. Jesus knows our situation better than anyone else. In silence, he will stand by us. In silence, Jesus will teach us his ways.

Holy Spirit preachers like myself are on duty for Jesus all day and all night. Jesus puts us in places to do his will. Sometimes people do not wish to be bothered. Or sometimes people do not understand the true workings of Lucifer. Jesus is continuously dealing with members of family to bring their gifts to the store house and watch Jesus work. Some people are held in strongholds and are in dire need of help.

War-torn country like Aleppo, Syria, that is continually bombed by Russia on a weekly basis, whilst everybody wait to see if justice from Jesus will soon be coming. Human beings fail to realize that the Syrian people really did not do anything wrong to Our Lord Jesus Christ. Just as the man born blind parents did not sin to cause his blindness. God the Father, God the Son, and God the Holy Spirit allows the Satan to do his wickedness, so that everybody worldwide must see the evil of ISIS.

The world looks on as though they are powerless towards Radical Islamism. Humanity knows that Jesus will one day come to fix it, when Jesus already gives to them 91 chemical elements to take care of the evil. When they keep stalling that means that they have not been paid a bribe to complete their mission.

Agnosticism is the belief that no matter what is preached on the God's Pulpit does not mean anything to main stream political technocrats. How dare you say that reason and scientific evidence should be the sole guides to finding truth? Who do you think you are? Jesus has never been to no earthly university. He has anointed preachers, evangelists, prophets, deacons to teach you guys that Jesus is still in charge. Jesus teaches them as he taught his 12 disciples. Jesus's school. One on one. Holiness versus, one who is shape in iniquity. That is what you all need the truth, the whole truth and nothing but the truth.

The Methodist Church is a Protestant denominational religious organization. It is a movement originated with groups of students at Oxford University. It was founded by John Wesley and his brother Charles Wesley, who followed him. In 1738, both brothers joined the Evangelical Revival of the 1700's. Where is Jesus in all of this? When Jesus does not send you, who did? Satan did.

Jesus pre-empts his cousin John who was baptizing his disciples before Jesus came. As soon as they met, John took Jesus in the river to baptize him. The Holy Ghost came down from heaven and alighted on Jesus head. This is my beloved Son in whom I am well pleased. Follow him! Where is the Word, that the brothers should have from the Holy Spirit, before they undertake an enormous job? Where is the Holy Spirit that possesses them?

Prophetic word came out of the mouth of John there goes the Lamb of God, whose shoe strings I cannot tie. God the Father, God the Son and God the Holy Spirit wants truth on his pulpit.

The Church of England is the symbolic head of the Anglican Communion. It is one of the world's largest Christian denominations. Anglicanism combines elements of both Roman Catholicism and Protestantism. In the early 1600's God the Father, God the Son, and God the Holy Spirit gives this church a mandate. In today's world they have become a weak church.

There is no such word as denominational. It is non-denominational. This church also is marrying gays and lesbians. An atrocity of life. It is good to say that you left the catholic church and form a new church. But now look at what you are doing. Jesus is saying that you must not allow big business to get into church's affairs. This is your failure. Boast about Jesus and not how much money you got to spread around.

Martin Luther German theologian and leader of the reformation, has founded the Lutheran Church. In 1521, his opposition to the corruption of the papacy and his belief in salvation through faith alone equaled his excommunication from the catholic church. His belief in remission of sins from purgatory through indulgences is far remote from the truth. There is no such thing as purgatory. There is no such place as purgatory. There is a heaven and a hell. For you to say that there is a place where the souls of those who have died in grace must expiate their sins—this is ludicrous. This is high treason.

Where is the scholar's humility? Where is his passion and love for the poor and the homeless? Where is his wife? In furtherance, where is his wife and children? It is all well and good to defect from the stronghold of catholicism, but did Jesus send you? If so prove it. Where is the Word? State time and place! Indulgences are evil. One must learn to live an austere life. One shall learn to love Jesus with all his might. Jesus is teaching us each and every day to coalesce with each other and break bread with one another.

Now the Lutheran church is marrying gays and lesbians just as their brother Episcopal (the Anglican Church). It also shows that Martin Luther was homosexual. He too had a mountain to clear and could not do it. Homosexuality is Satan, the devil living in you.

God the Father, God the Son and God the Holy Spirit does not want religious bodies on the earth. Jesus is patiently allowing this evil to dissolve themselves and kneel and pray. Jesus is raising up Ministries to replace denominations because Jesus is cleaning the house out. Are you listening? Now come follow Jesus!

To confess to one another is freedom of the soul. People are trapped in their mother's womb and the ancestors' graves at the cemetery. On the day of the funeral, the one who is seen getting up far too often is the one that never seized the opportunity, to forgive their mother or their father or their brother or their sister. Lucifer has just made an impact.

At the cemetery he or she would be real close to the grave diggers. The wailing person would be the first one to throw a piece of earth into the hole as soon as the casket is laid to rest. Then the wailing is louder and louder and louder as it turns into screams and shouts. No one has to come to this level when Jesus has given you every opportunity to confess and to forgive.

Others are seen laying the wreaths very carefully on the grave and fussing. They too has wrong the deceased and now has purchased a wreath or wreaths as a form of confession. And if you tell them anything, they become very mean and angry. That is why there are fights and abuse of loved ones at the funeral and sometimes revenged. Jesus is saying that lost time is lost time. When someone

PROPHET ALLYSON MICHAEL D'ESPYNE

dies their breath, which is their soul, leaves and goes to either heaven or hell.

The Pastor is there to see that the body of the deceased person is put to rest and to protect the body from Satan.

To confess to one another is like a beacon on a mountain top. Jesus is infinite. There is no sin that Jesus cannot forgive you for except, the sin of Blasphemy. This means to speak of God or a sacred entity in an irreverent, impious manner. To revile execrate. To sin against the Holy Spirit, is to curse Jesus out. Jesus is not shape in iniquity. Jesus is the true son of the true Living God. Without him we are nothing.

Jesus is speaking to professors of tomorrow. There will come a time when a student will come your way needing lots of help. The student would have just buried his love one. His memory is slipping as if going into a coma. Until you have buried your parents individually then and only then you should give that student to someone else who already has buried a love one. And because time is of the essence, work with wisdom and understanding.

To confess to one another takes trusting in each other. It is wrong to tell someone verbatim everything that someone just relate to you. It is wrong to write down the date and the time of the discourse. It cannot be used as evidence in the court of law. After exchanging each other's narrative one shall now bow one's head in prayer. Jesus is not playing house.

When two people say that they love each other, they should have that humble spirit. There is always an argument between two people. One shall keep one's mouth shut, whilst the other one shall speak. It shall not be debatable. Silence is golden. Jesus is the answer.

Some children confess their sins to their parents; come to find out they are all over Facebook. Parents must bear in mind that Jesus sees everything. Parents must bear in mind that Jesus hears everything. Parents must bear in mind that Jesus does not like ugly.

Jesus is saying that the sins of the parents will not fall on these children. As a result of this the children lose respect for their parents.

To confess to one another makes you a better person. It shows that you will not hide anything from anyone. It is integrity. Jesus is saying that integrity is a virtue that world leaders are greatly lacking. This too is the instrument of war. World leaders often believe that God, the Supreme God, owes them everything. This is a profound fallacy. This is deceptive. This is erroneous.

Jesus is constantly drawn into a dog fight with Satan, the devil, when it is not the time and the place for the Word of God is not given. People who are waiting for the end of the world to see or bear witness to this phenomenon will be disappointed. Jesus is doing all that he can do to ensure that families get to heaven, but families are weak and heavy laden. They are lacking in confidence.

The earth is round and not square was a problem with the world's greatest physicists. Until the journey of Christopher Columbus in the year,1492. The Then king gave Christopher a ship load of convicts because he never expected his return. But Jesus was with Christopher for in obedience he undertook his journey to discover the New World. When he got to the islands of Trinidad and Tobago, he saw three mountain peaks which he named "La Trinity". Then he stopped over to caulk his three boats, the Pinta, the Nina and the Santa Maria with the black tar. He made the pitch lake of Trinidad known to the world. Little did he know, that it is and indeed it is, the largest pitch lake in the whole wide world.

The discoveries of Christopher Columbus led Spain to colonize the islands of Trinidad and Tobago. The tiny islands measured no more than 1900 square miles. The gold and copper that they found in the island of Trinidad were all taken to Spain. Now the twin islands are a Republic.

Then he sailed West and discovered the New World now called "America". A vision that he had, since his youth. Jesus is constantly saying that nothing happens by guess. If Christopher Columbus did not follow his vision, then he would have lost the golden dust that heaven poured on him, in his mother's womb. His greatness. He did not steal fame.

To confess to one another is a breath of fresh air. Friday, October 14, 2016 at 8:30 a.m., I am walking with my parasol over my head in an easterly direction going to do the will of Our Lord Jesus Christ. It is fall and it is raining, when Jesus puts my gaze on the rising sun. It is like a horizontal line stretch out for miles parting the clouds as the rain drizzle right before my eyes. The temperature is about 69 degrees nice and cuddling.

Jesus is saying: Enough is Enough. Whilst the world is going left at speeds of 1,000 miles an hour, and everybody is on the train. Did they see what I see? No, they are too busy listening to music or texting someone or fighting over the telephone with their friends or their children. The day passes by and nothing gets done. They like to hear the sound of their own voice.

Jesus is as quiet as the mountains. If we will listen and pay attention to what he is saying in your mind, heart and soul. If you will fasten your seat belt and compose yourself and get some perspective, now Jesus can flow through you as the river Nile flows through many countries in all of Africa.

God the Father, God the Son and God the Holy Spirit makes us in his own image and likeness. A little less than the angels. What is your problem? Where is your focus? Do not blame Satan, the devil for your misstep! Jesus is saying that each human vessel is given a measure of faith. Where is your faith? It is as small as a mustard seed and grows and evolves into the largest tree in the entire world. The birds and the bees come and play in the arms of the loveliness of the sun.

The morning sun is there to lighten up the valleys in your life. Jesus is not your modus operandi. Jesus is teaching you, if only you will stop and listen. His teaching will not be anything close to what you have grown accustomed to. You must be born again by fire. You must have Jesus living in you. Now you are Holy Spirit fill. A new creature is evolving inside of you; there is conversation as never before.

Jesus came to give you power. Where is your power? Jesus came to give you a sound mind. Where is your sound mind? Jesus came to give you love? Where is your love? Lucifer came to steal and destroy as a roaring lion. Anything missing from the three--that means Satan got it. No excuses! God the Father, God the Son, and God the Holy Spirit is waiting for you to give you strength.

Grace and Mercy are at your front door. Just as the sun is stretching out its wings, between the clouds in the horizon, are you seeing it? Yes, we all have a choice either light or darkness. Jesus forces no one to come follow him. God the Father forces no one to come follow him. Holy Spirit forces no one to come follow him. You choose in love. The choice is yours. Procrastination is an evil.

It is all in the mind that when the Lamb of God woke you up this morning to see a brand new day, Jesus woke you up to do you evil. Jesus is saying: Enough is Enough. Self-control is one of the fruits of the spirit. You need to pray, pray, pray until you physically hear the voice of the Lord. You need to say thank you Jesus for seeing a brand new day. It is a new beginning for you if only you can pray unceasingly.

Some of you need to form prayer lines all across this country. Each one praying every 15 minutes or giving a testimony until the day is done. Jesus is saying over and over and over again you take of the homeless in your immediate neighborhoods I will surely take care of you. Ask him the size of his shirts and pants and go buy him precisely what he needs and you will see a miracle before your very eyes.

Jesus is speaking to me to tell you that he will always be with you especially, when darkness appears in your very lives and the palms of your hands you cannot see and there is constant pain in your ankles and knees. I am on my way. Hold on, Jesus is on the way.

We all are expecting miracles in our lives. Some of us are out of touch with Jesus. Some of us are blaming ourselves for things we did not say or do only to satisfy our frailties. Many of us fail to forgive ourselves even when we know that Jesus already has forgiven us time and time again.

To confess to one another is like the rain falling on my head. Jesus is saying that every living creature on the planet needs the rain to provide the essentials and necessities of life. Jesus says prove me. Jesus is saying that the falling rain is beating on the windowpanes. Jesus is doing all that he can do to get our attention. Are we listening? Do we have to wait for another?

Jesus is speaking in the narrative. The falling rain beating on the roof all night long is to keep you up with Jesus all night long. Jesus does not sleep. Jesus is constantly working with his heavenly father building a new heaven and a new earth. Preparing for your homecoming; giving you your heart's desires. Jesus loves to send signs. Jesus wants you to be resolute. Jesus wants you to be firm. Jesus wants you to be unwavering. Jesus wants you to be determined.

Jesus wants to bless his people abundantly. The falling rain is to wake you up early in the morning and get you in readiness for sunrise. There is something unique and beautiful and splendid about the rising sun. The early morning sunrise puts you in alignment with God the Father, God the Son, and God the Holy Spirit. A sweet, sweet perfume coming out of heaven through your nostrils. The angels keep you up all day and put you to rest whenever they feel to do so.

Jesus is continuously on the lookout for a few laborers in the vineyard. Jesus is constantly searching the hearts of men to carry out his promises made to his fellowman. Jesus is seeking out new vessels to undertake a good work in this world. Jesus is on the horizon keeping a watchful eye on his flock.

The falling rain is to prepare you for the future that is forthcoming. The future is ours to see. The future is ours to behold. The future is unfolding each day. The future is bright. Jesus is speaking to us in the rain drops that we see. Each rain drop represents 100 atoms in our bodies. Each dew drop represents 1,000 molecules in the atmosphere. With the rise of humidity comes the fall of less dew drop in the early morning.

Everybody is running around trying to fix and alter change. Jesus alone can fix it. When you play with fire you will surely get burn. When you want to play in the league of god you will get burn from Jesus. This is not a threat. This is the truth. Jesus expects you to kneel and pray anytime something goes wrong. Jesus does not want you to call the psychic hot line.

These sins become curses and curses become blasphemous too. There are families that are cursed with leprosy. Jesus will come and cure those members of the family that prays and seek his face daily. There are families that are cursed with cancer. Jesus will come and cure those members of the family that prays and seek his face daily. There are families that are cursed with leukemia. Jesus will come and cure those members of the family that prays and seek his face daily. There are families that are cursed with voodoo. Jesus will come and cure those members of the family that prays and seek his face daily.

This is to let you know that Jesus cares for everyone. Any failure belongs to you. Jesus is forever knocking on the doors of animism. The belief in the existence of individual spirits that inhabit natural objects and phenomena. The belief in the existence of spiritual beings that are separable or separate from bodies. The hypothesis holding that an immaterial force animates the universe. No matter what Jesus does people will still believe in the garbage that besets the world.

This practice is about 10,000 years old. It is to show that satan, the devil, will never give up. You better believe it! God the Father does not allow Jesus to kill and destroy any spirits, because the time for annihilation is yet to come. Some Christians lose sight of the fact that Jesus cannot be pushed by anyone for God is unchanging. Jesus is unchanging too. Jesus is saying do not tempt the Lord thy God IN VAIN.

Jesus is speaking out not only to animists but also to the many people who believe in cults, secret orders, witchcraft, black magic and all the evil that they can dirty their hands in the washing of their hands in blood.

To confess to one another is like the early morning sun showering its brightness all over you as you walk resolutely to do the will of Jesus. Tell me, when was the last time you did an endearment act? When was the last time you hug and kiss your 90-year old grandfather? When was the last time you visited your ailing grandmother? When was the last time you mailed out a postcard to any member of the family? Be truthful!

This is Jesus time to speak, because we have run out of gas a long time ago. Today is Saturday, October 15, 2016. We believe that we will become another god just like Adam and Eve taught by listening to Satan, the devil, in the Garden of Eden. The day you eat of that tree or touch a leaf from that tree or come close to that tree, you will surely die. One and only one commandment that is given to the first human beings on the planet. Today we are still fighting God. It behooves us to at least try. Now Satan, the devil got you.

This is what we like trickery. The sun pouring all over you means that Jesus is allowing you to see and bear witness for another day. Did you say thank you Jesus? No. You are your own man or woman. You do not have to listen to nobody. You are grown. You are a big man. Where is your humility? When last did you make a phone call to anyone? Do you have a life? Jesus does.

We speak about temperament: the manner of thinking, behaving, or reacting—the characteristic of a specific person. Who are you to judge? Until you have been washed by the blood of Jesus you will be continually walking in circles. You will never enter the promise land. Jesus does not conjecture. Jesus is not trying to do anything. Jesus lives. Do I have a witness? Thank God he lives in me.

The angels up in heaven see and hear everything that transpire on the earth. Few of us are able to see angels ascending and descending in the sky. When we tell others; they laugh at us. They call us crazy. Invariably, you can tell when you are among nonbelievers. They love to use the word crazy. Jesus is saying: Enough is Enough. It is all jealousy.

The early morning sun is the garment of Jesus spreading throughout the earth. We breathe in fresh air from the morning dew. We take deep breaths as we walk through His Majesty the King. Yes we serve a jealous God. We bring nothing; we take nothing with us. Jesus does not want us to envy one another. You see something that you like stop and pray to Jesus for that lovely pair of blue shoes. One day a miracle will unfold.

We become fearful that a new boss overseers us. We do not know his or her ways. We do not know how to act. Jesus is saying that he is in command of his ship. Jesus is saying that it is not a numbers game. Jesus is saying that the distinguishing mental and physical characteristics of a human are all about conception and not perception. God the Father, God the Son, and the God the Holy Spirit pours his uniqueness into you to make you different to the other person. You did not earn this. This is God's gift to you.

Jesus serves at all times. We want to serve him when we feel like it. We want to go to the house of the Lord whenever we choose to go. We want to change the dress code in the house of the Lord. We claim that it is antique. Well, heaven is antique. We want to change the vision of the church. Well, heaven is the triune god's vision. We want to be the first to orchestrate change. Well, heaven is unchanging.

To each his own. We show Jesus that at all times we shall have our way. Jesus garments spreading over us is a blessing; that is why early to bed, early to rise. Scholars have taken many children in the wrong direction. Scholars have dug deep and wide graves and have thrown many of our ancestors in the name of God. Scholars have burnt many a serving soul running for Jesus.

Holy Spirit preachers world over have the formidable task to take their followers to the threshold of the steps of heaven. Jesus is standing right there to open its doors for his children. Heaven will be a welcoming home for all his obedient children. There is room for everyone.

Let's sit at his table and have a meal!

To confess to one another is like becoming a soldier in the armed forces. What you see here, you leave here. It is a good and desirable thing to be optimal. We all have family in the armed forces. We wish them well and we keep them in our prayers. But as soon as word comes that he or she is dead, we begin to question Jesus. We forget who we are talking too. We turn and go the other way. We lose faith. We lose trust. We do not go to church no more. We become a loner.

Jesus is saying, you ain'tsee nothing yet. My prophets were beheaded for the love of Jesus. My saints were raped and abused in ways that you will not understand. My children been abused in the night clubs; on the highways; in the classrooms; in the hallways; on the buses. Jesus is literally standing there. No prayers in schools, or rather no prayers in public schools. Do not blame Jesus! Blame yourselves!

The road to Jesus is a narrow road. Few will take this road. The road to hell is wide and varied, many will take this road. Isaiah 2:4 And he shall judge among the nations, and shall rebuke many people; and they shall beat their swords into plowshares, and their spears into pruninghooks; nationshall not lift up sword against nation, neither shall they learn war any more. A statute representing peace in the world was erected in front of the united Nations building with some of this reading.

Jesus is saying that Jesus is the sign of peace. The world shall know much more world wars, because this is what the world wants. The world wants to take over your country and make your people slaves of that country. They want all your uranium. They want to control all of your network. They do not want capitalism. They want communism. Satan does not give up.

When you want to give in to the whims and fancies of a unbelievable world, here comes Satan. China will bow obsequiously before you with their so-called mark of humility. It is about time that we wake up and smell the roses of Jesus giving you that sweet, sweet, sweet, savor. They will love you for turning your swords into plowshares. They will love you to take your focus off of them. They will love you to come and sit and talk. Just rhetoric.

All communist countries are in cohesion with each other. They have built a strong bond that only Jesus can break. Jesus is saying that the good and bad people will live alongside each other. Sin has already entered the world. The law been broken thousands and thousands of years ago. Preachers that are under attack will fall for anything. Jesus is saying that we have not seen anything yet.

Soldiers returning home ought to be contrite. They have seen things that they need to share with their love ones. They will not be the same person. Families have to be strong and prayed up for their return. Cultures around the globe are different. Word means a different thing in each other colloquial vernacular. That is why you need to have Jesus living in you. You will surely take him wherever you shall go.

Yes we have to be patient with our love ones who have given their lives in service of their fellowman. It is an honor. It is an honor that must not be taken for granted. We have to ignore their screams at night. We have to abide with their loud or soft speech. We have to tolerate their change in beliefs and table manners. People do change. We shall not give up; we shall pray unceasingly.

We shall fight with all our might. Prayer changes things. The war movies are censored. Soldiers view and see everything in the raw. It is graphic. It is real. Jesus is real. Jesus is not going to bow down to any statute on the earth. Jesus is not going to allow anyone to steal one's dignity. The flood gates of hell are open for those souls. They will be lost forever.

Our veterans at the hospitals need more nurses. Our veterans who are disabled need your prayers. Our veterans who are shut-in need your love. Our veterans who are wounded in their soul need you to stand in the gap for them in every church that you visit for the first time. Jesus is watchful.

To confess to one another is like the sun being overcast by a cloud and now you can look straight into the sun without getting blind by the rays of the sun. Today is Monday, October 17, 2016. It is a little humid and there is an overcast in Shreveport, La. It is now nine o'clock as I head out to do the work of the Lord Jesus Christ. Jesus keeps me up when everyone is sleeping and there is tremendous conversation and sometimes laughter as though there are people beside me in a play with words.

Confession is good for the soul--an adage of tremendous depth. Growing up I will wander off to listen and hear seniors speak of their experiences. Conversations with them were far more rewarding than my peers. I remembered I was about 18 years old already working with the St. Vincent de Paul Society in my neighborhood. This particular young man, who I visited at least once a week, knew my entire family.

George knew my grandparents on both sides of the family. Though blind, he lived on the property that he managed for the white owners that trusted him. He stayed in a one-room that had everything. I distinctly remembered a quadruple table with a single chair and a black telephone. I believed that the table was of oak wood. We would be engaged in good, sound, clean conversation. He was excellent in civics. He knew everything and everybody in the New Town neighborhood. He dwelled in a beautiful, rich, upper part of my street.

It is ironical, that age for age, I have not found that and those cherished memories of a friend long gone whose funeral I never attended, because I was not there in that moment of his passing away. But in this moment, it has surfaced up. Jesus is saying that when human beings have moved on in their lives, we really cannot be everywhere like Jesus at the same time. And of course, no one ever telephoned me or come to the government Printing Office to deliver the news, which was only three blocks away from a dear-lost friend.

Jesus is zillions and zillions and zillions of megabytes in memory than anyone in the universe. Jesus remembers much more things than you could ever imagine. Jesus is a sense of humor, which he shares with you as you sojourn hand in hand with him on a memory walk. Jesus keeps your knowledge in his memory for you and returns the answer in visions on a day-to-day basis.

Jesus is forever young and his voice is forever youthful in a childlike tone. Jesus is speaking to everyone whom he has placed in positions of authority. He rallies them to shape their business for the future. Jesus takes them to task when they allow the devil to overshadow them. In decision-making Jesus plays a major role in innovations for the future belongs to no one else but Jesus.

Jesus is at all times with you especially when you are absorbed with family affairs and cannot separate yourself from the business of the day. In other words, leave the business outside the door, when you enter your home each day. It is called "family first."

It is now nearing noon time, and Jesus is saying that the world is seriously out of shape; it needs to come back home to Jesus, who has never slept with a close door. For Jesus's eyes is forever open and his doors are open forever for his sons and daughters to come in and go out as new creatures to show a dead world that Jesus never really died on the cross, but was put to sleep by his DADDY a miracle when the stone was rolled away.

Jesus is saying that the sun is not doing the work that is required of it to do at this point in time. Jesus is speaking to his world, which has become diabolical and overrun by satanic spirits whose job is to discredit the children of Jesus in a very sinister way in this month of Halloween (a month of devil worshippers) in all America.

Sad to say that parents of the secular world still naïve to believe that there is no evil in existence in this world. They look at evil as having fun. Yes, evil is having fun with the souls of your children, when they go from house to house and store to store dressed like somebody else, whose lives they would become in the future. Success does not mean like unto Jesus. Success does not mean like unto God the Father. Success does not mean like unto Holy Spirit. Jesus is saying that Halloween is Satan. The same Satan, who was thrown out of heaven, because he wanted to be Jesus and take his place and his seat in heaven.

To confess to one another is like the afternoon breeze blowing on you at speeds of 50 mph. Jesus is saying that the sun rolling all over you is his love for you that is exceedingly great and powerful. Jesus is speaking and is very careful in his delivery of the Word of God. When God has taken his time to mold you in his grace and mercy, do not expect others to embrace you. Do not expect your mother to embrace! Do not expect your father to embrace you! Do not expect your brother to embrace you! Do not expect your sister to embrace you! Expect the world to turn against you!

Jesus comes to save sinners. Jesus comes to silence the whoremongers, who will not give up their livelihood for the love of Jesus. Jesus comes with the breeze to teach you that he has to cover you with his feathers as in Psalm 91. Jesus comes in speeds to rescue you and change your direction as you walk with him. Jesus is never alone. You too will not be ever alone. Jesus angels are constantly at his side and all around him.

Trusting in someone is the peak of confession. Love conquers all. Jesus is talking and is repeatedly saying Enough is Enough and god alone knows that nobody is listening to the voice of the Lord. Heaven knows that one day their lamp will be without oil. Abraham trusted in Jesus and waited for his heir to his inheritance, a boy child named Isaac, at the age of 100 years old. We cannot even standup and wait for anyone or anything for five minutes.

The world would be in chaos as it is in chaos in this year 2016. The pundits, who are false prophets, that were not ordained by Jesus, to prophecy Word, would always be held in high esteem for the high office and position they now inherit or attain, as though it was given to them by appointment by God the Father, God the Son, and God the Holy Spirit.

Jesus is sometimes showing me the sun beating on the glass. Showing me together with the three in one as "We are LIfebeaters". For those of you who do not believe that there is life after death. Look at your babies, who affix their eyes on your every move! Tell me, what you see? That's Jesus letting you know that one day both of you will be in heaven one day. That's all it takes, just one day.

Some of you have aborted your child or children, because of peer pressure. Or sometimes, because of family pressure. Jesus is saying those children are happy in heaven with Jesus. Jesus is saying that the false prophets, who will come to you to tell you that you are a criminal or a murderer are indeed the criminal and the murderer of these times. Judge not or you will be judge.

Jesus is not going to let go of this subject. Far too often a girl child is raped by family or friends of family and the blame is put squarely on the young lady because she asks Jesus for a large family but then does not know what to do and how to go about doing it. On the other hand, family will know the thoughts and dreams of their children and take on the persons as husband. Lies! Lies! Lies!

The young lady cannot tell the difference. Satan comes to trick and to put us in strongholds so deep that we cannot even see the top of the hole that we were thrown into. No food to eat; no drink to drink; no one to turn to no matter what.

Jesus is right there at your side waiting for you to say yes to Jesus. Jesus is right there for you to call his name out loud. Jesus is right there waiting for you to listen to him gently speaking to you in the form of a favorite hymn that you will now begin to hum and hum and hum and hum until you fall asleep.

Then of course, you wake up in the dawn of the morning, only to behold that the morning sun has not even risen yet. Jesus is saying that Jesus got you. Jesus is saying that Jesus got all of you. Jesus is saying that Jesus has to spin you around to deliver you from the spirit that inhabited you, for you to feel all alone, when he is with you through thick and thin. There is nobody that will stand with you but Jesus. There is nobody that will take the shots of the fiery darts but Jesus. There is nobody that will bear your pain of your miscarriages but Jesus. There is nobody who can do you like Jesus, but Jesus.

To confess to one another is to take time and spend time with Jesus. How many of you are spending time with Jesus? How many of you love the Lord? Do I have a witness? Jesus is your witness. Jesus is your arms and your legs and your toes and your fingers. Jesus is your beginning.

Jesus is saying that as soon as you drop off the children at school this time is Jesus time. Time to relax and to have a conversation with your Lord! Time to allow Jesus to have a Word with his daughter! Jesus is saying that this is quality time and shall not be interrupted by no one else save your husband. Jesus is saying that this is what is wrong with the world we cannot put aside time to spend with Jesus. We too busy, giving our time to the devil, that is why nothing gets done.

Jesus is saying that time is Jesus and Jesus is time. We must learn to come to Jesus without the baggage. We must learn to come to Jesus without an agenda. We must learn to question him not. We must learn to say thank you Jesus repeatedly. We must learn to go to church to break bread with Jesus. We must learn to be contrite. We must learn to be more tolerant with each other. We must learn to speak the truth at all times. Lies are not diplomacy!

Jesus is sometimes allowing you to fall into diverse temptations. This is to make you resolute. This is to make you patient. This is to make you virtuous. Jesus is firm. Jesus has to make you securely fix in a position of respect for one another as yourself. Jesus is subtracting first before he adds to what he has already given to you. Jesus is shaping your adversities into an instrument of healing for someone else.

This is something that people do not seek from the Lord Jesus Christ. Jesus is saying that when you have become an instrument of anything that is of God the Father, God the Son and God the Holy Spirit. Jesus can use you effectively anywhere that he puts you to bring about a good work in Jesus name. Being an instrument is a great favor of the Triune God.

There is another thing that nobody wants to do that is to walk blindly in faith with Jesus. Remember that: Now faith is the substance of things hoped for and the evidence of things not seen. What is Jesus requiring of us to do for him today? Jesus already knows that we will be itching to ask him a lot of questions before we undertake this formidable task. We must learn to allow Jesus who is the Lord of our life to take control. We cannot allow flesh to lead, when we have to be led by the spirit of the Lord Jesus Christ.

We cannot allow fallen pastors to come into our lives to teach us how to pray. We cannot allow parents who have back-slid to come to dictate to us the wrongs and the rights of life. We cannot allow our congressmen and senators to come to show us who Jesus is when Jesus we have already eaten his Word. We cannot allow our so-called friends who hold high-paying jobs in the society to rule over us when we have Jesus speaking to us. Walking blindly is precarious.

Jesus loves danger. Jesus will not allow you to fall over a cliff. Jesus will not allow you to commit suicide. Jesus will not allow you to be killed by a passing truck. Jesus will not allow you to be beaten by anyone physically. Jesus will not allow anyone to poison you to death. You will always overcome.

There are a whole lot of preachers who have rejected Ministries from Jesus just because there was no money to be made from them. Forgetting that Jesus, who loves you with his whole heart; can give to you any amount of money that you will need in your lifetime, without you doing anything for Jesus. Jesus is our morning sunrise. Jesus is our morning sunset. Without faith we can do nothing.

Jesus is still saying Enough is Enough. Too often we want something for nothing. Too often we want to look for another and compare between me and you. Too often we rely on somebody's good word and good wishes because they are affluent in the society. In other words, we put them over Jesus.

To confess to one another is as solid as a rock. We become too emotional in our everyday life. We become too spontaneous in our actions towards others and get hurt thereafter.

9. To Persevere through the Mountain

At 12 years old, I won an exhibition to attend Woodbrook Secondary School. It was the first desegregated school that I had the privilege and the honor of attending. After five years of continual failures in all five disciplines, I decided to go to God the father, God the Son, and God the Holy Spirit and made a vow to attend church every morning for the rest of my life. A promise I kept.

Then one Saturday morning, on my return from the six o'clock Mass at St. Patrick's Catholic Church, one block away from my home, my mother (now deceased) came running to me to break the good news. She said, "that yesterday while she was walking down Tragarette Road; she ran into the government printer, her non-biological cousin, who told her that he is having a test at the office for an apprentice and that he will keep me in his mind." After hugging and kissing my mother for such a splendid job well-done, I immediately went into prayer in that moment. Thank you, Jesus.

A fortnight later, a letter came in the mail from the government saying "that a test will be given on the following Saturday at nine o' clock and only one person will be selected for apprenticeship." In that moment, I did not know what to do. In that moment, I did not know how to act. In that moment, I did not know what else to say or to do, so I gave it to the Lord in prayer.

That Saturday morning came faster than I envisaged. Being early for church meant that I would be early for the morning examination. Did I study anything? No, I did not. After a quick breakfast of scrambled eggs and toast bread with hot chocolate tea and condense milk, I proceeded to walk three blocks to the Government Printing Office, a familiar sight.

On arrival thee were at least nine people in attendance. Carefully taking my seat in the front nearest the aisle, Jesus quietness surrounded me. The math was elementary. The spelling test I knew every single word. I left feeling good, but a little speechless. On my way to the house, I soliloquy: only one out of ten.

On Monday, August 14, 1969, I reported to the government printing office to begin my tenure of a five-year apprenticeship.

The Jesus I knew then is not the Jesus that I know now. In this moment Jesus is speaking in that time Jesus was not speaking. Jesus is saying that this is a world of opportunity. And this is what America stands for: the land of opportunity. But sad to say, there is xenophobia.

Jesus did not bring me thus far to leave me all alone. I remembered as a Real Estate Agent at Prime Rentals in New Jersey, a young black woman, came to the office accompanied with her mother-in-law for me to take them to see some apartments. I recalled on the day in question, I took them to see a beautiful apartment owned by Mr. Goldberg, a very affluent white man. He is one of the wealthiest businessmen in all of New Jersey.

After taking these two beautiful black ladies to the apartment, from the corner of my eye I noticed a black man standing nearby who I assumed was the Super. Keys in hand, we ascended a flight of steps to the respective apartment. On opening the door, the young woman threw herself into me embracing me and saying that "I want this apartment now! It is near to the school that I want my son to attend"".

Immediately, I chauffeured the two ladies back to the office to write-up the contract. The young woman first-week's pay was enough to qualify her for the apartment. However, Mr. Goldberg started to drag his feet on the deal and would not return my then manager Mr. Monty's calls. Meanwhile, my client had already bought all the furniture for the apartment and had to spend extra money to keep them in storage.

Repeated calls failed. Then one day after almost two months in waiting, Mr. Goldberg, who was silenced because he knew that she was black and was wearing a mini skirt (so he was told by the super) called the office and gave her the first month rent-free for all her troubles. This was just the beginning of a new chapter for me.

A few months later, Mr. & Mrs. Williams, a young black couple, were interviewed by me and was qualified to purchase a house for about $400,000. The couple was black Americans and was very successful. They keep telling me that they have the cash to pay for the house. After careful selection of the house in the particular neighborhood and specific surroundings that they wanted to own property, we proceeded to the house as shown in the Real Estate Manual.

When we got to the property, it was the most gorgeous three-bedroom house I have ever seen and showed in my life. Owned by an Italian, who sat at the entrance to let us in and seemingly unconcerned, a white man in his fifties. The floors were hard-wood and well-polished. Clean as a whistle, ready to move-in, well painted and impeccable. The couple was in awe. On returning to the office, I filled out the contract and the couple gladly signed all the necessary paperwork. It was as it were a done deal--A Cash Sale.

Mr. Monty made many calls to the owner and none was ever returned. We lost $16,000. My commission would have been $8,000. This led me to make a decision of a lifetime. I felt the power of racism in all of New Jersey with one exception my boss, Mr. Monty.

Seeing is believing and touching is the naked truth. God the Father, God the Son, and God the Holy Spirit is put to wonder as to why we cannot get along with each other. Jesus demonstrated this with his twelve disciples. They were all of different backgrounds. Jesus taught them how to love one another. Jesus taught them how to get along. Jesus taught them how to share by the breaking of the bread.

Jesus is saying that human beings tend to be carved into their cultural heritage. Rest assure that even Jesus has a tough time in schooling one preacher in defiance of his culture. Jesus comes first. Jesus is not going to subject himself to the whims and fancies of the beliefs of mortals. Where were you when I and my Father was shaping the moon and stars? Who are you to tell me where to sit and where to stand?

Faith moves mountains. Where is your faith? When you come down with cancer, where is your faith? It is put to the test. To pass the test you have to move the mountain. To pass the test you have to not allow yourself to back-slid. To pass the test you have to give a true testimony. To pass the test you have to have Jesus living in you. In other words, you have to have the Holy Spirit. These are the crosses you bear, when you are not receiving Holy Communion regularly.

You come down with Leukemia. No problem. This is only a test. Why are you worrying? Do not allow doubt to enter into your heart! Jesus is waiting for you to say "yes" to the Lord Jesus. Far too often, the creatures of the planet that are made a little less than the angels take the Triune God for granted. Far too often, we allow vanity to get the better part of us. Far too often, we go window-shopping with our friends, and the next thing we do is to break the glass, because it became convenient for us to do so. This is stupid.

When the people of God are not healed by the Doctors that Jesus have put in your way. Then who are the false prophets. Of course, we are and not the Doctors. Are there any false prophets among Doctors? Indeed there are. Jesus is saying that having a sickness is not the end of the world. Jesus is saying that the family of the wise will come to the home and pray. Most times Pastors get together and pay a visit not just to their parishioners, but also to the sick in the community.

Jesus is saying that no man is an island. We must commune together as one for Jesus to come in. we must pay our tithes and offerings. We must hold on to our families and love them through it all. When you want to stand aloof, Jesus will not be there. When you want to show that you are worthy, Jesus will not be there. When you want to believe that you can make it alone, Jesus will not be there. When you want to change your family for rich friends and associates, Jesus will not be there.

Jesus is saying that I came often enough to wash you with the sweat of my brow. Jesus is saying that I gave you land, now it is all desolate. Jesus is saying that I gave you animals to rear and you ran away and leave them defenseless. Jesus is saying that you believe that you are the Morning Star. No you are not.

When your family is diabetic, this is the time to come together and pray. For those members of the family who are anointed this is your opportunity to run with Jesus, who is your crown for all ages. Jesus knelt in Reverence to his heavenly Father. We have done away with kneeling in the church. We look at it as though we are doing God a favor. Jesus is speaking out loud Enough is Enough.

Some churches have no kneelers altogether. Some church folk behave as though their a god is in command. Jesus knows that everyone has something to say, but sometimes you are better keeping your mouth close. Your time to speak is push back by Jesus. Your time to run with the sword is for another season. This is not about you, it is all about the love of Jesus in our heart.

In my Father's House there are many mansions. Where is your treasure? Jesus is letting you know that God the Father, God the Son, and God the Holy Spirit is not building you a mansion unless you have earned the crown of life for everyone to see as you sojourn the earth.

Your mansion on earth will not be compared to your mansion in heaven. The solid concrete will be replaced with 24 karat solid gold. Jesus made 91 chemical elements for us to use on the face of the earth. The same 91 chemical elements will be used in heaven. Your windows will be diamond. Windows and doors will automatically open the moment you draw near. Jesus and his heavenly Father is building you the best the very best in heaven.

This is why you have to remove the mountains in your life. There is much too much hate in this world. The hate in this world has grown into many, many mountains. It starts in our dearly beloved neighborhoods. Too much shootings are heard in the surroundings. Too much playing with weaponsare seen before the very eyes of our children. Too much boastfulness are among our fellowmen. Too much discord is in the immediate family.

Jesus is waiting for you to take it to the Lord in prayer. Jesus cannot do anything until you pick up your cross and come follow him. There is much work to be done but the laborers are few. Jesus knows that you are fed up, but then you must learn to let go of the evil that has enslaved the family for centuries. Until you let it go, Jesus cannot come in to rescue you.

We talk too much. Jesus knows what needs to be done. The tongue can and will get you in trouble. Learn to speak when you are spoken too! Avoid becoming reticent! Watch your mouth! The tongue can set a whole world afire. One word can tear buildings down. One word can start a war. Much less a world war. Jesus knows that you need rest. Come rest in Jesus!

God the Father, God the Son and God the Holy Spirit is busy creating and building a new heaven and a new earth. This means that we should be more vigilant. More astute! Rendering our hearts to God and not to Caesar. Jesus is showing me that families put the evil in the steel and the mortar as they resurrected a house before the eyes of their families. Then children and grandchildren wonder why the house came tumbling down.

We have made the National Lottery our god on the earth. We go to bed every night with the hope that we dream numbers for us to go play. And since we can carry our children to the casinos to hear and to see where the money came from is this a good example for us to purport. Jesus is saying Enough is Enough.

The Golden Rule is do not do unto others what you would not want them to do unto you. Jesus is saying that this rule of law of the highest is not respected by almost every single human being. Look around you and judge for yourselves what the world is unfolding before our very eyes. There is no doubt in our minds that Jesus walk the face of the world. There is no doubt in our hearts that Jesus performed many miracles. There is no doubt in our souls, that Jesus did not raise Lazarus and others from the dead. What is your problem? I am pretty sure that you have seen him.

We subject ourselves to be last and not to be first. We allow others to lead us astray. We forget Jesus, the almighty conqueror is our Savior. We forget Jesus came to redeem us and to take away all our sins and wash us in the precious blood of the Lamb of God.

In 1996, I landed a job as a Unit Manager in Glenwood Memorial Gardens. This cemetery was situated in Broomall, which is next to the City of Philadelphia. It was one of the cemeteries owned by one of the largest co-operations in the whole world. This cemetery was not making any money. For the year 1995, the cemetery made just about $30,000.

A program was put in place to revamp sales. All previous customers were called and given a *quid pro quo.* Then knowing fully well that this is a commission paid only job, I decided to go door-to-door in the early summer month of July. Driving my 1988, Dodge Dynasty, I parked on the first street in the City of Philadelphia. It was about nine o'clock in the morning, a beautiful day.

Brown being my favorite color, I was all spiffy in a pin stripe three-piece suit. Brown and yellow bow-tie with all leather laced brown shoes. My hair was jet black and shining with grease and well-groomed back with a part on the left side. Coming from a family that paid attention to detail, my shirt was white with gold cuff links with shanks. My favorite cologne was anything expensive.

At 12 noon, I quit the field to attend to one of my afternoon's appointment. It was pretty nearby, just a few blocks over. The family needed a head stone for their beloved parents. In closing the deal, I would ask the family for referrals after I have written up the contract. Then you would always know when you have done a good job.

Dinner was served. Families respected me as I respected them and there was never a dull moment.

Closing out the year 1996, brought me a new job as Sales Manager of another cemetery. The name of this one was called "The Cemetery Beautiful" It was about a half hour's drive from this location.

In the early month of March, 1997, I received my income tax check of about $3,000. I decided to treat myself with a brand new 1997 Cadillac: Sedan de Ville. The color was cotillion white. I won a prize as an early customer to install a brand new telephone in the car and the long-awaited North Star System. Getting around now was as easy as one two three.

Every morning I was early for the six o'clock Mass at the Broomall's Catholic Church. On this particular day, I heard the voice of Jesus as I opened the door to take my seat in one of the pews. Jesus is saying open your Bible on page 3 and read. I looked up in the horizon, and placed my eyes in the direction of the voice and saw no one. Taking my seat, I opened my brand new Jerusalem Bible on page 3 and there was the confirmation. Genesis began on page 3. I felt a tap on my shoulder from one of the parishioners who said, "we do not read a bible in the church". This I knew, but in obedience to Jesus, I did.

Returning to the cemetery, I could not put away the Bible not even for a moment. Wherever I go, I will stop and continue to read the Word of the Lord. Sometimes in the cemetery beautiful, I will hide myself in the mausoleum and read from where I left off. I read with such passion, not missing a coma, or a full point, or a name the entire book in just three months. I repeated this every three months.

In retrospect, I recalled reading the Bible on my own. I could barely read two or three pages at a time. I remembered not remembering where I last stopped. It took me a whole year to read the book. My recollection of anything was very little. But when Jesus took me through the Bible, I connected with some things easily for the continuation of the story to the story was some ten or twelve pages away.

PROPHET ALLYSON MICHAEL D'ESPYNE

If I fall asleep, Jesus will come and gently wake me up to continue the reading of his Word. One day as I was door knocking I met an Evangelist by the name of Drewnell (who is now deceased). She was instrumental in showing me the other side of the mountain. Little did I know that she was already spoken to by Jesus to take me around and teach me some things that I needed to know. She will take me to basements that black preachers were using for churches.

One morning, probably about three, I had a vision of myself feeding birds. When I woke up I did everything to unravel this vision with very little success. One Saturday morning, I heard someone knocking on my door, as soon as I opened the door, there stood a beautiful young couple asking me if they could stop by and take pictures of their wedding at the cemetery beautiful. My answer was yes in the affirmative. They thanked me and laughed and went away.

In the summer time, the cemetery beautiful is frequented by couples who stopped by to take pictures in the midst of beauty. The street signs are well lettered and clearly visible day and night. Friends and families come to visit with fresh flowers to replace those in the copper vases that adorned each and every grave on the plain. The grass is always green and there are perennial trees that flowered all year through. The grass is cut at least twice a week. The landscape is magnificent.

In the mornings, when I am taking my stroll along the black pitch streets; I observed that there are no pot holes. There are no gravel on the roads that are left behind by the caretakers. In the canals there are no broken bottles, leaves, cans of any kind to take away the natural beauty of an impeccable sight to behold. The painted signs of each section is carefully lettered in large print and placed in an area of visibility.

People in single file come by in their cars and open the door but remained seated in silent prayer. Meticulously, reading their eyes as I walked by in silence. Some people be it man or woman young or senior would stopped by the mausoleum and placed a single flower on the outside door of their beloved grave. This is what I left behind, a piece of heaven to answer my call to preach the Word of Our Lord Jesus Christ on St. Simon's Island, Brunswick, Georgia.

Jesus is not about platitudes. Jesus is speaking to me and saying that the whole world needs love. Jesus is sharing with me his thoughts and his understanding of truth in all its facets. Jesus already knows that the same way the world did not receive him; they would not receive me too. Jesus was stoned. Likewise I would be stoned too. Jesus was beaten with a cat-o-nine tail. In the same way, I would be beaten with a cat-o-nine tail.

Jesus is real. After becoming a Minister, Jesus took me unto himself and spinned me like a top and emptied my soaring temples that pained me for forty years. The cold came out of my mouth at about three in the morning in my single bedroom apartment. With mop in hand, I placed my Bible on the counter top of the kitchen. I was instantly healed by God the Father. Eighteen years to this day, I feel no pain. I can push my fingers into my temples and feel no pain. Jesus is real. Yes he is.

Jesus takes me wherever he wants me to go. As Jesus is processing the information in my head, he is already taking me to a sight that I would not want to be a part of. Jesus will often say that you have to see it with those two big beautiful eyes that I give to you. And in humor Jesus will say that He has two big beautiful eyes too.

In the month of February, 1999, I received my income tax check of about $600. Immediately thereafter, Jesus took me away from Brunswick, Georgia. Jesus is speaking to me now for much longer hours. Jesus keeps saying to me that he will one day put me in black. Black is a color that I really did not like. But I never questioned him.

Jesus is increasing his speaking even in my sleeping time. All day and all night long. Jesus is speaking to me whilst I am speaking to someone. When I am having breakfast, Jesus is picking out the menu for me. If it is not available, I will pause for him to tell me what he wants me to eat.

Jesus is not speculative. Jesus does not compromise. Jesus allows the false prophets to run the world in the way they see fit. Jesus allows Satan, the devil, to have his way with people who really do not care for the children of Jesus. God the Father, God the Son, and God the Holy Spirit is and will be at all times in control of both heaven and earth. You better believe it.

Jesus wants his people to listen because the world does not have ears anymore. The world leaders use diplomacy as a lie and would never have a contrite heart. False prophets are everywhere. It does not take you long for one to pass you by. They speak words of flattery. Empty vessels make the most noise. They are puffed up. They speak in circles and at the side of their mouths.

A good example of all of this is the President of the Russian Federation, Vladimir Putin. Russia is the world/s largest country in area. It covers a large part ofboth Europe and Asia. It has coastlines on the Arctic Ocean, Baltic Sea, black Sea, Caspian Sea, and Pacific Ocean. Russia landmass in area is 6,601,669 square miles. This is the reason and the only reason, why rebels of the world go to Russia for help.

Take a look at Aleppo, which was a beautiful and striving City of Syria. The rebels of Syria are backed by the might of Russia. When they launch their missiles and drop their bombs on Aleppo, they do not care who they kill or what they destroy in their pursuit of their own self-interest. Selfish or excessive regard for one's personal advantage or interest. is the motto of Russian philosophy.

What do they want? They want Syria's other mineral products include gypsum, limestone, salt and sand. Why do they want the gypsum, because it is used to make plaster of Paris. They also want the crystals that are called satin spar. The Russians would take all the satin spar and polished them and used them as gems on bracelets, rings, ankle bracelets and chains that beautiful women love to wear around their necks. It has become a favorite gem in esteem Russia.

Take another look at it again! Vladimir Putin wants all of Syria. He needs eyes, nose, ears and mouths. He is just as ambitious as his namesake Vladimir Lenin. He will do anything to conquer Syria and use it as his footstool. It will make him immortal in the eyes of his people--another great one that Russia will produce. He will stop at nothing, because he already see and hear the fear that the world has for him. He is another demigod.

Jesus is saying, that when we take our eyes off Jesus, and do not listen to his every word, as he speaks to us in that childlike gentle tone, then this is what we allow to happen in our human globe. Then it trickles down into our schools, and we wonder why our children are fast becoming violent in the streets of all America. They watch these bombings on National television. They see every graphic thing.

Sunday mornings the very parents are not taking them to church. They are off to some football game. Jesus is saying, where are your priorities? These are precarious times. We behave because we are all present in the house at dinner time that this will last forever. We behave because we wake up seeing our parents every morning that this will last forever. This is deceptive. This is erroneous.

When your neighbor house is on fire you throw water on yours. Jesus is saying that we must take nothing for granted. This is our error in all America. We take our mother for granted. She will make a list of the things that she wants us to take care of before the week is over. We memorize the list and we take off to play football. The week has passed we have not done any of the chores listed.

Three weeks later, your mother walk down the steps and trip over a fallen branch that you have stepped over for the past three weeks. Now she is in the hospital, a single parent caring for four children. Is this how you intend to grow up in a society of culture where every child does this or something similar to a parent or parents? Do we really care? Really!

We live in a society where the rod is taken away from the hands of parents. When a child is scolded, he is free to call 911. Did the child afflicted himself? We say that we love Jesus; we surely have to prove it. We would not like Jesus to put a scolding on us. The effects would be far remote. That is why Jesus gives us parents to do the scolding.

When the secular society has to frame laws as stupid as this one, then we know for sure who truly loves Jesus.

We view the aspects of life differently. We will all see Jesus passing by before our very eyes. Yet in all fairness, we will see something and miss something that somebody else sees in that moment in time. Jesus is saying that each human being is not equally gifted as his counterpart. Jesus is emphasizing our uniqueness. A son may be the spitting image of his father, but his character is not his equal.

The physical aspects of the mountain that took your gaze as you drive by in your SUV might resemble another mountain that you see nearby. They both share similarities in everything but there is something that will be unique every leaf on the tree will be different.

In 2002, whilst living on the streets in the City and County of San Francisco I attended one of the Church of God in Christ services one Sunday morning. In attendance was a young preacher, who introduced himself as Reverend Espy. We became friends in an instant, after a few days, he invited me out for lunch and confessed to me that he had asked Jesus to send him some help and he believed in all earnest that I was the one. Immediately, Jesus response deep within me accepted him as a brother.

This young preacher was the Minster for the youth. He had his own cleaning business, which he inherited from his deceased father. Minister Espy is married and has three children. Together they have two young ladies and his baby son. He and his family lived in another County.

We would meet at least twice a week, because his business took him everywhere. Whatever concerns he had on his mind, be it business or his social and family affairs, the Lord Jesus would allow me to shape his future. He was faithful and attentive and very honest in his deliberations. Oftentimes, he would want to buy me clothes and Jesus would take me away from his generosity.

When he became a Pastor, he invited me out to his home to witness to people in a nearby park. For the first time, we had the good fortune to work together and reach out to the downtrodden and the homeless, that we encountered that Sunday afternoon. It was indeed a prize of heaven from above.

The Christmas of 2003, Minister Espy invited me to spend the day at his home and then we all journeyed to his sister's home for a family reunion. As soon as we got there, we both anointed the house room by room. I had the opportunity to meet his sisters and brothers. Jesus is saying that as Christians we do not show our immediate brothers and sisters the love that we ought to show in front of our children.

Minister Espy and his wife preached out at the Community Centre in his neighborhood. Every Sunday, he and his family was always punctual at every service. One Sunday, he gave me the passage to take the metro from Market Street to the very last stop. There I took the bus to his home to have breakfast and then proceed to the Community Center. I spoke briefly from the pulpit on the subject of Prophecy.

After spending an evening with my brother and his wonderful family, he dropped me off at the metro and gave me enough money to be back on the last Sunday of that year December 31st 2003. On that very morning, the Lord Jesus kept me up all night. I took the first metro out bound to the very last stop. Falling asleep was pretty obvious. When the tube pulled in, I grabbed my black coat and my black bag and proceeded to take the bus outbound to his home.

God works in mysterious ways. After a hearty breakfast prepared by my brother, we left for service at the Community Center. Minister Espy preached as never before, on his athletic career that was mired by unfortunate circumstances. His athletic career in the 100 meters came to a halt. After the service on our way to his home, he told me, "that he is having an afternoon service at his home and I will be the main speaker."

My theme was "Nobody loves Jesus." Jesus chooses the theme for me and speaks through me whenever I have to speak his Word. In that moment whatever I say is all the Word of the Lord Jesus. After repeatedly scolding Christians for not doing the will of Jesus and not walking forthrightly with integrity and dignity worshipping the one True Living God, Jesus brought the service to a close.

Immediately thereafter, a young man came forward and said to me that he was going out that New Year's morning and kill a whole family. We prayed for him and his family. Is Jesus real? Yes he is. Then why are we laughing at each other's failures? Satan teaches us false pride. Satan shows us the dark valleys. Satan takes us to these soothsayers for prayers and anointing of evil. Until we continually give thanks to Jesus for every single thing that has happened to us, is happening to us, and will happen to us we will always fall prey to PRIDE.

In March 2004, the Spirit of the Lord took me to Dallas, Texas. At noontime, I assembled in the food line for the homeless. Dallas a city of mountainous icebergs, reminded me of a ghost town. The buildings stood tall with wide spaces surrounding them. I felt uncomfortable as I felt in the food line. After a lunch of beans, rice, cabbage and meat loaf, I proceeded to perambulate the city.

Walking is not just the best exercise for one, but also it is a profound gift of wisdom. Jesus is speaking to me as I turn corners and climb large sidewalks. Jesus is showing me around;teaching me the meaning of silence, darkness, stillness, wastefulness, wantonness and darker sides that we do not want to talk about. When we are stuck in our emotions, because things are not going our way, call on Jesus.

Spontaneous is a happening or arising without apparent external cause; self-generated. Jesus is saying that we as a people cannot be withholding secrets from our love ones. We as a people cannot be hiding deeds from our love ones. We as a people cannot be two-faced with our love ones. We as a people cannot be turning the soil of evil on our ancestor's grave to obtain much success. We as a people cannot be ruled by our emotions.

The city took me through dark and lonely places leaves scattered on sidewalks. Pecans twice the normal size I will crush beneath my feet, as I sleepwalk to oncoming huge buildings in my wearisome eyes. Looking up I saw a black large print painted sign on a white background saying something about a heart hospital. Getting hold of myself, and carefully pacing my footsteps on this dark night, I counted eight blocks of a monster of a hospital of the likes I have never seen.

Jesus is reminding me about the vision that I had of a split step in front of a two-story residential house. The vision meant that I would be leaving San Francisco en route to Dallas. It also meant that I would not be staying there for too long either. Whatever work Jesus had prepared for me was not forthcoming. Jesus will remind me in quiet conversation and humor that I have a whole lot of work to do for him. I knew that that was true, because I walked blindly in faith for Jesus.

One day about three in the afternoon, Jesus says to me to tell the preacher that he has been running too long from me. I went over to the Minister and said precisely what Jesus said to me. The preacher paused for a while and in a spirit of humility confirmed exactly what the Lord said. In addition, he said with a contrite heart that he ran from Jesus for four long years, until he was cornered by Jesus. Jesus mercy and grace flowed over the preacher and he replied, "that Jesus gave him this beautiful church."

Everybody has a story to tell. Jesus wants families to get together in silence and pray. Jesus wants offices to stop and pray in silence. Jesus wants parks to be used by the communities in fellowship of respect and pray. Jesus wants churches to keep their doors open after services for those, who wish to pray in silence. Jesus wants his angels to come around you and pray with you in silence.

Jesus is saying that we do not need eight blocks of a heart hospital. Jesus is doing his work to cut down the hopelessness that exists among Christian folk. Saying that you are a Christian does not mean anything to God the Father, God the Son, and God the Holy Spirit. Jesus is busy about his father's business. Jesus is showing you that doubt and fears and lasciviousness has nothing to do with being a Christian.

Many a time, parents go to their graves with their troubled little ones deep down in their hearts. That's a prayer. Many a time, childless women go to their graves wishing that they would not be turn down by Jesus, because of their little faith. Many a time, fathers who wish for sons and did not get any but daughters turn away from Jesus, because he did not give them a son. Many a time, unwedded mothers turn away from Jesus, because he did not give them a husband. Many a time, young people become easily betrayed by an evil employment system and blame Jesus for the injustice. Many a time, children give up because their parents never made it pass elementary school or even high school and yes, blame God too.

Jesus is saying that eight blocks of a hospital is wastefulness. All those wide gaps between buildings are wastefulness. Jesus is showing up the wastefulness of Dallas, Texas. Jesus is saying that when he sends his whirlwind into the far corners of the earth, and allow his homeless children to take cover close to or on the sides of these buildings for want of no room at shelters, Dallas will undoubtedly pay for it. Jesus cares for his children more than the wisdom of an earthly world.

Jesus is constantly reminding his architects not to build those structures for kick-backs, or pay for play in any given society. Jesus is not in awe with a whole lot of things that the world takes for granted. Jesus is reminding them in visions and appearances not to fall prey to corruption in high places. Jesus is about his children roaming about the streets day and night with hands outstretch asking and besieging others in a humble way for something to eat.

Jesus will bring every knee down regardless of their beliefs at a time when we feel so strongly about our accolades, distinctions, self-worthiness, seats of prominence in a created world of self-will. Jesus is grossly appalled, when people say that they love Jesus and then turn around and kiss the ring on someone's finger. Jesus is speaking through little children about things to come whilst everyone discard a word of wisdom. It's not about you. It's about Jesus.

The streets in Dallas are wide and varied in instances of rebuke. Jesus is saying that it is easy to admonish the children for they are your biological children. Then what about those children that you see roaming the streets day and night? Jesus is very much aware that this is not your problem. Then whose problem is it? It is easy to say love your neighbor as yourself. Then who is your neighbor? It is easy to point fingers in other people faces. Until one day the same finger is pointed back at you.

I remembered at age 32 that I needed to do more work for Jesus. I sat down carefully with myself to figure what must I do for inner peace. After careful consideration, I decided that on Friday's I will visit the poor house in the town of St. James, Trinidad—a place I knew very well. Already a legionary in the diocese of the Cathedral of the Immaculate Conception, I felt that I must add this one to the list.

My first Friday evening as I parked the car and got out of the vehicle, the scent of the surroundings was so awful, that Jesus kept me from vomiting and strengthen me to do and fulfill one of the desires of my heart. On entering the first male ward, I decided to read a prayer for my first brother and the prayer was from my little testament pocket-size book. I Peter 3:17 For it is better, if the will of God be so that we suffer for well doing, than for evil doing. Jesus is saying that this is not just for the City of Dallas, but it is for the City of Dallas.

Jesus is reminding me that God the Father, God the Son, and God the Holy Spirit and I, the Prophet, are Lifebeaters. It is not about me. It is about Jesus. Dusting my shoes in quite a few cities are not a pleasant thing to talk about, but the truth must be spoken. Jesus is not going to leave heaven, to come down on the face of the earth and do the work of his Sons and Daughters. Jesus is about strengthening them to finish a good work.

In furtherance of a booming City and County of San Francisco, I remembered walking the streets at night and seeing great big dumpsters full of fresh bread standing tall outside of hotels. Idly waiting for the pick-up truck to come by and take them away. I humbly recalled sidewalks literally plastered with food thrown away when that food could have been given to shelters in the immediate vicinity.

Jesus does not go to sleep. Jesus will put seeds in the palm of his hand and allow the birds to come eat out of his palm hand. Then suddenly, one day you wake up to find trees growing on your estate that were never there from inception. Did you see the birds coming your way that windy morning? Yes you did. Did you see them on the plains of your field? Yes you did. But did you see the birds regurgitate the seeds on the plains of your field. No you did not. That is how Jesus works with wonders of his realm of mystery.

Jesus gives you the desires of your heart. It does not matter of the status of your parents. It does not matter of your beginnings, whether rich, middle class or poor. Once you press on in Jesus not caring about the fiery arrows that one day will come your way. Once you put others to the test and not allow them to put you to the test, then Jesus will at all times be there. Jesus is standing right there at the side of you, and because you did not see him standing right there with your natural eyes, you believe that Jesus is not there.

Jesus reads and knows our every thought, action and sincerity of heart. Some people carved their names and draws hearts on trees in wishful thinking. Is Jesus in the midst of this action? Did you hear from Jesus before you carried out this action? Jesus is saying that he speaks to you first and until then you are on your own.

We are too busy wanting things to go our way and that is why we get caught up into ourselves and become cynical. If at any time what we say came to pass, then we believe that we are greater than the prophets of God the Father, God the Son, and God the Holy Spirit. Forgetting that there are clairvoyants and psychics that think the same way too. Jesus is awesome. Yet everybody has made this Holy Word their doormat. They have become abusive to His Holiness.

Jesus is steadfast in his out pouring of his Holy Spirit on all peoples of the world. Jesus is not a silent bystander. Jesus is not going to stand idly by to see a world that God the Father, God the Son, and God the Holy Spirit become disingenuous to the greater evil of the world. Jesus is forever young and do not resemble Satan, the devil, who appears with horns on his head and would not say his name when he is doing you all the evil.

Staying at a shelter one day in frisco, a colloquial name for San Francisco, We all saw fried chicken on waiters going through one of the side doors of the kitchen. Half an hour later, we assembled by the hundreds for dinner at about six o'clock in the evening. We realized that they would not open the door for entrance to the diningroom, only to find out that they were quickly cooking meatballs and gravy.

This is why at some shelters the rich people would bring their expensive steaks already cooked. Their cakes would be numerous to mention. A band playing and oftentimes a soloist singing paid for by the rich family, that is present at their offerings. They would humbly stand in prayer and thanks giving, making the homeless not feel like a vagrant or a bomb names that is often thrown at them, from the mouths of the technocrats. Ice cream would be served and the rich family would be exceedingly happy to bring hope to the hopeless.

Jesus is forever present when the rich folks shake the hands of the impoverished miscreants of the society, who are blamed for every single crime that takes place in the society. Someone will say, "that a vagrant was seen at that store shattering the glass windows." Most times that is not the case. Then the police officers would go to the respective shelters at night, to arrest whomever the description fitted.

Jesus is not about painting a wall white. Jesus is not about painting a wall blue. Jesus is not about painting a wall purple. Jesus is about bringing an awareness as never before. The university is on the street at night. Each individual is seen at night by someone's eye or eyes going about their business as nobody's business. The undergraduates are on the street at nights, taking mental notes as their eyes survey the good, the bad and the ugly in the society.

It is ironical that the events of the night do not make it in the publications of the town, city, parish or province of our society. The newspapers would be very careful in reporting homicides, especially in cities like frisco, because of the tens of thousands of visitors and tourists from around the world. There is no reporting of point blank shootings and killings in restaurants as seen by the unsavory in the community.

There is no reporting of drugs being sold in restaurants on a daily and nightly basis. There is no reporting of drug raids and drug rings in their distribution both day and night. Jesus is saying that some of these events are known, but nobody cares of the innocent bystanders and children with parents, who are seated in these very restaurants not knowing that their safety is at risk.

Jesus is looking at the clock on the wall. It is an example for peopleof all walks of lifethat time is running out. Human beings far too often become unbelievers because of peer pressure. They withhold information that is vital for the well-being of all and sundry just to benefit their so-called friends. Jesus is saying it is not about you, it is about Jesus. It is not about your acquaintances, it is about Jesus. It is not about your siblings, it is about Jesus. It is not about your mother or your father, it is about Jesus.

I remembered going to the library, after having breakfast in the food line with the vagrant children of God the Father, God the Son, and God the Holy Spirit. After waiting for 15 minutes in front of building for the doors to open at nine o'clock, I know that I have to depend on Jesus to keep my eyes open when the clerk beckons us in. Taking my seat on the third floor on the very table that housed all the reference books, including the encyclopedias, which were my favorites, I begun to read. Before you knew it, the chair was pulled from under me and the black police officer looked me straight in the eye and threatened me.

The police officer standing six feet four inches tall weighing about 260 pounds, in his early forties, told me most emphatically to go outside and take a walk and then return. This I did. He also reminded me that those books were not for me to read. Really! What Jesus is saying is that nobody cares, because the society as a whole sit in referenda and make all these laws and policy making so that the bombs must go along with their truth no matter what.

Jesus is vociferously saying Enough is Enough. Jesus is boisterous, noisy, vocal and loud. Jesus is looking around and seeing human beings cuddling animals and cleaning up after them. A change society putting up signs for the disabled. Schools erected for the blind and the deaf. Groups of people representing certain hospitals are seen picking up money for the children who are born with cancer. Marches formed by the elite of the society for cures of various types. Yet the homeless, the children of Jesus, are treated like the venom of the world.

Jesus is saying that the homeless is growing in population as the days go by. Jesus is saying that the more society is against his children that have to run and hide from so-called family and friends because of their objectivity on life will feel the wrath of God. Jesus does not care about tenets. Jesus does not care about statute of limitations. Jesus does not care about the gods of the earth.

The world is made for Jesus and Jesus does not need anyone's opinion. This is Jesus world. The people of Jesus will hear one voice and come follow him wherever he shall go. The earth will vehemently criticize everything that Jesus says from the mouth of his Sons and Daughters of truth.

The City and County of San Francisco have the longest lines and the most shelters that I have seen in all America. What is Jesus saying? Jesus is simply speaking about the scars of the society. The long and lonely nights make you hungry especially when you are looked upon as a foreigner. The dark and dampness as the season changes from summer to fall make you reminisce as though it is actually taking place in this moment.

Where is your home as you walk along the side streets not to be observed by the police? Where is everybody as you pinch yourself knowing that by the grace of god he has brought you thus far? Soliloquy as you pass by families standing in front of their homes, as if to say that Jesus never ever forgets anyone or anything, since the creation of this world. But the world wants you to believe that Jesus never put his hand out, and ask someone for a drink of water, or a loaf of bread, or a share of his meal, or to spend a night at his home.

Jesus is working in silence on the inside of his children. Jesus does not have to put a painting on a wall; change it dailyfor someone to pass by and take notice of it. Jesus is not seeking friends on the basis of the Triune God. Jesus is not making a movie on scientology. Jesus is stating categorically that science is not Jesus. Believing in science will not get you into heaven. Believing in physics will not get you into heaven. Believing in philosophy will not get you into heaven.

The children of God have to align themselves with God the Father, God the Son, and God the Holy Spirit on the insides for Jesus to begin a new work in them. It is all well and good to stand by the curb and give out tracts looking good but Jesus is not on the inside. It is all well and good to say that Jesus is the answer, but where is the proof. It is all well and good to tell someone that you loving on Jesus, but every time you pass the dog that stands in front your neighbor's house you stand there and tease and provoke a creature of Jesus. It is all well and good that to say that Jesus is your Lord and Savior, but what have you done for Jesus lately? Jesus is like the adage: the proof of the pudding is in the eating.

10. To Stand for Jesus

Judges 14: 14 And he said unto them, Out of the eater came forth meat, and out of the strong came forth sweetness. And they could not in three days expound the riddle. Jesus is saying that there are too many hands in the compromised world. The planet already knows that God the father, God the Son, and God the Holy Spirit does not compromise. But the enemies that be are not going to give in to Jesus's autocracy.

Jesus is extremely busy in adding to the heavens new windows and new doors to accommodate the very few that are standing for Jesus in every corner of the globe. And Jesus said unto them, Out of the eater came forth meat. The leadership of Russia is Vladimir Putin. He is building new regimes across the globe as never before. He is using the computer system as a distraction to secretly pass on information to his soldiers whom he uses as diplomats across the planet.

Vladimir Putin main objective is to befriend the Kazakhstans, who are the largest producers of uranium in the world. Hemust regained autocratic control of this territory to keep him at the helm of Russia.

And Jesus said unto them, Out of the eater came forth meat. Jesus is saying that we live in a world of governments who think only of themselves and their immediate families. Presidents who will literally sell their souls to the devil for that high chair. They and their cohorts will go all out to lie, cheat scheme, rig, turn the tide and make vile promises. Jesus is saying that Enough is Enough.

Standing for Jesus in this world does mean obedience to his Word. It is the same as Jesus talking to you and commanding you to go do something for him. You are standing at the corner waiting for the bus. Meanwhile, there is a blind man with stick in hand, obliquely opposite you silently waiting to cross over the busy highway. Jesus gives you a command to go to the blind man and walk him over.

You immediately turn around and go over to the blind man to do precisely what Jesus told you to do. Holding his hand, you carefully walk him over to the other side of the road and point him in the right direction. A feeling of joy possess you. In that moment you really do not know what you have just done for Jesus. Jesus is laughing and is on his way to bless your womb that was sterile so the doctors say to you over and over again.

Seven years later, your husband is becoming a very happy man because he too was obedient to God the Father, God the Son, and God the Holy Spirit. Jesus never promised you that when you do this deed of virtue, he is going to bless you with a child. But in your seven years of waiting Jesus would have sent you Prophets to let you know that one day you will have a baby.

As soon as the baby is born, the church will at all times remember your story. Wherever you and your husband go people who are bless with the gift of wisdom will come around you and bless you. Yes, there are some people who are doing good deeds practically every day of their lives. And when you look at them, they wear the hat of suffering. They quietly go about doing good and nobody really says anything good about them.

You go to the hospital to visit your love one, they are there opposite praying for the sick who is not their family. You wonder why they do not own a car. Whyare they seen daily catching the bus? Why are they quiet and helpful? You go to them and ask them to come with you to give blood for your mother. There is no hesitation; there is a kind word. Your enquiring mind is running at a speed of 300 miles an hour.

At the hospital their blood is running and flowing smoothly. Yours on the other hand is dripping. Jesus is silently talking deep in your mind but your problem is that you ask too many questions. Invariably, your true friends are giving you an example of the childlikeness of Jesus. Jesus is working on you, whilst Jesus is moving them into deep wisdom and understanding.

Your Pastor most times is the same as you. Your Pastor is given the same flock by Jesus in the form of a Ministry to bring the church to heaven. The flock is not anointed by Jesus to understand the undertaking of a mystery of faith. Every Pastor is blessed by Jesus to run a Ministry that he is transformed to run. This makes him unique. This makes him the king of his house.

And he said unto them, Out of the eater came forth meat. Jesus is saying that there are teachers who were told by Jesus to go and become a school teacher. Some of these teachers have a rugged mountain to climb. Some of these teachers are watched by cameras in and out of school. Some of these teachers have been taken to court. Some of these teachers are working under tremendous pressure by standing for Jesus.

One of Jesus ministries is teaching. Jesus is not playing with no teacher who pretends to be called to the office of a teacher whether secular or anointed for the pulpit. Teachers are transparent. Parents put their trust in teachers. Teachers have a mountain like Mount Everest to climb. The students that are slow in the classroom shall not be humiliated. The students that do not have the shine on the ball are not to be provoked into anger to see what he or she is truly made up of.

Teaching is Jesus. Jesus is speaking about his twelve disciples, whom he love. The youngest John was only a lad when he was told to follow Jesus. Immediately John did as he was told and commanded to do. At night, John will tie his cord on Jesus cord so when Jesus wakes up he will wake John up too. But, John a lad, could not have gone anywhere with Jesus who was deeply anointed by His Heavenly Father for a greater work.

Jesus in his humility will arise early and untie the cord of John without waking him and at the same time deepen his sleeping time because he was not ready to undertake the enormous desire he had in his heart. Jesus will go out and come back and they would all still be sleeping. Jesus only slept one hour a day. The angels would come and put Jesus asleep, while they took guard of the Son of the King.

The time came when John had to stand for Jesus. After breaking the bread and giving thanks to his father Jesus was taken by the soldiers to be crucified. Everyone except John fled. John bore witness to every singular thing with his eyes filled with water as he held on to the arm of Mary, the mother of Jesus.

With every lash of the whip on the body of Jesus, John felt in his own body. With every fall with the cross, John felt in his own body. With every stab and piercing of the crown of thorns on the head of Jesus. John felt in his head for Jesus. That is why John's account will at all times be felt by readers worldwide, because he was there bearing witness for Jesus.

We were not there present. That's why we are doubly blessed. Jesus is saying that teachers must take all of this in their classrooms on a daily basis if they want to see the face of Jesus standing in their classrooms continually. Jesus is saying that this will be a phenomenon. Jesus is having a conversation with just a few teachers around the globe.

Children have a tremendous amount of respect for their teachers. Teachers shall not allow Satan to come shake their tree in the classrooms. Teachers shall not become fearful of any student. Jesus took charge of twelve apostles. There were no fist fights. There were no stabbings. There were no murders. There were no arguments. There were no quarrels.

None of Jesus's disciples were schooled in the field of theology at any given university. None of Jesus's disciples had to study psychology to become a preacher. None of Jesus's disciples was taught by anyone theology but by Jesus himself. Jesus is saying that to obtain truth one must have truth spoken to them from an appointment confirmed from on high.

Churches today cannot stand for Jesus because their ideologies have been theorized by a scholarly secular world. A world of misfits that God the Father, God the Son, and God the Holy Spirit never appointed to those prestigious positions. Heaven and earth shall be in one accord with the Triune God.

Teachers shall be in tune with the Word of Our Lord Jesus Christ. Jesus is showing me that quite a number of teachers have not fully read the bible in all its entirety. Interpretation does not belong to you. This is for your Pastor. Satan is everywhere. You cannot take Jesus for granted. Satan will be constantly around you, because he was invited by you and your family to take a seat at your table.

And he said unto them, Out of the eater came forth meat. Jesus is always at the forefront of everything. Jesus is never changing. Jesus is taking a whole world back to the days of Samson. First appointed by God to overthrow the Philistines. These people were the Sea Peoples who had fled the Aegean area around 1200 B.C. They dwelled in the cities of Gaza, Ashkelon, Ashdod, Ekron and Gath. A philistine is a person who is smugly indifferent or hostile to art and culture.

The Aegean civilization arose after the people discovered how to make bronze. Consequently, the people became highly skilled in architecture, painting and various crafts. Their narcissistic life became apparent in the eyes of Jesus. Soon afterwards here comes Samson anointed and appointed by Jesus Judge of the Israelites. Obedience is heaven first law.

Samson is a man full of integrity which is seemingly lacking in a whole lot of Presidents, Prime Ministers and leaders of a so-called free world. It is all about them seeking their own self-interest. It is all about them. It is not about Jesus. Now Jesus is showing me the flesh that they will tear from the bodies of a sickening world. They believe that they are impervious.

In 2003, I recalled going to a social worker, who was assigned to help the homeless in their time of need. He quickly searched for the forms and did not make any promises to me that this would eventually work. Frequenting his little office and answering all his questions which he summarized. He allowed me to sign all the necessary paper work and wished me well. He told me to return to his office in the next three weeks.

After three weeks, I kept the appointment and behold good news came our way. He was so happy that the state was not going to charge me for a new green card. His first naturally. Thanking him vociferously, I sped off to the Immigration Office, which was a few blocks away, to get an appointment to replace an already expired green card, that by now was well over a year.

That morning, Jesus woke me up real early. I was numbered among a few early birds. Sitting in the waiting room and hearing and seeing everybody leaving me all alone made me feel like Samson being left alone to fight the philistines. Only in this case she was not a philistine; she became angry with me, because I would not take full citizenship as she wanted me too. Yes it was free. Jesus requires his Sons and his Daughters to be obedient to his voice.

And he said unto them, Out of the eater came forth meat. Jesus is showing me a whole wide world running away from the whole truth for a lie. Standing for Jesus requires strength in his Word. Jesus will one day tell you to go buy a bouquet of flowers for your wife. You on the other hand, ignores Jesus because it is your wife and not the wife of Jesus. Jesus is sitting in the back seat of your car, whilst you just filibuster the command of Our Lord Jesus Christ.

Unaware that Jesus is behind you, you race to the light which is on red and make a left turn into oncoming traffic. The results are obvious. The whole world thinks just like you. The world does not want Jesus in their everyday decision-making.

Jesus is thinking of the many missteps that he has not brought to human beings, since the beginning of Adam and Eve. Jesus knows that this is what each individual wants him to do. They believe that the litany of sins that they have already committed has doomed them for life. They believe that Jesus is a sham. They believe that Jesus is a hoax. They believe that Jesus is spurious. They believe that Jesus is meretricious. They believe that Jesus is feigned. They believe that Jesus is not genuine.

Jesus is showing me the many times they put a gun to their heads, and when they have pulled the trigger the gun is jammed. Jesus is showing me the many lies they have told on their deceased fathers and mothers just to get money out of the kind hearts of their fellowmen. And in parting they will say that they will never forget you.

Jesus knows every action. Jesus knows every contrite heart. Jesus knows every tongue that want to say honey I love you. Jesus knows every hand that wants to shake your hand is not clean. Jesus knows every tear that is shed is not real. Jesus knows every hymn that is sung did not come from the mouthpiece of Our Lord Jesus Christ.

And he said unto them, out of the eater came forth meat. Jesus is saying that the alcoholics feel disparaged. It is easy to belittle someone lying at the side of the street inebriated. It is easy to deprecate someone that you used to care for. An alcoholic is someone who is afraid of the charismatic Jesus. He often wonders, how Jesus did that? For the life of him, he feels afraid of the dark, when left alone to sleep. He will speak aloud in his sleep as the night goes by. Often seemingly happy as he walks the street late at night and will ask you to point him in the right direction.

Standing for Jesus is an ingredient that is given from above. It is not how much work you do for you to go boast about yourself. It is all about Jesus. The only begotten Son of the True Living God, whose name is Jesus. We all come to Jesus with baggage. Some of us come with much more baggage than others. Some of us believe, that we got it made, because we did not do half the things that others have gotten away with.

We come home from work tired as usual and barely made it to the tub. That hot or warm water made us feel good. Already eaten dinner, we rolled into bed. We dreamt dreams all night long. We had a vision, a dream and a nightmare. Immediately thereafter, Jesus wakes us up. We remembered nothing. We are all perplexed. Jesus is saying that if it was that important Jesus would have been in your memory all day long. Why not let it go?

Can Satan bring dreams and visions? Yes he can. But he will never say his name. The devil does not want you to know that he brought you a vision, because he has not gotten your soul yet. Jesus will continually say his name even while you are rising. Jesus is drawing you out to go do something that you have thrown into the sea of forgetfulness a long time ago. Something that you have discarded completely from your memory; something that you are afraid to bring to your remembrance.

Jesus is walking upright, because we do not walk upright due to a belligerent past. Someone stop you to ask a question; you do not stop by reason of a guilty past. You do not want that person to remind you of your wrong doings. What are you afraid of? Of course Jesus found you out. Well it is the same way that Prophets, Pastors, Evangelists and people of wisdom will find you out. What are you ashamed of? What is this feeling of distress?

Standing for Jesus heals a whole lot of pains that we carry with us everywhere. Sleeping with that bright light over the bed at night does not prevent the attacks of satan. It is not how do we stand? It is when do we stand? Right now! We have been sitting down far too long. Since Jesus came on the face of the earth to this very day, we have been sitting down.

We believe that since we can plug in the microwave and heat something up that we have arrived. Well, we ain'tsee nothing yet. We believe that in as much as we can put a man on the moon we have arrived. What we fail to see is that the earth is enormously full of sickness, debt, fear, with no real direction. On bending knees, come to Jesus! He is our savior. He is our redeemer. He is our morning star.

Standing for Jesus brings you in alignment of his truthfulness. Jesus always says be not afraid! Our lives are dictated by what we read in the newspapers. We wake up in the morning and the first thing that we do is to go fetch the newspaper. We forget to say thank you Jesus. We fall asleep at night; we forget to say thank you Jesus. We fuss and fight with our wives and children; we forget to say thank you Jesus. We get a raise in our income; we forget to say thank you Jesus.

Jesus knows our every weakness. Jesus is speaking to me about things that we discover in us that we are not prone to do. But are we sure in the absolute? Could it be a desire in your heart? Take a look at the mountain peak! Who formed it? Jesus did.

Standing for Jesus is in giving of our tithes and offerings. Jesus says should a man rob me. Jesus expects us to give ten per cent of our gross earnings to the church. Jesus says that when you give, he will open up the gates of heaven and pour out a blessing unto you.

And he said unto them, Out of the eater came forth meat. China is the largest producer of steel. They supply Germany, South Korea, Japan and the United States of America, who by the way are the largest importers of their steel worldwide. Isn't it ironical that Christian America imports almost everything from a Communist country? A country that only has two per cent of Christians. A country that Christian folk cannot roam freely. A country that does not have free and fair elections. A country that is about to wage war with all Americans.

Jesus is saying that freedom can only be gained through the precious blood of the body of Our Lord Jesus Christ. Samson who was born with the Spirit of the Holy Ghost, which is Jesus, was given one law. No alcoholic beverage of any kind! No strong drink of any kind! No wine of any kind!

Yes, we are all aware of cyber war. The Pacific Ocean is presently mined with bombs all along the ocean floor. They use steel as a camouflage with thick weeds hidden under rocks that will spark a light when a signal from a cell phone will be depressed.

II Chronicles 7:14 If my people, which are called by my name, shall humble themselves, and pray, and seek my face, and turn from their wicked ways; then will I hear from heaven, and will forgive their sin, and will heal their land. This is what a whole wide world needs to do. This is what America needs to do. A Word of Wisdom from the mouth of the wisest human being--one of the Sons of God--Solomon.

Jesus dwelled in Samson the same way as Jesus dwelled in Solomon. Everybody wants Jesus to live in them. Everybody wants Jesus to forgive them of their sins. Everybody wants Jesus not to use the rod of correction on anyone. Everybody wants Jesus not to pass judgment on their families. Everybody wants Jesus to remove any sin that will annihilate a member of their family.

Jesus does not think like human beings. Whether we come out of the same parents, our DNA will at all times be different. Jesus is forever in the present. The future belongs to us. We are of the earth, but want to be numbered among Holy Peoples. We are mortals. Heaven consists of peoples that are immortal.

When Solomon lived people came from all over the world to see and speak to him. They must have asked him which God did he served? His answer would have been God the father, God the Son, and God the Holy Spirit. Jesus is saying to each his own. God does not force anyone to accept his Son Jesus. But Jesus expects his brothers and sisters to stand firm on the Word of God.

Jesus healed ten lepers. One day whilst Jesus was baptizing his people, one of the lepers came to him and said, "thank you Jesus". It is amazing after all these wars that some people are still naïve. There is no safe haven on the earth. Jesus is your safe haven. Jesus is your peace deep within you. Jesus is your going out and your coming in. Jesus is your alarm clock. Jesus reminds you of your appointments.

Jesus retorted where are the other nine? Are the other nine significant in this world? Jesus is humbly saying that the other nine behaved the same way as brothers and sisters treat each other on a daily basis. Nobody cares! Jesus is equally saying that when you are driving through a very populated inner city, you will see and you will hear the clicking of heels in a whirlwind of truth.

We see Jesus everyday and still does not recognized him. The birds in the air; who feeds them. Each day there is a new born baby that enters into the world. The sun comes up bringing joy and hope to the most vulnerable in the society. The baby waves at you as you pass by. Someone is opening a church door to go pray for someone else. A celebration of a wedding anniversary that Jesus presided over some twenty years ago. A child receiving a distinction in physics that no member of the family has ever achieved.

Jesus is laughing deep within and showing me the many faces that exist in the worldthat eyes have not seen, because of peoples' cultures and humble beginnings.

Jesus is saying that prayer is lacking in the homes of Christians. First thing in the morning, everyone rushes out of the door before assembling to pray. It does not matter what book or verse is selected by anyone for prayer. Prayer is like the glucose in your body. Prayer is like the Vitamin A that the body needs to break down in to a liquid that is taken throughout the brain. A cleansing of your heart and a drawing out of what the body does not need via your intestines.

Is this the world that Jesus expected us to build? Not really. The Word still is eyes have not seen. Jesus shows his love in the very word that we pray. Jesus wants families to pray in the mornings. Jesus wants families to pray in the noontime. Jesus wants families to pray in the evenings. Jesus wants families to pray in the midnight hour. Jesus wants families not to give in to satan.

Prayer is the lifting up of the mind and heart to God. Jesus is saying that it did not end there. Where is your soul? Until your soul receives the prayer and starts back talking to you, you have not done anything yet. Far too often people take prayer at face value. They believe that they know everything. When last has Jesus spoken to you? Jesus is speaking right now to you and you have not heard him. Jesus uses your little children to speak to you. They would say something that go like this "Daddy" please do not forget to pass and pick me up. And this you will take very personal. Upset!

Your anger means that you are upset and distressful of life's day-to-day dealings with you. God is Omnipresent. The Word of God says pray unceasingly. That means do not give up. The race is not over until you receive the CROWN that is placed on your head by Jesus. This is not the valedictory function that you attend after 40 years of hard work. This is not the accolades that you plastered on the walls of your house to make you feel good. This is all about Jesus.

Jesus is still in the keeping business. When your mind is not fully made up about anything? Give it all to Jesus! Jesus will come to you and bathe you in his preciousness. Then he will continually burn your feet with the fire of his love to keep you from falling. You will notice that you do not have indulgences. Your patience and your tolerance have increased tremendously. You are more relaxed as the days go by.

Jesus is standing by the river and looking at me and is showing that not many Christians are baptized. Romans 10:9 That if thou shalt confess with thy mouth the Lord Jesus, and shalt believe in thine heart that God hath raised him from the dead, thou shalt be saved. This is like John 3:16. This also is gospel. Jesus knows that people have a hard time believing in the Word of the Living God. Especially if they were thrown under the bus by someone, who had a seat on the pulpit.

Forgiveness is prerequisite to love. Jesus is continuously thinking. Adam and Eve had a problem with forgiveness. Jesus knows that humankind feels wronged by having to pay the price of the sin of Adam and Eve. Jesus knows that Christians too have a problem with interpretation of this very Word. Some preachers believe because Jesus died for the forgiveness of sins then humankind cannot sin no more. These are all New Testament preachers. It is easy to say that your sins are forgiven, but where is your forgetfulness. You are still holding on to something. That something is sin.

There is crime every day of our lives. How dare you say that your sin has been forgiven? People are seen killing people every single day of our lives. Wars waged against peaceful nations. Satan is at the forefront. American soldiers have to be deployed in dangerous countries. God alone knows how long there stay would be. Families destroyed by bombs from evil people, who have given their souls to the devil. Presently, the world is in chaos. There is no forgiveness.

Everyone wants to be a leader. Once they can make bombs and proliferate guns and weaponry; it is their right to assume the office of a leader. They are not presumed innocent until proven guilty. Jesus does not care about such people, who go around maiming and killing innocent people in the name of Radical Islam.

There are so many homes that have been ravished on the question of forgiveness. Jesus is waiting for those who cannot find it in their heart to forgive their own siblings over something stupid like an unpaid debt of a car. Even though the parents had interceded time and time again, pleading forgiveness through the blood of Jesus.

If my people, which are called by my name, shall humble themselves, and pray, and seek my face, then there will be no wars, but deep respect for each other. The entire world is muddled by a few dissidents, who want to become demigods on the face of the earth.

The teachings of Jesus are insurmountable. Jesus impartiality took him to China and Russia and they in turn took the word of Jesus throughout the world. Jesus is speaking to the ears of the most vulnerable in the society, that the hour has come for your removal from the streets of all America. Jesus is tearing down the walls of injustice in the court houses that have done this tremendous wrong.

Jesus is sending his angels to strengthen the few that will make this possible. The few will be like diamonds shining in the darkest moments of your life. The few will be like philanthropists donating everything they have towards human welfare and advancement in the inner cities of the most run-down neighborhoods of society. Jesus also is raising up a few prophets who will be mightily bless by

God the Father, God the Son, and God the Holy Spirit to add to the Halls of Justice.

Seeking the face of Jesus is a step in the right direction. This is like a staircase from the earth directly to the doors of heaven. Could you take a step at a time until you get to the top? Jesus is saying that one step is equivalent to a measure of faith. Where is your faith? We often hear stories from our parents that granddad had these dreams of building a business from the ground up. These dreams had never flourished into fruition. Yet these desires are passed on from generation to generation to generation and nobody is listening to the voice of Jesus.

Granddad did not achieve his desires, but he left behind the faucet that keeps dripping and dripping and dripping. Is anybody listening? Your grandfather's word did not go void. Satan came and stole the word from his heart. It is up to the family to take the beacon of light and persevere up the stairs with all your might until the doors of heaven are open unto you.

Jesus is on the horizon looking straight into your eyes to strengthen you to accomplish all the desires of your heart. Meanwhile you are becoming mistrustful to do the work that Jesus set forth in your life. You are forever doubting the love of Jesus in your heart. Your confidence is weakening and weakening and weakening as the days go by. Jesus can no longer speak to you because your feet are not firmly planted on the ground.

We have borne witness to so-called great ones in our immediate surroundings. Who boast of their debut as an actor/actress on Broadway in Manhattan, New York. Now, what are they doing? Working at Family Dollar. Doing something that they have no passion for! Jesus is right there waiting to take them up the staircase to heaven, but they would not listen. Sometimes they would offer you good advice.

It is easy to climb up stairs that have rails on either side or stairs that automatically take us up to the top, which they called elevators. The stairs from earth to heaven do not come with rails and are not earthly elevators. Keeping your eyes in Jesus eyes and staying focus on the prize will get you up there. And when you get there members of your family will see just what you did and will come follow too.

Someone has to become the leader, even when the real leader does not want to undertake the task. Jesus is about blessing the family. Too many families cannot be traced back to more than three or four generations. Some people befriend people only to find out one day by a visiting cousin, that those people are your family.

Seeking the face of Jesus takes us into trouble sometimes. As soon as we have the Holy Spirit deep down in our hearts, our lives begin to change. We stop smoking. We stop drinking. We stop gambling. Friends and family do not want to associate themselves with us anymore. They will taunt us. They will ridicule us. They will scoff at us. They will insult us. They will jeer us. They will leave no stone on turn.

Jesus has not gone anywhere. Jesus is still in the saving business. Jesus is on the job. Steering at the wall trying to figure out something in our lives is not the answer to fulfilling our dreams. Jesus body has been broken up to feed each and every soul that exists or have existed in this world. When there is something missing call on Jesus? Jesus alone can fix it.

Seeking the face of Jesus brings tears to our eyes. We wake up in the morning and there is no food in the pantry. We open the refrigerator and all we see is a bottle of water. We open our wallet and there is no money, but a bunch of credit cards that have all been maxed out. This is not cause for panic. Jesus alone can fix it. Calm yourself down, and go take a shower! Pick up your Bible and call on Jesus! Jesus alone can fix it.

Jesus is showing you through it all that he is everywhere and all you need to do is call. There is no food in the pantry. This means that whatever you are doing is not working. You need to start going to church and give yourself totally to Jesus. You need to watch your mouth. You need to get with the pastor and confess all your sins in a peaceful way, with no animosity, between him and you in a spirit of goodness. You can take along your best friend with you.

There is no food in the refrigerator. People of visions often wake up in the night with tears in their eyes wondering, why me Lord. Why not you? Jesus is saying that Jesus never wakes up in the day or night and says, why me God? The crucified one endured it all. The crucified one took the nails in his hands and the nails in his feet. The crucified one took the crown with sharp and very sharp thorns that pierced his head. The crucified one took the lance that pierced the heart of Jesus.

There is no money in the wallet. Just take a walk to the front door and look outside. The car is gas filled. The insurance on the car is paid up. The tires are not smooth. You can still get to work and borrow some money until payday. Jesus is reminding you, that you need to stand up for the workers, when there is a genuine reason to do so. Stop being too firm with your colleagues!

Seeking the face of Jesus becomes a nightmare. Phantasmagoria steps in, which brings a feeling of illusions or deceptive appearances, as in a dream or as created by the imagination. Jesus is saying that illusions are dreams that comes directly from satan, the devil, and not from God the Father, God the Son, and God the Holy Spirit. Yes Jesus can and does bring dreams and visions too. But in the former scenario, there is fear and wild imagination. This son or daughter of God is called by Jesus to serve one day on his pulpit.

The enemy will at all times scream and shout in your head to discourage you from taking up your appointment with Jesus. The evil will constantly fight with you to tear Jesus out of your soul. Jesus wants you for himself. You also are blessed with one of the fruits of the spirit, which is called longsuffering. Your willingness to put up a fight is tantamount in depth of your wisdom.

Jesus is saying that nightmares also are feelings of helplessness, anxiety and sorrow. The death of a loved one lingers in our mind, heart and soul. If the death was traumatic or sudden, your pastor needs to be called to the house as soon as possible. It is easy for someone to deal with the death of a loved one who has had a long or a very long illness. But sudden death brings great sorrow. Jack just left the house and got killed while crossing the street near to his home. The one that would feel this the most would be the one that Jack had just spoken too.

Most times that one is unable to even go to the funeral, because he keeps blaming himself for the cause of his best friend's death. He constantly makes excuses like I could have delayed him or I had a gut feeling that something bad would have happened to him. Emotions are unimportant in either kind of a death. Jesus is saying that human beings must learn to let it go and give it all to Jesus.

Sorrow is like the root of a tree. It will keep you shut-in. You will turn greyheaded in a very short space of time. Your body weight will start dwindling. You will lose interest in everything under the sun. Life will matter not to you any longer. The house will one day fall on you, if you do not seek the face of almighty God.

If my people, which are called by my name, shall humble themselves, and pray, and seek my face, and turn from their wicked ways, which are evil or immoral; playfully malicious or mischievous; severe and distressing; highly offensive; obnoxious. Jesus is saying that nobody loves Jesus. Christians are constantly threatening to kill someone or to stab someone or to maim someone.

Jesus is showing me groups of young men scattered all across the country putting together plans, bombs, guns and signs to go after banks in neighborhoods that nobody knows their names. Women are meticulously scrutinized and handpicked for these robberies. Though dangerous they all believe that they can pull it off without leaving a trail behind. Wearing of masks are considered inconsiderate. Their main goal is to get in and out in seven minutes.

What have brought this on in a society that boasts on their being impartial? Mass incarceration of the underprivileged; professors at Community Colleges not truthfully giving students their just reward. Jesus is saying that students who are doing their best to return thanks for the opportunity that was extended to them feel deep pain and remorse in their hearts.

Society tramples on its own head when they turn against the children of Jesus. Jesus is showing me himself washing at the riverside. This is to say that society runs the risk of millennials shying away from a grotesque world that they had no hand in shaping. They in turn will never forgive or forget the pressure that is put on their backs in a world of sin and shame. They see through the eyes of tomorrow. They judge and form their opinions in a pungent and caustic way. This is like a carpenter choosing the furniture of a shining wooden floor. His face he sees, and nothing else matters.

When someone comes into a world that had been built from centuries of wars and they are trapped in a war of Isis then they see total failure. They see that they are the ones that will be thrown into a war, that they never saw forthcoming. They see strife, beheadedness, rape, refugees, turmoil and unrest. Graphic killings on the television by the Russians, who maliciously continually drop bombs on Aleppo, Syria.

Jesus is the only one who can fix it. How many politicians go to church on Sunday mornings? Yet they call themselves Christians. How many judges go to church on Sunday mornings? Yet they call themselves Christians. How many lawyers go to church on Sunday mornings? Yet they call themselves Christians. How many doctors go to church on Sunday mornings? Yet they call themselves Christians.

Society owes millennials the whole truth and nothing but the truth. We are all trying to fix a world that is ravished by evil through self-will. We show it by our total disregard for church. We display it in our everyday lives. We demonstrate it by procedure and reasoning by putting together chairs and tables and television sets.

When someone falls sick at the house, we call the doctor. We will not call the Pastor, because we have not been to church in a very long time. We just missed Jesus. At night one of our sick parents telephone us to come over and pray. We say that we will be right over and never show up. We just missed Jesus. One of the children at the house wake us screaming and cover in blood from a running nose. We telephone the doctor to come over. We just missed Jesus.

These are the lessons we intend to teach our children in a world that has gone left serving other gods and reaping exactly what they have sewn. Jesus is only called to the house when all have failed. Jesus is only called to the house when a spouse is given up by the doctors. Jesus is only called to the house, when all hope is lost and nobody does not know, what else to do or who to turn to.

We should have known by now that self-will is like procrastination. Deep down in our hearts we know that Jesus loves us. We have seen our grandmother still healthy at age 100 and it scares us. She tells us stories how Jesus will always come to her in her time of need. One day she felt that she was leaving without saying goodbye and Jesus came through the window and healed her just like that. Yet we procrastinate no matter what.

If my people, which are called by my name, shall humble themselves, and pray, and seek my face, and turn from their wicked ways of stealing and money-laundering, then Jesus can come in. In all America cars are stolen every second of the day. Gangs are formed in basements, at the parks, and even on the job. Jesus is saying that the youth falls prey tp gang leaders, who pays them top dollar for every luxury car that is brought in.

America shall at all times be paying attention to the youth who are the future of tomorrow. It is time for the meeting of the minds in all major cities. There are youngsters who are born gifted in innovations but are scared to tell anyone. Conversation between peoples from different walks of life will ultimately draw these gifts out, so that the state and community can flourish.

The youth will go to every neighborhood and steal any and every car that they can get away with between the hours of midnight and five o'clock in the morning. Then they strip them and put an ad in the local newspapers. Jesus is saying that crime does not pay on earth as it is in heaven. The youth does not need role models. The youth needs love and understanding; something that is lacking in the communities.

Young people need to discover themselves for themselves. They need to tear things apart and without help reassemble it back together again. They do not want a tap on the back. They do not want innuendos and slide remarks. They must win your trust. They need to be left alone.

Human beings that are not endowed with the blessings of God the Father, God the Son, and God the Holy Spirit are usually used by the devil to mess up a good thing. Jesus is the whirlwind of love. Jesus chooses his children and plant them in the countries that he wants them to strive. When you are not gifted to see and observe Jesus gifted children then satan can use you to abuse Jesus precious little ones.

Sometimes there can be too much instruction. Sometimes there can be too little. What Jesus is simply saying is that the road is not for the swiftest, but for the one who can endure it to the very end. Jesus is going about his father's business as he did on the earth. Jesus does not need anybody's help. All Jesus wants you to do is to be watchful and do as he says do.

Young ladies that become pregnant also must bear in mind that Jesus loves you. There is no need to panic. There is no need to get rid of the baby. There is no need to put the child up for adoption. You are not obligated to put your child in foster care. It is not necessary for you to go and commit suicide. Jesus is saying that he will at all times send you help, because you are at the hour of need.

Schools are a necessary asset in a growing society. Schools must reflect that which is necessary in teaching and training for Jesus's children to have a job in their desired discipline. Inventors must give some of their time and knowledge in the training of teachers in their product and manufacturing business. This will give students not just an incentive, but the hope that they will get a job when they graduate from school.

This also will give assurances to the parents, who have sacrificed their long working hours at their respective jobs, to put money away for their children's education. This also will send a clear message to would-be detractors, who might want to change or break up a good thing. Jesus is saying that satan is always right there when a good thing starts to grow.

A growing society requires a textile or textiles industries. Jesus is watering the lawn of the earth to bring about a much needed American textile industry. Doing everything and anything in the clothing industry to help boost our economy for our people. In this way, we would not have to depend on China for raw materials or clothing. We can manufacture our own machines to get the job done all across these United States of America.

There is a requirement for a textile or textiles industry. We do not need to import clothing from China anymore. We can with Jesus blessings open up industries all across America that will benefit our people in the future. We can create and build our own machinery. We have all the necessary ingredients in our country to become proactive and innovative.

If my people, which are called by my name, shall humble themselves, and pray, and seek his face, and turn from their wicked ways of committing adultery. Jesus is saying that the society is like a soap opera. There are very, very, very few examples of true love in existence. The planet is emasculated and eroded by so many false doctrines across the continent that gave rise to hate and bigotry.

There are too many single parents. There are too many children growing up with just one parent. This is foolhardy and it is not cute. Most of the time, the one parent is the mother of her children. The father on the other hand, is incarcerated for God alone knows for how long. The society is responsible as a whole to kneel before Jesus and pray for forgiveness of the sin of incarceration and the breaking up of each and every family under the sun. How dare you bring about suffering to Jesus's children? They have done the society nothing wrong.

Who do you think you are? Jesus is speaking to all of America and is saying without candor that this world does not belong to anyone, but the True Living Son of Almighty God. His name is Jesus. This is Jesus World. Jesus is saying that Jesus does not care what happens to those who repeatedly breaks and flouts his heavenly laws on earth as it is in Heaven.

Some preachers are married to the church as the catholic priests and nuns are married to the catholic church. This is sacrilege. Marriage is one of the Ministries of God the Father, God the Son, and God the Holy Spirit. It is not an institution. It is one of the Ministries of Jesus. It is not political. It is one of the Ministries of God the Father. It has nothing to do with the Judiciary. It is one of the Ministries of the Holy Spirit.

Some doctors are married to their profession. This is sacrilege. What is sacrilege? It is the violation or profanation of anything sacred. Where two or three are gathered in my name, I am in the midst. Jesus is saying that children are all innocent. Children are the ones that will suffer, and when they become adults they would teach their children the same foolishness. The doctors also are false prophets.

Some lawyers are married to their profession. This is sacrilege. Jesus is saying once again that Marriage is one of the Ministries of Our Lord Jesus Christ. Be respectful! Children look up to doctors and lawyers and see something of a gift of goodness, faithfulness, humility and love all wrapped up in one and could go off in a tangent. Jesus is speaking loud and clear that these times are not to be taken lightly. It is impervious.

This morning October 31st, 2016, marks the end of Halloween. The most evil month of the calendar, yet a great cross-section of the society including the media bears witness and adoration for and committed to the whims and fancies of Satan, the devil. This is why Christians will at all times be held accountable for the bringing about witchcraft. Human beings must cease all playfulness. It is not about candy. It is not about having a good time. It is not about dressing up the children in adoration of satan, the devil. It is all about Jesus.

Jesus is saying that our bodies are made in the likeness and image of God the Father, God the Son, and God the Holy Spirit. It is imperative. Jesus is the one who bled on the Cross on Mount Calvary. Jesus is saying to all parents that the tricks of the devil will ravished the earth until he comes. We must not allow him to prey on us in ways of a broken record of a sacrilegious life.

There are many fun things that we can do with our precious little ones. We can take them out to the Zoo. We can take them out to the movies. We can take them out camping. We can take them out to the park and go jogging as a family. We can take out to ski. We can take them out hiking and teach them how to hunt and survive in the mountains without carrying food with along.

Indeed, there are a lot of things that we can do as a family, together with friends other than masquerading the streets of inner cities. Unless of course, society takes the whole month of October, and walk the streets humbly for Our Lord Jesus Christ. During this period Christians can give out tracts in adoration of Our Lord Jesus Christ. Or, fellowship with one another in unison with the Triune God.

Jesus is saying that it is about time that all America take responsibility under God and strive not just for life, liberty and the pursuit of happiness. But the remembrance of living as a family as Jesus did on the face of the earth, thus fulfilling the Word of Jesus, I am who I am send thee. Jesus earthly father was Joseph and his mother was Mary and he had brothers and sisters.

Proverbs 22:2 The Rich and Poor meet together: the Lord is the maker of them all. Jesus is speaking to the whole wide world, that there is no place on the earththat the Word of God did not cover. Jesus had already condemned the adage: an eye for an eye and a tooth for a tooth. Jesus had already condemned, the stoning of a child to death regardless of the crime he had committed. Jesus had already condemned the beheading of human beings by anyone under the sun. This is and will always be, is well over 2,000 years ago. Jesus is Lord and master of us all.

11. To Gain Humility By Fasting

Everybody wants to gain heaven without suffering. My best friend Robert roamed the streets of Baton Rouge, Louisiana. Each day he would go to the Super Market and purchased a can of beans, a tin of sardines and a two-liter bottle of diet Pepsi soda. Jesus is saying that one in every ten-million citizens in all America will actually be adopting this way of life. Jesus is now addressing the Military, who has to roam the streets of Isis in the very near future. Take heed of this practice!

Jesus is showing me that only a few would at all times be standing in alignment with Jesus. On Jesus's return to the earth, he started a fire and placed on the grill two handfuls of fish, fresh fish to feed his twelve apostles. Jesus in essence was teaching them a lesson in humility by fasting. All they had that day was just one meal. Then Jesus went into instructing them in the direction that they must go after he dismissed them.

The same applies to Robert. Jesus is instructing Robert on a day-to-day basis precisely on what to eat and what to drink. Human beings does not want Jesus to become the narrative in our daily lives. Every morning we ought to have two eggs, two to four slices of bacon, a beef biscuit, a cup of oatmeal and a cup of coffee with four milks and six sugars. This is the typical breakfast for all Americans. Jesus is saying that humility begets love.

My yoke is easy and my burden is light. This also means humility. We quarrel each and every day of our lives concerning matters of heavenly business. Jesus has never turned his back. The professors in theology at all universities do not have the gift of humility. All they could teach you are guidelines in obtaining the fruit of the spirit. It is laughable, when universities cannot come up with any professor who possesses the nine fruits of the spirit.

Could you imagine, Jesus comes to the earth right now, what will happen when he starts pointing out the dirty sheets left on the insides of important people? Jesus is showing me people that talk in circles and will duck every question that is posed. People that spoke of transparency when Jesus already knew everyone's mind, heart and soul. Jesus is constantly knocking on the doors of his pastors to get out there and do the work that you are anointed to do. Robert remembered one day he was speaking to a Pastor outside his church. The Pastor asked him where did he live? Robert's reply was that "he lived on the streets." The Pastor retorted in humility "I wished that at least one of my Ministers could spend one night on the streets."

How many Ministers on the planet would have said precisely or verbatim what was enunciated? Jesus is showing the pitfalls of the highest creatures under heaven. The animals cannot speak, smile and laugh, but are obedient to Jesus's every Word. The animals cannot think or reason, but are obedient to Jesus's every Word. The animals cannot act, play musical instruments, but are obedient to Jesus's every Word. The animals cannot play basketball, football or baseball, but are obedient to Jesus's every Word.

The angels are in heaven dancing and singing because they know that time is drawing nigh. Whilst we, who are a little less than the angels are cornered by the devil, to do all his evil deeds as we lay quiet in the grass for the most opportune time. We oftentimes blame Jesus by saying that God is not fair. We look up into heaven daydreaming; hoping that one day we will see Jesus eating and drinking ice cream and cake.

Robert recalled [people questioning him about his articulate word. It is the same thing that they do to Our Lord Jesus Christ. How many times shall God the Father, God the Son, and God the Holy Spirit says do not question me in the Bible? Human beings treat Jesus as they treat their teachers in the classroom. They continuously question him. What does Jesus portend to? Jesus takes the telephone off the hook.

Jesus allows us in America to go to church and question the preachers. Jesus allows us when we meet Prophets on their journey to ask them questions. Jesus allows us to question Evangelists who travel around the world bringing Jesus's good news. Jesus allows us to fall in the company of people of wisdom whom we can question. Some of us have been raised by a great uncle or aunt, who was blessed with the gift of wisdom. Some of us grew up in orphanages and were blessed with teachers of wisdom. That is why there is no reason in the absolute to entertain any thought of the devil to question His Holiness, Jesus.

How many of us would like to be modest: having or showing a moderate or humble estimate of one's merits and importance which is free from vanity, egotism, boastfulness or great possessions. Practically every home you go into you will see awards plastered on the walls. A cabinet full of trophies displayed for everyone to see. University degrees hanging on the walls. Jesus is saying that being capricious is a real danger.

Some people may not be able to carry out Robert's menu of the day. Some may be able to eat two meals a day and hopefully still receive the gift of humility. The Bible says that some will receive 30, some 60 and some 100. To obtain the gift of humility one must surrender their all. It is easy to say that Jesus is not impartial. Are you fair?

Your brother John owes three months and calls you for assistance. You tell him to come over to your business place and he will get the sum total. He reminds you that he is low on gas and will have to borrow $20.00 worth of gas to get to you. You reply to him that you got his back. Needless to say, that when he pulls in you take off and tells him that you will be right back. It took you eight hours to return.

Your brother John is very happy to see you, but you become very hostile to him because you remembered as a child a very long time ago, that he came into some money, and you asked him to borrow

$100.00 and he told you that he could not lend you any money. To this day he never explained you why. You begin to remind him of that vivid situation. At this time, your brother cannot recall anything like that so now you withhold your hand.

John left quietly without a murmur. He got into his 1968 chevy with doors that can hardly close. You on the other hand showed total disregard for the love and kindness that your brother John just displayed in front of you. As far as you are concern he had this coming a long time ago. To satisfy yourself, you called on your other brothers and sisters and told them everything. The irony is that they all remembered but poor brother John he could not. Jesus is saying that families must know when to put love over ego.

Jesus is saying that surrendering your all is not an easy thing to do, but Jesus is equally saying that by trusting in him he will come to strengthen you. Can you plunge your whole self through Jesus? Can you dive off the side of the swimming pool straight to the bottom, and only surface up to the top after you have struck rock bottom? Until you let go and go through all the storms of life you will not see the face of Jesus.

There are people that you meet each day of your life and do not know the sweet name of Jesus. Once Jesus has cleaned you up and is now showing you off to a very selfish world this means that you have become a new creature. Wherever he has allowed you to bear witness to his lost children is a mark of his abundance wealth of joy that breathes new life into the nostrils of the forgotten few.

There are no guarantees given to Sons and Daughters that God the Father, God the Son, and God the Holy Spirit takes out into the wilderness to do a magnanimous job. You owe it to Jesus to surrender your all to him. You owe it to God the Father to surrender your all to him. You owe it to God the Holy Spirit to surrender your all to him. You owe it to your wife and children in the foreseeable future to surrender your all to Jesus.

Some people will fast all day long by drinking orange juice and at the end of the day will have a full dinner. Did Jesus teach these folk how to fast? Or did they learn this from someone else? It is easy to go do your own thing. It is easy to follow someone's lead. It is easy to become a follower and not a leader. It is easy to lay up treasures on the earth. Learn to wait on Jesus!

Jesus is not about directing your path up a rocky mountain to throw you off a cliff. Jesus is not about you trying to convince someone to go the way of the beast. Jesus is not about the trials and the tribulations that you are encountering presently. Jesus is about these end times. Jesus is about the book of Revelation. Presently America is about to be served notice.

Homelessness is an atrocity of the 21st Century. There is only one natural thing that is lacking in all America and that is diamonds. Can Jesus bless America with diamonds fields? Yes he can. But where is your modesty? Families are sleeping on the streets of America. Families are dividing up because of homeless living. Parents have to give up their children to foster care, when all they need is loving-kindness.

To gain humility by fasting on bread and water for 24 hours, three days a week (Wednesday, Thursday and Friday) is just like the catholic church in defining sin as venial and mortal. My best friend Robert did this for 16 years, when the good Lord Jesus stopped him and put him on a path of fasting. Jesus is saying to young people, who want to get by through the efforts of their parents, or the death of an uncle or an aunt leaving behind a Will, a financial blessing towards their future. You have to do much better than that.

Jesus says pick up my cross and follow me. It behooves all young people who call themselves Christians to go pray and fast. In this way you would not have to think, where did your money come from? Can satan, the devil, give you money? A whole lot more than you think. Your job is not to fall prey to the tricks of the devil. Does he has tricks? Make a 360 degree turn and tell me what you see? Chaos!

Jesus is speaking to everyone under the sun that the moon will one day be losing light. Be not afraid! Jesus is your bright morning star shining on you both day and night. Jesus wants to take you through the storm that is coming your way. Young people have dreams to become a great one. Could you walk the walk to talk the talk? You need the strength of Jesus to take you through the iron curtains of life. This got nothing to do with Instagram or hashtags.

Fracking is the process of extracting oil or natural gas by injecting a mixture of water, sand or gravel, and certain chemicals under high pressure into well holes in dense rock to create fractures that the sand or gravel holds open, allowing the oil or gas to escape. When you do not fast as Jesus wants you to fast, you will become another disaster to global warming.

The scientists around the world have unified themselves together with the catholic church to give their opinion on global warming. This is not a tenet. Jesus is saying that he and only he alone holds all the answers to anything and everything on the earth. It is easy to go build a cathedral thus making yourself look good in the eyes of your so-called beloved friends. Politics have no business in any church.

Jesus is saying. Do as Jesus do! Jesus cousin John was beheaded by the king for freedom of speech. This is one of the freedoms that is granted through the mercy of Our Lord Jesus Christ. It is not how much work you do. Jesus and his cousin John had already given their lives for you. You cannot tarry along. You cannot say to Jesus "keep a spot for me." You cannot tell someone in the line "hold this place for me." You cannot allow Jesus to play second fiddle to you.

Jesus is saying that the keys of life are shaking before your very eyes. The doors that a century of Christians should have opened are now yours to open. The footprints of Jesus that were left behind for they to follow has been avoided for fear of death by a nefarious people. Churches were closed by these people and threatened at the point of death. Everybody went into hiding. Prayers were said under the breath. Homes were burnt to the ground. Hundreds and thousands of Bibles were burnt.

When a people do not want to follow Jesus, that is a sign to dust your shoes and fervently follow Jesus. Jesus fasted for forty days and forty nights. Very few human beings on the face of the earth could accomplish this feat. It is very easy to look out at the waves breaking and backing away from the rolling water touching your feet. Jesus is saying that the quicker you undertake fasting the better your grades will be.

Fasting is not a cure for any disease. This is a time to relax and to read your Bible slowly and to encourage your friends and your family to pray, before they leave your presence. This is a time for reflection and perspective. Remembering that Jesus was never sick is a prerequisite to good health. Jesus is saying that it is easy for a camel to pass through the eye of a needle.

Jesus is saying that fasting is not a prerequisite to good health. Fasting is the interaction of the Triune God. For when you are fasting, the mysteries of God comes and overpowers you to direct your path. You are at the station waiting for someone coming in on Amtrak. The arrival for your best friend is nine o'clock eventide. It is now that hour and the green light is not on. You start to wonder to yourself if anything is wrong.

Jesus is saying that, is that a normal behavior or is it a condition. Jesus is saying that panic is about terror. Wondering is about nervousness that keeps you pacing the floor and mumbling prayers beneath your breath hoping with the help of Jesus that everything will be alright.

Satan, the devil, is already panicking for his hour is drawing nigh. Jesus is showing that the earth is closing in on the devil. Robert is constantly smiling as he goes about Jesus's business on one meal a day. Fasting deepens your love for Jesus. Sometimes it feels as though Jesus is carrying you along the way, for there is peace deep down inside your belly. A peace that only comes along, when Jesus enwraps you in his arms.

To gain humility by fasting is an excellent achievement. You would only know that you have achieved this when Jesus sends his children to surround you with words of wisdom. For wisdom is the breath of humility. Turning the other cheek when someone strikes you with a fist is the breath of wisdom. Being talked about by your peers for adamantly following Jesus is the breath of wisdom—the breathing ground of humility.

Jesus is about saving lives when you fast. Your good friend is in a car accident a million miles away. You do not know about the accident until the good Lord allow you to meet him at your sister's house. Your buddy is telling his story about his accident whilst crossing a bridge too small for two cars. The night is past three in the morning. There is no moonlight. The oncoming vehicle light is dimmed and he is coming towards you at a terrific speed. You opened your door and threw your body over the side of the bridge into the river.

Jesus is saying that you have saved your brother's life without even knowing that through your fasting Jesus held him up from breaking his neck. Every path you take is not for yourself. When you come to a junction and there are six roads, you will pause and wait for Jesus to direct your path. Fasting keeps you waiting no matter how long Jesus takes to come your way.

It is sad, when a Pastor that has never fasted is telling the church, that Jesus says that he is putting the church on a three-day fast. What can he really teach the church? Jesus is really showing up the Pastor. Does the church see this? Jesus knows how to put a wrinkle in the face of his Sons and Daughters sermons on Sunday mornings. Jesus knows how to let the church see the shortcomings of their Pastor.

It is easy to thread the needle when you have 20-20 vision. Can you thread the needle blindfolded? Jesus can thread the needle either way. Jesus has lived on the earth for 33 years. Jesus did everything in that 33 years. Some of you are postponing fasting because you take pleasure in indulgence. Some of you are postponing fasting until you have made up your mind. Some of you are postponing fasting because you cannot give up that steak. Some of you are postponing fasting because you cannot give up fried chicken. Some of you are postponing fasting because you cannot give up pork chops.

Jesus is saying that you cannot fast whilst being pregnant. But you can surely fast after the pregnancy. Wishing for a son or wishing for a daughter before you undertake fasting is like playing Russian roulette. Do not tempt Jesus! Jesus is not the one. You want your children to end up in heaven with you. What are you doing to see that this great day will come to pass? Or have you given up before you start?

You have asked Jesus to gift you to become a doctor. Jesus gave you another gift. He never told you that you were selfish. He never told you that you would never make a good doctor. He never told you to go and give it your best shot. He just gave another gift. Your grandson before he came into the world, a Prophet stopped by years ago and told you that Jesus is going to gift you a son who will become a doctor. His word came to pass. Now you are a proud grandmother and humbled.

Jesus is speaking of the many times you have stumbled and fall but has never been taken to the hospital. All you know is that you have fasted but Jesus never really gave you the answer to this mystery. Jesus is keeping you humble for others to see the fruit of the spirit operating in you as you traverse this earth. Jesus knows what he is doing as he takes you up the tallest of staircases for any human being to ascend.

I Corinthians 7:5 Defraud ye not one the other, except it be with consent for a time, that ye may give yourselves to fasting and prayer; and come together again, that Satan tempt you not for your incontinency. Jesus is saying that out of the cartels come gangs and out of the gangs come drug dealers.

In Mexico there are at least 12 cartels. And these cartels have their own planes in and out every state of America. Then the gang one by one comes aboard the aircraft to make deals and be given what the cartel chooses to give the gang. This is like the perennial flowers in the fields. They do this in a very systematic way. Their hours change every full moon on the calendar.

In this way the cartel can see you for miles in the distance coming towards the aircraft and can get out of their real quick. Jesus is talking about fasting to an incontinent group of cartels. When a people, who belong to Jesus want all that they can get out of you, they start playing with your mind. There is always someone in a high-ranking capacity, who can tell the cartel to change his or her landing at any time. And this is why the police with limited physics knowledge cannot intercept their link, which is linked to Russia.

The cartels have discovered that fracking by American oil companies around the world have caused death to the unborn in their own countries. There is a price that America must pay that nobody wants to talk about, which is open war between the cartels and the White House. There is open war between the armed forces of the United States of America and the cartels. There is open war between the coast guard and the cartels. There will always be an open war between all America and the cartels until restoration is done to each and every family that was hurt through and by fracking.

The Mexicans will at all times use the borders to traffic drugs in and out of America. Their mission will always be to get back every penny, that their ancestors were robbed, when they sold those lands to America for next to nothing. And just like Radical Islamic peoples, they will feed their children and their grandchildren from generation to generation till the end of time.

Defraud ye not one the other, in relationships with each other. When two people, male and female, form a relationship with each other, before you know it, the cheating has already begun. Boy meets girl and as soon as arelationship is formed, here comes the lies. Cheating is the main ingredient of single-parent families, in every town, city, parish or province.

Cheating also is the main ingredient that results in quarrels and fights between married couples the world over. But as soon as the police are called in the wife starts changing her story. Is this because she does not believe in the word called divorce? Yes it is. According to her church teachings divorce is a dirty word. It's a stigma. My Bible tells me that divorce is one of the Ministries of God the Father, God the Son, and God the Holy Spirit.

When young people are forming relationships in churches, this is the time for the Pastor to take an interest before the baby or babies come along. Some Pastors do not believe that they should get into stuff like that, especially if the parents of these young people are not paying their tithes and offerings. On the other hand, some parents do not care how the babies come.

Consequently, some fathers do not care if their daughters have children for every man on the street. All they think about are the returns they will get on their income tax return. As far as they are concerned those children are their grandchildren and they would love them to death. One of the biggest lies that has ever been told. They used the system for their own selfishness.

All these are reasons why there are so many broken homes in the society as a whole. Pay a visit to any inner city that is overpopulated! What do you see? A single mother with four, five, or six children taking them to school, whilst pushing a carriage along the dangerous streets. Where is the husband? In prison. Where are her parents? Do not want to be bothered! Is this the kind of society that Jesus wants on the earth? When much is given much more have to be returned to Jesus.

Defraud ye not one the other, except it be with consent for a time. Jesus is saying that some people do not know what is right or what is wrong. Especially, if the culture in their surroundings are only teachings of New Testament interpretations. These preachers who are self-willed and are schooled by a professor, who really does not need no introduction, go out and rent these huge buildings that hold thousands of people. This really is not preaching. This is playing church.

Some people do not want the Pastor to anoint them with oil when it is absolutely necessary. Some people do not want the Pastor to lay hands on them. Some people do not want the Pastor to interpret their dreams or visions. Some people definitely do not want no Holy Spirit Preacher. Some people do not want Pastor's vision for the church. Some people do not want grape juice for Holy Communion. Some people do not want to be baptized or plunged in water at the church.

Jesus is saying that these are the people held in strongholds for a time. These church builders need to fast in order to attain humility. In order to know the whole truth and nothing but the truth you must read the Word of God in all its entirety. You need to eat the scroll. Jesus does not bend to any tree, because these new testament preachers provide the best band in town. Playing hymns for hours, before the congregation in nostalgia, while they stand in awe with all the instruments of a big band at some night club, do not make you a steward of Our Lord Jesus.

And these said preachers will one day aspire to become president of America and have their parishioners politic for them by going door-to-door to win an election that means absolutely nothing in the sight of God the Father, God the Son, and God the Holy Spirit. When you are called as a preacher to the highest office in all the earth and want to settle for a lower office then you really do not know the Lord Jesus. You just like every defeatist person on the earth. You want to look good wherever you go.

Wisdom does not exchange height for lowliness. Wisdom is consistently on course for Jesus, turning and twisting around in circles, for Almighty God. Jesus says that I am the good shepherd. Not that I am the president of any country. I am the beginning and the end. Not that I am the prime minister of any country. I am the king of kings and the lord of lords. Not that I am the king of Morocco. I am Jesus the True Living Son of Almighty God. Not that I am a supreme judge.

When preachers who are called by God to preach his Word bow their heads down, because they were not called to astute an office as a lawyer or a doctor, or some foolishness that society upholds over you, this means that you have been caught with the word consent for a time. Jesus is showing me that there are scholars, who have never been to academic schools world over. There are scholars, who have never been to music schools. There are scholars, who have never been to acting schools.

Jesus whilst on the earth did not have a house to call his own. He was on his master's business. Satan will at all times in every conceivable way get you for idly standing by. Jesus puts a ring on your finger. How many rings you see on people hands? When Jesus was crucified on the cross on Mount Calvary, was there any ring on his finger? Jesus came on the earth to do his father's will. Not to play the fool and conjecture and sway from his responsibilities. Jesus is not a fooland that is why preachers fall, because they want an easy job.

As the earth closes up for satan to have less ground to cover, Jesus is not playing with the gift or gifts he has put in his preachers. Jesus is not playing with anybody. Preachers who are walking the streets with empty pockets shall remember one thing under the sun. Jesus loves you the more. Preachers who are being stoned by passersby as they go about their father's business shall remember one thing under the sun. Jesus loves you the more.

Women preachers, who are called to preach the Word and are denied a seat on a male Pastor's pulpit. The hour is coming for those who feel that it is not right for a woman to preach on a pulpit. Jesus is saying Enough is Enough. And every measure you measure will be measured unto you. Jesus is saying that the pulpit is the office of God the Father, God the Son, and God the Holy Spirit. Everyone shall govern themselves accordingly.

Defraud ye not one the other, except it be with consent for a time, that ye may give yourselves to fasting and prayer; and come together again, that Satan tempt you not for your incontinency. My best friend Robert has now lost himself into the wilderness of downtown Baton Rouge.

Jesus is showing me as I wend my way down the streets of Shreveport, Louisiana, that the sin of incontinency is far greater than I can ever imagine. White people, who put their parents in nursing homes, and abandon them to the incontinent of the perverted staff therein, are just as guilty as the uncontrolled staff. When you tell your parents that you love them and they fall ill, it is your duty to take care of them till death.

In Africa families are more united than the rest of the world. Parents raise their children in their homes until they become adults. They in turn get married and move into their parents' home and raise their children. In this way, nobody gets lost and the legacy will continue for generations to come. The children are there for their parents. They treat their parents with the utmost respect. The grandchildren grow to see and continue this love at first sight culture into the next generation.

In America the culture is quite different. Parents kick their children out at 18 years old. They will do everything like the birds in the nest tossing out their young ones. Some parents begin to put their children with their friends' children thus forming an early marriage. This is incontinent.

Jesus is saying that the children become more grown quickly with very little experience of a real and changing world. Whenever they lose their job, they become a nightmare. Very few of them can return to their parents' homes to face a very hostile environment. Interrogation after interrogation after interrogation? Then the name calling begins. Failure! Then the parents get into the faces of their children.

Consequently, the children find a job or any job and are very happy to move out into a ruthless world. Jesus is saying that were these children ever thought fasting? Of course not, neither were their parents. There are far too much conjecturing among peoples of America. Nobody lives by guess. You have to give an account of your stewardship. Jesus wants to roll out the red carpet for you to walk on the run way to a heavenly prize.

Jesus birth is one of struggle and moving from place to place because his foster father Joseph had to be obedient to God the Father, who entrusted his Son to him. Pharaoh, who was possessed by Satan, the devil, knew of the coming Messiah. Pharaoh's job was to find Jesus and kill him. This king of Egypt stopped at nothing in his search to seek the True Living Son pf God the Father.

God says in his Bible to prove him. Isn't this enough proof to a Christian world to lay down their arms and their ammunition, and fast to attain this phenomenal fruit of the spirit, that is given to all of us freely? The fruit is humility. We need this in our everyday meals be they breakfast, lunch, dinner or dessert and a few cookies and a hot cup of black coffee.

A baby in the womb is never given a slice of bread with peanut butter and jelly. A baby in the womb is never given baked beans in mustard sauce, rice and fried chicken legs with wings. A baby in the womb is never given jumbo, pork loins, turkey legs smoked, and briskets. In the belly all he or she tastes is milk. But did his mother drink milk? No siree.

All the food that the baby's mother has been eating during her pregnancy had to be converted into a liquid and fed to the baby via a cord. Human beings take too much for granted. They allow scholars to get away with murder. Their very conscious are beating in their heads, the conscious of Jesus. Jesus sends a Prophet or Prophetess over to your house to have a word with you. And your first response is that "girl I have been thinking about you all day long". This is Jesus giving you a sign.

We allow ourselves to be run over by a bunch of crooked uneducated university scholars, who have no conscious. No etiquette. Never giving of themselves in a total way, continually slandering and bashing the frailties of good honest, hardworking skilled peoples. Jesus is consistently using a dear friend to nurture some of you hardheaded folks in the society.

Jesus is assembling his world in groups of threes and fours in the immediate family. Jesus is lovingly giving of himself, but everyone is too busy to stop and to think about their loving Savior Jesus. Gone are the days of occupied chairs and tables at the home of the family. Everyone is too busy going after monetary gain. The lanes at the drive through restaurants are fully occupied with long lines of cars slowly going by.

This clearly shows that families are not eating and drinking around their tables at least once a day. This reminds me of the great state of New York. Husband and wife is working different shifts. As soon as he gets in first thing in the morning, his wife had already left for work. They may or may not meet to spend the weekend together. This is ludicrous. Jesus does not want this kind of living in his earthly house.

We got to slow down and put things in proper perspective. Jesus worked with his Dad Joseph, who saw his wife Mary, the mother of Jesus all day long. Mary worked nowhere. Everybody wants to be independent. Where are the family values? Fathers have jobs out of state. God forbids something happens at the house, where is Dad? A million miles away. Did God the Father, God the Son, and God the Holy Spirit created this? No.

We want to create our mess and then wonder why Jesus is taking so long to come and fix or straighten out this mess that we have crated. Jesus says to prove me. Jesus never told you to allow Satan to make a fool out of you. You created the mess. Jesus will not come to fix your mess. Jesus is holy. Jesus will not do what you can do for yourself. Jesus will undoubtedly be with you only on the occasion that he sees fit.

Jesus never wakes you up in the morning and tells you to go do two, three, four, and five jobs just to meet expenditure. You cannot and must not hang your hat higher than your hand can reach. All these are more reasons why the sun never goes down for some of you. Your children do not know you anymore. They go out to find love in places unheard of. Your daughters have become grown and pregnant, because you were not there for them.

Joseph had one job. His trade was Carpentry, which he taught Jesus. Joseph and Jesus were well known in the small town. The people often refer to Jesus as the Carpenter's son. God the Father uses his earthly family as a prime example of a beloved good family. These principles have changed tremendously over thousands of years. Jesus is never changing.

It is easy to derail yourself and go off in a tangent. All it takes is ego. Jesus says that when you need something;yousimply ask Jesus, then you shall wait for Jesus to give you that something. Is this hard to do? No it isn't. Keep your focus! Do not go to compete with your neighbor! He is just an example of Pharaoh, the devil. God the Father does not make any mistakes. At all times he is true to his Word.

Joseph job was to keep his eyes on Jesus. Mary's job was to take care of the rest of her sons and daughters, because they were not as well behaved as their eldest brother Jesus. Of course Joseph had a rod, which was used most of time by his loving wife Mary. We pick up the newspaper every day and we see runaways. There were no runaways in the house of the family of Jesus.

Joseph and Mary did not have to call someone over to the house to stay with their children. The family is very important to God the Father. There is laughter and a total giving of oneself to each other. There is comradery, each one taking a special interest in one another. There is a chore for each one to do and finish at the end of the day. There is singing and relaxation for the rest of the day.

Jesus is showing me the outcome, and in this moment of time, he will allow me to give you the result. Joseph's job of keeping his eyes on Jesus was not as easy as some of you may think. The authorities searched for Jesus everywhere. Sometimes at the dead of night, the family had to move on to other towns and cities, before they came to a tiny town called Nazareth.

A whole lot of us would not have passed the test that was given to Joseph and Mary. God the Father did not care about the weather. God the Father did not care whether the mountain was rugged or not. God the Father did not care whether Joseph and Mary had a good night's rest. God the Father did not care whether a motel or a hotel was in the town or city before they lay down to sleep.

To gain humility by fasting is not ours to give. We love to go to the movies with our children. As soon as we leave the movie house the rain begins to fall. We do not stop to think or even ask ourselves a question. We hurriedly race to the car and off to the house. Did we at any time ask the kids, if the Word of Jesus was at any time in the movie? Or do we feel all so self-satisfied, because we have fulfilled a promise.

Jesus is saying that the more we inject the life of Jesus over and above our authority of parental care, in areas of our lives that seem fruitless, is a beating of Satan, the devil, out of the heads of our precious ones. We are all aware that Jesus is the answer. Where is our humility?

On reflection, we were at the movies enjoying ourselves with the kids eating popcorn and drinking soda. What happens outside of the realm of this audience? Nothing really! Jesus is saying that there is a lot going on even in your immediate surroundings. After the movie, your children will have a different view of everything, both off and on the screen.

Jesus is casting a net before my very eyes to show that Americans do not want anybody in their lives who remotely disagrees with their culture. Yet they all claim to love Jesus. Does Jesus really, really, really, really, really, really care whether you love him or not? He does not. Remember that there is a heaven and a hell! God the Father, God the Son, and God the Holy Spirit blesses all America and all Americans with the prophecy that was told a long time ago. Jesus is not and will not change the Word of God

When we fast as a parent, we shall speak in the ears of our little ones that we are fasting. They in turn will want to fast. They too will have a whole lot of questions to ask. This is your hour of reaping something that Jesus is already sewing in that moment. Your child or children will remember this one little thing that you may one day forget. The power of God does not tell you the exact time and the exact date. Jesus keeps the score in his head.

Jesus is not a mind reader. Jesus is not a fortune teller. Jesus surrounds you with his angels and his saints. Jesus will come to you, to remind you and strengthen you, as you walk with him on a dangerous road to heaven. Some of you were involved in an accident. Your car spun and then came to a sudden halt. You stayed there motionless not knowing what to do? The minutes flew by as the flashing of lights surrounded you.

Jesus is saying that your calmness is Jesus. In that moment of need the angels came and stopped the car. The saints were the people who came to help you and take you to safety. It is about time for people to put things in proper perspective and put an end to day dreaming. Jesus is talking, but we want to talk the same time that Jesus is talking. At the accident, who showed up first, Jesus.

Until we put Jesus ahead of us and everybody behind us, we will never ever see the humility of Jesus in that moment of grace and mercy. The doctor, who is in and out of your room shows the face of Jesus. The nurses who are checking and checking to see that you are coming along just fine; monitoring the readings, whilst they are taking your pulse are the saints of God the Father, God the Son, and God the Holy Spirit.

We love to sing and dance only because there is a whole lot of money to be made in these professions. Can we take the arrows by day and the arrows by night? Jesus knows what we are seeking? Most times the answer we cannot take. So we go do the evil with the soothsayer. Then we try to justify the evil that we did for the rest of our lives. Are we teaching our children evil or are we teaching them good? Must we wait for another one!

We compare ourselves with our neighbors. We drive around our block to show everyone that we have a brand new car. We speak big words and we do not know how to spell them, and most of all do not know the meaning of the very word. We get into debates without an introduction, because we want to be noticed. We will never take No for an answer.

Jesus is setting up his building blocks on the planet. These blocks are a reminder of the souls that did not make it to heaven. The families that are told would have to do as Jesus says do. We can play hide and seek only for as long as Jesus allows the devil to do his thing. There will be no surprises for any family, when they get to heaven. All loses would be painted on the door of everyone's heart.

Jesus is showing that to gain humility by fasting is accepting his creed to the bitter end. There is no relenting by God the Father, God the Son, and God the Holy Spirit. Jesus is not going to give up his wrath on the souls and the hearts and the minds of human beings. He is continually showing the light in the eyes of his blind fallen flock, who dwells in the valley of the shadow of death.

Jesus is not going to stand in the way of those, who are seeking the devil for monetary gain. When you are doing evil, evil will attend you. When you are doing good, good will attend you. Good will not go where evil is. So for those of you that shall steal for the rest of your lives, and lay blame on Jesus, down you will go. You do not have to fast one day a week. You do not have to fast two days a week. You do not have to fast three days a week. You can fast just one day a month.

Humility once had, will open up doors for generations to come. Your child or children will be prosperous. Sickness will not overcome you or your precious little ones. The tree of success will take root and a legacy of fruitfulness will continually flow as the wind that blew your hat off your head in the early hours of the morning. Or like the nightingale singing his melodious songs in the tree by your window.

After dinner your wife says to you honey and falls asleep. What do you do? You tuck her in and make your way to the kitchen sink to clean and tidy the place up. Jesus intercepts you on your way down to the kitchen sink and shows you something that you would have never thought about. After exterminating all the bugs in the garage, you still had time to meticulously clean the sink and its surrounding areas.

Jesus is drawing you in the covers of his wings. Reminding you of your infancy, when you would have rolled off the bed, if your mother was not awaken by Jesus to fetch you by her hand and tuck you under her. Your mother would have given you those stories especially when you think that you have grown. Humility is truly a wonderful gift. How many times in your life that Jesus had to come to show you the way? Do not stand there scratching your head! Many times over.

Jesus came to show you that your name is already written in the book of the saints of heaven. But of course, you are still there throwing the dice on the sidewalk. You lost all your money. Your week's pay package lasted but few hours. Next week same old, same old, but Jesus remembers the tears of your grandmother. God the Father, God the Son, and God the Holy Spirit had shown your grandmother, a long time ago, what would have become of you, if she does not begin to pray for you right now.

Some of you have to come home all covered in blood. We believed that we shall settle this dispute only one way, the violent way. We keep hearing the Pastor's voice ringing in our head, as we make our way to the battle ground. Jesus is constantly harassing us long before a fist is thrown or a knife is wielded or a shot is fired. Oftentimes, we allow our colloquial fame to stand in our way.

Jesus is saying that earthly fame means nothing in the sight of God, when it is not given from above. God the Father, God the Son, and God the Holy Spirit appoints you to the office of fame. Jesus will come and teach you how to achieve and harness this special gift. Fame carries the gift of humility, for where there is true humility love will follow. Fame without love is a stench in the nostrils of Jesus.

To gain humility by fasting is not as easy as kissing hands. The devil sees and hears your prayer being offered up to Jesus. He assembles his minions. They will come after you to devour you. They will tear you apart limb by limb. They will tell lies on you. They will torment you as a bird of prey chases after its most vulnerable creature. They will come after you for your money.

Jesus is showing me that only a few make it to this mountain. Boulders will be thrown at you from mountains high. Everywhere you go the police will come and seek you out. You will receive the beatings in your head for the love of Jesus. Your peers will roll you in the mud. Your preaching time will be taken and given to someone else. When you think that it is the end, it is now the beginning.

To gain humility by fasting is like love that is unforgiven, but yet forgiven. Jesus is speaking to the mantras of this planet. It is easy to speak or write in favor of support. It is easy to support a falling housing industry, when you are part of plot to put it back together again. It is easy to advocate Hinduism, when their priests give you a word that you shall repeat often, to gain entry to Jesus's wealth in the form of meditation.

Jesus does not say that after every action there is a reaction. Jesus says that serving a multitude of gods will not get you into heaven. Jesus is saying that there are no short-cuts to the kingdom of heaven. It is easy to say what the heck. Jesus is speaking to the people of this world, that your soul is much more valuable than temporary platitudes. Jesus is showing me, that there is no human being before you, or after you to create a soul or to make anything infinite.

Jesus is walking around his planet with his garden of angels who praises him all day long. When praises go up blessings come down to rest on top of your head. God the Father comes with his great broad golden spoon and stirs the gold that sits on top of your head. The liquid gold is pure gold running all over you. To protect your feet, he puts on a pair of golden shoes. There is no man on the earth that can protect your entire body like Jesus.

Jesus is opening the door to his truth to spread to the East, West, North and South. He is not giving his truth to a body of people that cry the hail mary full of grace. He is giving his truth to a body of people, who mumble and repeat mantras. He is not giving his truth to a body of people, who say one thing and turn to do another. He is not giving his truth to a body of people, who speak only when forced to do so.

Jesus is standing on the side of the road that nobody wants to occupy, when the wind reaches 100 miles an hour. Fasting is not for pleasure. Fasting is not to keep you in good shape. Fasting is not going to bring about good grades in the classroom. Fasting is not going to make you a famous football player. Fasting is not going to improve on your singing. Fasting is not going to win you the presidency.

The true soldier for Jesus fasts without an agenda. His mind is totally blank. Jesus comes to him in silence to stir up the fruit of humility that sits in his belly. This soldier is unaware of the stirring up in his belly. Jesus is not about emotions. Satan is full of that. Jesus is about winning the soul of this young man, who in turn will go off into the wilderness to seek and win souls for his Lord.

We love to have in our hand the Bible, when we are giving out tracts. Pastors must have the Word of God sewn in his heart, before he undertakes a mighty job. Satan knows whether you are full or empty. Pastors should at all times use both hands to give out tracts, whilst allowing Jesus to use them effectively. Jesus says let there be light and there is light. Jesus is the light of the world.

Who are you? Hopefully a child of Jesus. Have you ever been bruised by satan? If yes is your answer now you are on the way to glory. In order to do a magnificent job for Jesus you must have been lost. Did you move any of your mountains in your life? You are better off accomplishing this great and enormous feat with the help of Our Lord and Savior Jesus. Consequently, Jesus will equip you with the weapons to remove the evil in people's lives.

Jesus is shaking his head for the young people of this world still, if even Jesus comes, will not understand. Too much evil has been done and the list goes on. The few doers of his Word grow tired and weary as time goes by. Jesus keeps them strong by strengthen their souls and opening new roads for them to cast their net to win more souls for Jesus. The race is not over. The road has already been cut, but only a few is on the road. We do have a mighty long way to go. Fasten your seat belts!

Jesus does not want you to look at the clock. Jesus wants you to steer Jesus deep down into his eyes, and keep it right there until Jesus keeps your eyes forevermore. Jesus is all about perseverance. Jesus is all about temperance. Jesus is all about seeing in the foreseeable future. Jesus is all about pointing you and pushing you up with his hands to sit on the mountain peak. Jesus is all about you viewing the magnificence of his creation.

To gain humility by fasting is eating the Word that Jesus puts into your mouth and speaking without fear the truth about God the Father, God the Son, and God the Holy Spirit. There is no other way, but Jesus's way. There is no other highway, but the highway of Jesus. There is no other bridge, but the bridge of God the Father, God the Son, and God the Holy Spirit.

12. To Worship Him And Him Alone

Revelation 1:17 Fear not: I am the first and the last.

18 I am He that Liveth, and was dead; and, behold. I am alive for evermore, Amen: and have the keys of hell and of death. Jesus is saying that for too long and much too long, that worship had been lost from the House of God. God the Father, and God the Son, and God the Holy Spirit together with the entire universe, do not need human beings to help us in anything.

Jesus is showing me that to worship Him and Him alone is a command in the absolute. Christians love to do things their own way. Christians love to test Jesus in every way possible. Christians stop at nothing in their quest for earthly accolades. They must put their souls to chance no matter what.

God the Father says in his Word where two or three is gathered in my name, I will be in the midst. This is a challenge for most young preachers, who see Jesus as the only one to have been given everything, when Jesus is just another son of God. In other words, he is our eldest brother.

Jesus is the great high priest that God the Father chooses to build his entire universe around. We have our free will to do what is right or what is wrong. Jesus does not force no one to do anything that he or she does not want to do. The origin of Adam and Eve in the Garden of Eden became the first test of human beings in obedience.

In the Book of Genesis God the Father created first Adam and then Eve. Adam the first male human creature that was formed from the dust of the earth sat one on one speaking to Jesus. Jesus will teach him his first command. Do not eat the fruit of this tree or touch the leaves or pass near this tree!

As soon as Adam figured out that he was lonely, he began to allow Satan, the devil, to torment him on daily. Jesus already saw the interaction of Satan, who came in the form of snake, mocking Adam in every way. God the Father, and God the Son put Adam in a deep sleep. God, the genius of geniuses, takes a rib out of Adam and forms a miracle of one of the most beautiful women in all the earth.

Jesus awakes Adam out of his slumber and tells him to tell his wife the command. Eve on the other hand, fell in love with the snake for his home was a lonely one housed in the tree. The devil will show Eve his knowledge of wisdom; his knowledge of heavenly angels and saints. Then one day as Eve came out of the hot spring water, there was the devil teaching her that she could become another god, just as knowledgeable as he is.

Satan convinced Eve, the woman, to eat the fruit and she would become greater than himself and her husband Adam. Eve smiled and ate the fruit. Immediately she ran to her husband with more fruit to show him that God the Father, and God the Son lied to them. The next day Adam saw his wife rise and stretching herself out came to the belief that she was right. Eve is not dead. Eve is alive.

Consequently, they both filled their bellies with the sweet tasting fruits of the forbidden tree. However, Adam realized for the first time that he was naked. Hearing Jesus coming towards him in the wilderness, he and his wife hid in the bushes of the garden. The sin of Adam broke the law because the law was given to him. Eve on the other hand, suffered in pain of child bearing. This was her punishment for listening to the devil.

Adam and Eve both were sentenced to death. All their siblings were now shaped in iniquity. Human beings will always be shaped in iniquity. This means that we will be sinners until death. A thought that a whole world hate and despised God the Father, God the Son, and God the Holy Spirit for, for they did nothing wrong. Jesus is saying Enough is Enough.

Understanding the mysteries of this universe is not given to earthy peoples, but to preachers, prophets, prophetesses and evangelists who are obedient to His Royal Highness. It is our duty to humbly come to the throne of God. It is our one-way ticket to heaven.

Your free will is not given to you as a means of revenge. Jesus is saying that to know him is to love him. You cannot serve Jesus unless you have met him face to face. Jesus is not someone passing by your window every morning on their way to work. Jesus is not the mail man that comes to the house daily whom you never saw. Jesus is not the milk man standing outside your window that you wave to without coming out to speak to him.

Jesus converses with his sons and daughters and also secular peoples too. Jesus is nothing like mainstream journalists and journalism. Jesus is not what you see is what you get. Jesus is the Alpha and the Omega. The beginning and the end, for there is no other. Jesus is not monotheistic. Jesus is the only way to heaven. Jesus is the main ingredient.

Jesus wants the whole wide world to pray for their enemies. Jesus wants each individual to think of himself or herself as a force to be reckon with. Each human creature is liken to one of the stars up above. Your quest is to rise as high or higher. Let no one ever tell you that you cannot make it to the top! Tell the bullies that Jesus says that their hour is coming sooner than they think so cut the foolishness out!

In life some of us have many rivers to cross, many bridges to mend and most of all to wipe the tears away. Jesus is showing me that the tempest of a whirlwind can be removed through worshipping him and him alone. It is easy to say that Jesus can fix it and you turn around and walk right out the door. Jesus is showing me the many sins that you will not talk about. You stand in line to pay the bills whilst hating every moment that passes by.

Jesus thinks of you long before you could ever imagine. You are owing three month's rent on the apartment. Your aunt calls you up in the middle of the night to tell you that she will be right over. Immediately, you get up and start cleaning the house to save yourself from an embarrassing situation. As soon as you put the broom down, the doorbell rings and here you come running to open the door and let you aunt in.

Jesus is the one that brought your aunt to your doorstep to give you a financial blessing. Before you can open your mouth, she counts out twenty hundred dollar bills. This is more than enough to pay the rent with extra money to go shopping. In furtherance, her visit was short and she never said to you that you owe here anything. Saying goodbye to you was like a breath of fresh air from the morning's dew.

Jesus never ever tells you that you owe him anything. Jesus wants you to give him adoration. Speak about Jesus everywhere you go! At all times dance for Jesus when things are going wrong. Sing alleluia out loud even in the marketplace! Jesus loves you first. If you fail to do something in the morning, do it in the afternoon! Jesus is saying that you shall not give in to the tricks of the devil.

Jesus wants to heal your whole body. You must learn to relax and lift the name of Jesus by deepening your soul with the fire of his love all over you. The more the devil fights you, pray Psalm: 150 till you fall asleep. Jesus will come to you and drive away all evil thoughts, words, missteps and wanderings of your mind. Jesus will come to you and spin you around to take you in a new direction.

Jesus is nurturing you by feeding you with his daily Word of the Lord's Prayer. This is a prayer of protection wherever you may go. Jesus wants you to pray unceasingly. As soon as there is a sick member of the family, pray the our father. Your friend calls you up on the telephone after losing his job, pray the our father. Your children are at school taking a test, pray the our father. Your husband calls you from the job and is having a bad day, pray the our father.

We have to learn to pray spontaneously. To become this way one needs to read his or her Bible daily. This is prayer in action. Anytime someone calls you to pray, Jesus will overtake you and put a word of prayer in your mouth. Jesus also will be harassing you from time to time, as your children harass you all the time. Jesus knows and forecasts your whereabouts in visions and dreams, lovingly showing you that he cares for you.

All these are instances that Jesus begins to show you as you walk untiringly on the road to Damascus.

Revelation 5:1 And I saw in the right hand of Him that sat on the throne a Book written within and on the backside, sealed with seven seals. The beloved disciple John, who was exiled by God the Father, God the Son, and God the Holy Spirit on the island of Patmos, one of the Dodecanese Islands, off the South West coast of Asia Minor. Jesus comes to John walking on the sands of the seashore bringing with him fresh fish to fry. Meanwhile, John the disciple that loved Jesus takes out his book to write about the things to come.

Jesus is saying that his Word will not be well-received by the non-Christian world. Christians must bear in mind that they have to walk a lonely road from the earth to heaven. Jesus will be at their side as they walk along with their brothers and sisters bringing with them only those that heard the voice of Jesus. Walking with Jesus is an awesome moment.

John hearing from God the Father in the midnight hour speaking to him in a language, that he had never heard before, kept him up all night long till he ate the fried fish with his eldest brother Jesus. The Lord is my Shepherd I shall not want resonates in the heart of John, as he gazes on the forever youthfulness of Jesus. An image of fire surrounds his figure from head to toe. A spirit of graciousness and locution emanates from Jesus's mouth, as he speaks slowly and gently to John.

Jesus is saying that they rejected me right before the eyes of John and that is why he was chosen to write about the things that are to come. The other ten disciples fled and ran away into the wilderness of the trees. In the intervening time, John pulled away from Mary the mother of Jesus and took his seat under the cross. Mary observing this ran towards the cross as the lance, thrown by a Roman soldier, pierced the heart of her beloved Son.

Some of us, who called ourselves Christians, would have done the same thing that the other ten disciples did on that sad and lonely day of the crucifixion of Our Lord Jesus Christ. The savior of the entire world was ruthlessly killed for the whole truth and nothing but the truth. Whereas and although this was in the past; still exists to this very day. In these end times Jesus is not playing with his Word and his translation of his Word.

And I saw in the right hand of Him that sat on the throne a Book written within and on the backside, which is the Book of Revelation. Whereas the book of revelation is given to one man, who was crucified within, as he sat under the cross of our Savior, so one man had to be separated to write the writings of Jesus. Jesus is saying that to achieve something great or as great as requires the strength of Jesus.

A preacher is the representative of Our Lord Jesus Christ on the earth. He is anointed by Jesus to do a phenomenal task. Sticks and stones may break my bones but the Word of Jesus will bring about miracles. God the Father, God the Son, and God the Holy Spirit does not care whether you serve him and him alone. All those who want to serve mohammed, buddha, a gods, priestess, soothsayers, psychics, apollo, delphi, mediums, quida, sorcerers, black magic, wizards just to name a few—do this at their own peril.

Jesus is firm and that is a mark or trait of one who is obedient to God the Father, God the Son, God the Holy Spirit. Jesus is showing me the many sufferings of men and women that stand for Jesus. A Christian has to leave a legacy of strength for his siblings, children, grandchildren and great grandchildren. A Christian has to show love beyond compare in a loveless world. A Christian has to worship Jesus in every way conceivable.

For God so loved the world, that he gave his only begotten Son, that whosoever believeth in him should not perish, but have everlasting life. The same John that spoke this prophetic Word is now given the right hand of Jesus. Worship him and him alone will take you to glory. Jesus wants to deepen his love for him. For it is not by works, thus saith the Lord.

Jesus knows that the whole wide world will come after you to tear you apart from holding on to the hem of Jesus. God the Father, God the Son and God the Holy Spirit will take you through your darkest moments of life's valley of human weaknesses. Your child born handicapped is not that you have sinned against Jesus. People, evil people, shall at all times keep their mouths shut.

John is taking a look at the physical aspects of the body of Jesus. God the Father is showing John precisely what is going to happen to his frailty body. His grey hair and baldness would be no more. His wrinkled body and slow moving fingers as Jesus dictates to him the writing and meaning of the times. The aspects of the moves of Jesus seems so effortless as John is beholden by immortality. An aspect of life that we would not or never see even in our lifetime.

Immortality is not just greatness. It is awesomeness spread out to infinity. The sun sheds its light on you at noonday. You see yourself standing on your head. A view of Jesus standing on your head, in the aspect of the sun shining all over you. This is worship. It is not three-dimensional to say the least. This is greater than physics. Physics is just one per cent of the greatness of God the Father, God the Son, and God the Holy Spirit. In Jesus there is no equal.

Worshipping God and him alone takes a very special human being to run this race and not to be overtaken by the devil. Jesus is showing me the many soldiers that have been wounded by the devil on their way to immortality. Their trials and tribulations were undoubtedly taken for granted. Their peers would silence them whenever they take the pulpit to speak the Word of God. Their time for speaking would be 15 minutes. They forgot that the same Jesus in the book of revelation is the same throughout the Bible. They forgot that Jesus miraculously changed five loaves and two fishes into thousands of loaves and fishes before a congregation of thousands in the wilderness. His sermon was longer than six hours.

Jesus is shaking his sword at those who viciously go after Sons and Daughters doing the will of the Almighty God. Jesus is saying Enough is Enough. His blood on your hands is worth annihilation. His blood on your hands is worth doomed to hell. His blood on your hands is worth your name, which is not recorded in the book that is found in the right hand of Jesus.

Jesus is sticking his foot out before my very eyes as he deepens the Word of God in me. His Word many have tried to steal from East to West; from North to South. Jesus does not care what mortals do on the face of the earth. For without him they are nothing. They take his Holy Communion and sprinkle the blood of killed animals on the sanctity of Jesus before eating the bread of life. Woe beyond those that desecrate the body of Jesus.

The rolling hills and plains of Europe are equivalent to the enormous wisdom of human beings. Jesus is showing me the Arctic. The region that is near to the North Pole. This area will one day be feeding the very planet that we exist in today. There will be a time for Homo sapiens to reap what Jesus is presently sewing. The miracles of tomorrow will come out from both the Arctic and the Antarctic aspects of the world.

The world is viciously seeking the creation of superficial chemical elements. The scientific world is bombarding other elements purely for their fame. Jesus is constantly diving off the rock into deep waters to get their attention and focus on his Word. The planet does not need any substitutes. Jesus requires us to stay within the natural chemical elements which he has created for us to use.

No one can compete with Jesus the risen Lord. Jesus is always sharing his stories with the youth. Especially after, he had a very long night of homework. Jesus will communicate a message of peace and love in the form of an oracle. The youth enjoys the mysteries of God. Jesus is searching the youth to give him wisdom and understanding. Jesus is keeping young men and young women up at night showing them the mysteries of God the Father, God the Son, and God the Holy Spirit.

Jesus is gently taking some young soldiers away from the indulgences that have befallen their parents and their friends. It is to show them that it is not how much work that you have put in for the Lord. Jesus gives his gifts to those whom he chooses to freely bless. Too much emphasis is placed on hard work. Too much emphasis is placed on academics. Too much emphasis is placed on loving your neighbor as yourself. Too much emphasis is placed on studying. People seem to forget that Jesus holds the answer to all your needs.

Jesus writes his Bible for each one to read. No one has to have academic achievement or achievements of any kind to be able to read and understand the Word of God. All you need to do is to worship him and him alone. Then Jesus will come and anoint you to read his Word.

Worshipping Him and Him alone is awesome. Jesus is waiting for you to pull the rug from under the feet of your enemies, who blatantly rule over you, Jesus is showing me an open door ajar. Some Christians treat people the same way as they treat them. John's birthday is coming up on November 16, 2016. For my birthday John bought me a brand new suit costing $240. So in return, I will buy John a brand new suit for the same price.

Jesus is healing someone somewhere in most likely a different part of the world. And of course, this will not make the news on any news channel. But does this stop Jesus from healing anyone, regardless of their service to him or not to him. Take a look at the mountain of sun coming up in the distance and striking you in your very eyes as if to say now I got you. Is this the thinking of Jesus? Yet everybody blames Jesus for everything.

Lazarus whom Jesus raised from the dead sat on the outside, sitting on the sidewalk with his hand out begging for his daily bread. The owner of the building a trillionaire would continually stop to give Lazarus something, that is equal to zero and not even one per cent. For one per cent is equal to more than 100 million dollars. Jesus is saying that the Triune God does not have to think before he acts. This is purely human and not divine.

Jesus cannot think the way you think not even for a moment. The door that is ajar is just like you. You sit on a chair having a cup of coffee looking at the morning sun. Yousee someone whom you do not like coming your way with their breakfast on a waiter. You stick your footout and the guy trips over and breaks his leg. Immediately you get up and go racing to your car, since nobody saw what you just did.

Jesus is saying. Are you a Christian? Yes you are. Then why are you doing the job for Satan? The rich man that gave Lazarus nothing also was a Christian. His soul has been annihilated. His name is not written in the book of life, which is the book of revelation. Jesus does not care whether you accept this or not. Jesus is all about truth. Jesus does not care whether or not you have read the Bible.

Abraham gave his ten per cent to Jesus. Who have you given your ten per cent to? We love those who agree with us. We worry about the things that we cannot change. Do we have wisdom and understanding? This is precisely what you need. But you do not want it, since it comes from God the Father, God the Son, and God the Holy Spirit. It does not come from any monotheistic god. It is easily given to you by asking.

Jesus is showing me the craftiness of Satan. As soon as the election is over, now everyone is changing their tone and their ways towards the elected one. Jesus is unchanging. You either worship him and him alone or die with satan and his cohorts in hell. Jesus is not playing games with the minds of men. The mainstream media of America did this to the minds of all Americans. God does not steer anybody along the wrong path.

Journalists who pride themselves as shrewd without the wisdom of Jesus will one day pay the price for their cunningness and adeptness in their writings. Woe beyond to you! Thou shall not call thy name in vain. You shall not slyly use word to denounce others that holds a different aspect of a view or views of the setting sun. You speak and write the truth vociferously. Your pen is not mightier than the sword.

Jesus does not care about your mortgage debts. Jesus does not care about your filthy accolades. Jesus does not care about the seat you take at so-called high-powered gatherings. All Jesus cares about is your distribution of the whole truth and nothing but the truth. When you are not welcome, quit the job! Jesus is not running around with his tail between his leg. Jesus stood and took it all.

The gift of a prolific writer is given from above. Be you a Christian or not, God does not care. Jesus gives his gifts to whomever he chooses. These gifts could be used to do the work of satan, the devil. Or the gifts could be used to honor and glorify the name of Jesus. God the Father, God the Son, and God the Holy Spirit does not force anyone to worship him in spirit and in truth. That is undoubtedly your decision. You are the master of your own destruction.

It is easy to say that you worship him. The devil worships him too. It is easy to say that you are one of the Sons of God. Satan is one of the sons of God. It is easy to say that you are a believer in the name of Jesus. Satan is a believer in the name of Jesus.

Jesus is making it abundantly clear that you have to become a doer of the Word. Satan and his cohorts will not become doers of the Word of the True Living God. A Christian lives the life of Jesus. A Christian has to be obedient to Jesus at all times. A Christian has to learn to swallow his pride. A Christian cannot be scornful and condescendingly proud. A Christian cannot stand aloof.

Jesus is saying that these are the pillars of worshipping God in the spirit of his loveliness. The people have failed Jesus in so many different ways that they do not want to admit. People want you to forgive them first, before they forgive you. People want you to rewrite all their wrongs before admitting their wrong doings to you and your family. The word sorry has lost its true meaning.

Jesus is flipping things over and throwing things out. We tend to take life too seriously. We choose our friends on impulse. We reluctantly go about life as if life will take care of us and not being in the service of Jesus. We engage in too much rhetoric and gossip. We do not care what we say or what we do. We spend whatever little we have on our fears and worries. We cry over every conceivable thing.

Worshipping Him and Him alone is a gigantic step for some of us. We do not know how to act when we confront greatness. We take offense if our dress is torn as soon as someone knocks our front door. Jesus is not about our torn dresses or our holes in the soles of our shoes. Jesus is all about the saving of our very souls.

You do not want to go to church because you do have a new dress. You do not want to go to church because you do not believe that Jesus will forgive your many sins. You do not want to go to church because you believe you will not make it to heaven. You do not want to go to church because you believe that satan will get you anyhow. You do not want to go to church because you do not want to stop drinking alcohol. You do not want to go to church because you had a fight with your Pastor. You do not want to go to church because you cannot give up crack cocaine.

As soon as we are committed to the hospital, we get scared. Everyone must know the number of our room and the floor that we occupy. As far as we are concerned, we are already dead. We are faithlessly, faithlessly, faithlessly, faithful. Our visitors have to go buy the food that the doctors are trying to discourage us from eating. Even Jesus can no longer speak to us.

Did you make out your Will Daddy? He will always nod his head in the affirmative. Though everybody knows that he will surely die, if he does such a thing. Now Jesus is reading the newspapers. Something that we continuously hide behind especially, when we are seated on the porch. All these are the tricks of satan, that we have adopted over years and years in our communities.

We go take out the garbage because our boss is coming over to our home. We go cut the grass with the lawn mower just to make our wife happy. We accompany our children to the football game to see if our neighbor Charlene will be there with her children. We are busy painting the house since Christmas is on the horizon. We are busy changing the curtains in the living room only to please our visiting neighbors.

Worshipping God the Father, God the Son, and God the Holy Spirit is not you trying to become somebody. Jesus is sharing what has been given to him by his heavenly Father to his earthly brothers and sisters. Jesus could have kept the whole planet all to himself and allow God to build us all a separate world. But Jesus through his love for us decided to share heaven and earth with his brothers and sisters.

Could we see through a towering inferno? Of course not. Well Jesus is saving the best for last. Some of us are angry with Jesus who likes surprises. We will wear our parents out just to know the entire menu for the next day. Come to find out that our parents do not behave like Jesus. It is not yet Christmas, but we have already broken and played with all the toys that we have received.

Jesus allows all these things to happen to us, for us to know that there is a vast difference between the Triune God and mortals. Jesus has to teach us all these things before we enter heaven. Jesus prepares us from the day of our birth to the day of our earthly demise. Jesus takes us through the metamorphosis of life.

God the Father, God the Son, and God the Holy Spirit, is very much disenchanted with the news media for using their offices as a tool for the whims and fancies of other people's beliefs. You cannot be a Christian and push other people's beliefs of non-Christianity. You let them find their own forum to vend their own feelings. You cannot be mammoth and be Jesus. We must learn to be strong at all times through it all.

God allows us Christians to show love at all times but we chose to follow and agree for fear of reprisals. This is Jesus world and Jesus is unchanging. You teach by actions and not by reactions. It is foreboding and utterly divisive to belief that there is no hell. That is your tenet. Jesus is saying and saying again that Jesus alone will show the entire world who is the Ruler.

Some people are willing to die in their quest in finding out all what heaven is doing at this very moment in time. Some people are willing to die for Isis. Some people are willing to die for their families. Some people are willing to die for their wives and their husbands. Some people are willing to die for their country. But how many people are willing to die for the whole truth and nothing but the truth so help you God.

The story of Solomon, the wisest man that had ever lived on the earth showed us the true power of wisdom and understanding. Yet we ignore truth no matter what. We will all prefer to believe a lie over the true Living Word of God. We cannot take the truth. We must not have the truth. This is our world. Now let God come out from his hiding place and wage war with us.

Solomon had two young ladies brought before him claiming that they are both mothers of the same child. In today's world we have DNA and we believe that this judgment is 100 per cent right and justified. God the Father, God the Son, and God the Holy Spirit does not care about earthly fixes over heavenly cures. Jesus's wisdom in the belly of Solomon chose the rightful mother who was willing to give up her baby over death. Truth is what we do not want.

Jesus is clearly showing that we do not want law and order. We must be able to go to the store and pick up anything and walk right out with the merchandise. We do not care about the sufferings of others in their obedience to God the Father, God the Son, and God the Holy Spirit in bring about the true gift of worshipping him. The gift of love which is sharing a gift or gifts that Jesus well up from their bellies to bless the whole wide world.

I Corinthians 13: 4 Charity suffereth long, and is kind. Jesus is saying that in heaven there are angels and saints. This means that there are leadership roles in heaven. When society wants to change the role of heaven and earth to suit their own agenda this is anarchy. Does everybody really want to go to heaven? I do not think so. Does Jesus really care? Jesus does not care.

God the Father, God the Son, and God the Holy Spirit is busy building a new heaven and a new earth. Jesus has already showed signs by allowing rocks to fall from heaven. These rocks or meteors are signs from Jesus that he is on schedule in keeping his promises. We must all learn to walk in blind faith. We prefer to walk the street with a rod at the side of us, taking us wherever we shall go. Jesus is repeatedly speaking to us by using the voice of our parents.

Charity suffereth long, and is kind is a replica of Jesus's crucifixion on the cross. They spat on Jesus every time he fell with the cross. They stoned Jesus as he walked along the steep and winding road. They mocked him by saying that since he had healed and brought a man back to life; he could free himself. They cursed his mother, brothers and sisters out. They called them ladies of the night.

Jesus heard everything from the cross, as he is hearing the same exact words from his so-called brothers and sisters on the planet. It has become the status quo. Jesus is saying that it is easy to come home each day of our lives and make believe that everything is all right. It is easy to see the rain coming and decide in that moment that there will be no rain. It is easy to know that Jesus healed you yet you will tell everyone that you have healed yourself.

Jesus has heard all these innuendos and is still alive to speak the truth. Is Mussollini, the Fascist leader of Italy, still alive? Is Adolf Hitlet, a Nazi political leader of Germany, still alive? They are all dead. Jesus is risen, Alleluia. Jesus is saying that everyone has to give an account of himself.

Heaven is a place for those that have been criticized for standing up to the false and incorrectly called stylistics of the modern world. The people in high places are now having a funeral in the White House. Jesus is saying that heaven controls all earth no matter how anyone may feel about God the Father. The rain falls on the good as well as the bad. The sun will come up each day but now there will be a different sunset.

To worship him and him alone is a task for the majority of people on the planet. There will always be excuses after excuses which all pan out to be failure. For those of you that do not believe that we are presently living in the End Times—shame on you. Jesus is moving on. Yes you can do like in the movies, come running to see if you can come aboard on the last carriage.

This is no time for crying here on earth. God the Father, God the Son, and God the Holy Spirit had already cried on the cross at Calvary. Be reminded that there will be no tears in Heaven! Jesus is showing the little children to whom you do not give much credence to, that Jesus has had Enough with even their parents. Jesus is at least speaking to one person in each country. Because Jesus does not need a whole bunch of fools listening to one another.

Jesus wants everybody to listen to one voice, which is his voice crying in the wilderness. Jesus is all about worship. Fun and games that have swept the past, have given rise to Jesus. Because when people are told to go do something, they procrastinate. They keep listening to friends and families that will get hurt on account of what Jesus had already told them to do.

Jesus does not care about friends and families; he cares about worship. Hundreds of years have gone and hundreds more will pass by, before one finger does precisely what Jesus wants the entire world to do. Jesus is about not asking anyone to come follow him anymore, because Jesus is moving on. Jesus is not about remaining silent, because this is not the hour for silence. This is Jesus world.

Revelation 16:16 Speak Armageddon! A movie was made about Armageddon Jesus is denouncing that movie.

Jesus is looking at the massacre of his children all over the globe. Whereas: we are talking politics. His children are targeted by Radical Islamic regime in Syria daily, whilst we are talking politics. Politics in this case has become genocide. Jesus is not playing. You came into this world naked; you will leave naked. Where is your worship? Afraid that you are in Muslim territory and cannot exercise your Christian duty! Jesus is never afraid.

Jesus is not an anomaly. But Jesus is about breaking the most difficult in the society. From the top to the bottom need to be broken. From the front door to the back door need to be broken. From the left to the right need to be broken. From the North to the South need to be broken. From the East to the West need to be broken. Jesus is the architect of every mountain.

People believe that their spouse, who had committed suicide by taking a gun and putting it to his head and pulling the trigger had gone to hell, had been misinformed. People believe that the death of their still-born child means that satan got the child, had been misinformed. People believe that the one, who had been raped is as guilty as the rapist, had been misinformed. People believe that since Jesus did not stop him from pulling the trigger means that satan got him, had been misinformed.

Too many churches have already discontinued Sunday Schools on Sunday mornings. It is all well and good to say that it is not found in the Bible. Jesus is laughing at the fools that do not know his Word and that is one of the reasons, that worship is only found in very few churches. Human beings continually believe that the traditional churches hold the truth, when Jesus himself came to overthrow the very churches that existed in his reign at the time. It is common knowledge that churches existed before Jesus walked the face of the earth. They were all untrue.

Jesus is showing me the screams and the yells of parents to their children day after day. Is this because the children have bad parents? The society has a lot to pay for. The society holds the very answers to this problem. The society has all the ingredients but just would not do it. Worshipping Jesus is like running two marathons on the very said day.

Jesus is showing children using shields for the Isis regime in their war against Mosul. Does anybody care about God's children? Jesus is about pulling the boat out of the water with no one in it. In this way, he can tilt the boat over to examine every inch for holes that are about to be formed. Thus placing pitch from the island of La Trinity.

There are about 500 hundred different versions of the Bible. Every church has a scholar, who believes that since he has a PhD in Theology, this gives him the right to rewrite a new version. Is this a complaint of Jesus? No. Jesus is purely about worship. Jesus wants everybody to worship him and him alone. You do not need a degree to worship him. You do not need an NBA ring to worship him.

When Noah, who was one of few human beings that was obedient to Jesus, believed to himself that it was time to come ashore, made certain that he was in the absolute. He took out his beloved raven and released him with a smile. Immediately, the raven came back to let him know that he could not fall asleep on water. A few days later, he released him with a smile of Jesus. He heard a tap on his window and opened the door to see who was tapping. He ran to his usual position and welcomed his raven who had a twig in his mouth.

In our society today or in all of our societies across the globe, how many obedient souls are there? This is one of the reasons why Jesus came to dwell among brethren, so that they cannot blame anyone but themselves in choosing heaven or hell. The choice is yours. We are all individuals. We are all unique. Going to heaven will be a marvelous choice.

Jesus is saying that holding on to Jesus wherever you can find him is a form of worship. For in the event of a situation or a calamity one can easily backslide and be overcome by temptation. We have experienced a very tough day at the job. On entering the house, a letter is opened and all the money is gone. You sit there motionless hoping that this never happened. You go take a shower and behave that there was no letter.

The next day you pretend that everything is all right. But your best friend Jesus comes along to let you know that you was disobedient to his very word. You stand there on the job as though you have seen a ghost. Ignoring Jesus as he passes by showing you that grace and mercy will see you through. When you are surrounded by a bunch of disobedient people, you also will become another disobedient soul.

Your father is busy at the house helping your mother out with the chores of the day. He sees you passing by he says "John, go purchase these few items listed on this piece of paper right now!" Immediately, you get offended and taking the paper you decide to drive off with his car to Houston, Texas. The hours had passed by before your parents came to the conclusion that you were up to no good.

Your father decided to call the police and reported his car stolen. Within the hour the police pulled you over and charged you with theft of a vehicle. Your excuse to the police officers is that you would never ever steal your father's car. Then for heaven sake, what did you just did? Jesus is saying that the sins of the parents did not fall on their disobedient and ruthless minded son. Jesus does not ever give up.

God the Father, God the Son, and God the Holy Spirit, is not going to allow any human being to draw him into a dog fight. In heaven there are laws that even the Triune God adheres to. So who do you think you are to believe, that you can ever come to heaven to do what satan your king did? Nobody knows your name! Jesus is there tilling the soil providing food for you whether you like him or not.

Jesus is showing me that the tundra that exists in the Arctic, he will one day break to provide the world with much more oil, natural gas, and fossil fuel another wonder of the world. On the Antarctic, Jesus will be releasing more copper, gold and tin. These are the chief reasons why human beings cannot dwell in these places. When God is working no man can enter.

All these discoveries concerning the Ark of the Covenant and the Garden of Eden are false and denounce by our Lord Jesus Christ. Many will come in my name but are sheep in wolves clothing. You will know them by the fruits they bear. What fruits? The Fruits of the Holy Spirit are nine (9) in number. Do not be swayed by scholastic achievements!

To worship him and him alone is liken to a child on his mother's breast who takes all the nourishment out of her in the form of milk. This purity in action is Jesus way in showing worship in its simple form. Though abandon children will grow up without this maternal gift of a mother's love, Jesus will always be there waiting to extend a heavenly embrace. There is no reason to point fingers or to regret the day that you were born.

Suffice it to say, Jesus did not always had his own way, when his parents had to get up early in the midnight hour to depart to wherever his heavenly father is leading his parents. Bear in mind that life does not cater to anyone's feelings! If Joseph and Mary were not obedient to God the Father, Jesus would have been killed on many occasions. Mary had to flee with Jesus wrapped on her breast.

Soldiers at every turn looking for Jesus, whose parents with infant in hand sometimes could not even stop to change the diaper of Jesus. Languishing in the heat of the day only to take shelter under a shaded leaf; moments of desperation wanting to overpower the one-singular family of hope and love in a ruthless world. Images of prejudice thwarted the faces of those that were not relatives or friends.

Jesus felt every pain. Jesus felt every anguish. Jesus felt every swear word. Jesus felt every disappointment. Jesus felt every torment. The experiences that his parents had to go through Jesus felt. It is easy to say, that you were not there in that moment in time. Yes you were there, because you are experiencing the very same things that have thwarted your efforts.

We live in times when young people feel that they are invincible. We live in times when young people feel that they can get away with anything. We live in times when young people feel that they can cheat their way through exams. We live in times when parents do the math for their children throughout their whole adult lives. We livein times when brothers go take the exams for their siblings even at university level.

Jesus is clearly showing to an audience of this world that he is the only way to salvation. For those of you who are still waiting, you are waiting in vain. For those of you who have not received the Holy Spirit, the time is now to seek out an anointed Holy Spirit Preacher or Pastor. For those of you who are comfortable with your self-will

Pastor, do not try to dissuade those from seeking the Holy Spirit Pastor.

For the many Christians who have procrastinated by putting off baptism, until they are about to die, Jesus is saying that no one knows the hour of the coming of the Lord. Jesus wants you to know that he is able to do the things that you have tried to accomplish on your own. Jesus is showing me the empty vessels in your life. Vessels that need Jesus to come and fill up.

Jesus is laughing because his hour has come to speak the truth to all humanity. A truth that will divide some of our people. A truth that will heal the wounded soldiers of Christianity. A truth that will dig deep into the minds, hearts and souls of human kind. A truth that will uphold all heavenly laws. A truth that will break every stronghold. A truth that will bind every demoniac person, people or thing. A truth that will not surrender to ambushes of satan. A truth that will live on until eternity.

Fear is man's greatest enemy but the gift of Jesus will overcome all fear. Jesus is still in the healing business. Jesus will tear every dividing wall that families have put up against other families. Jesus is putting an end to all slavery East, West, North and South. Jesus is putting an end to systemic slavery seen or unseen. Jesus is putting an end to every high bridge that has separated both the rich and the poor. Jesus is putting an end to just a wealthy few.

Jesus is speaking from his Throne of Grace that houses God the Father, God the Son, and God the Holy Spirit. Jesus is saying that one of these days in the near future, movies of heaven will be shown in the sky in the midnight hour. People would not have to come out into the open air to view the magnificence of heaven. The movie will not be eclipses of the moon. The movie will be precise. The movie will be Jesus.

I remembered in December, 1998, when the Lord Jesus kept harassing me about putting me in black. Jesus allowed me to start packing all my colored suits in the trunk of my Sedan de Ville. In early

February of 1999 after receiving my income tax returns of about $600 (six hundred dollars), I left Georgia via Pennsylvania.

Taking the Route I 95N knowing fully well that the trip would take me 12 hours nonstop. Jesus began to harass me after about two hours of driving. Jesus would make me pull over and open my trunk as though he is physically doing it. Then he would overpower me and start throwing out my suits on the ground. Immediately thereafter in utter amazement, Jesus would calm me down and repack the very clothes that he had just thrown out.

As soon as I entered the City of Philadelphia, Pennsylvania, I took my car to the Motor Vehicle Inspection Site. Receiving my successful clearance from the site and wearing new 1999 stickers, I then proceeded to my best friend house in the beautiful city of Philadelphia (the city of brotherly love). Embracing Drewnell after about a year was my last gift of seeing and meeting a most beautiful and wonderful Pastor.

A few hours later, Jesus was once again taking me out and moving me on to East Orange, New Jersey. After two hours of driving, I embraced my son and kissed him for the last time. Reminiscing on how he looked at five years old to how he looked now from a High School Portrait is a novelty. I would always remember Junior. Consequently I would sleep in my car and move around a town that I knew best. Till one day I woke up at a familiar place and my ride was repossessed. Jesus reminded me immediately of his profound word, that one day he will put me in black and how was I dressed in a black sweat suit.

AUTHOR: PROPHET ALLYSON MICHAEL D'ESPYNE

Printed in the United States
By Bookmasters